P-V

# Medicine
## and
## American Growth,
### 1800-1860

**Wisconsin Publications in the
History of Science and Medicine
Number 5**

**General Editors**

William Coleman
David C. Lindberg
Ronald L. Numbers

# Medicine and American Growth, 1800-1860

James H. Cassedy

THE UNIVERSITY OF WISCONSIN PRESS

Published 1986

The University of Wisconsin Press
114 North Murray Street
Madison, Wisconsin 53715

The University of Wisconsin Press, Ltd.
1 Gower Street
London WC1E 6HA, England

First printing

Printed in the United States of America

For LC CIP information see the colophon

ISBN 0-299-10900-3 cloth

ISBN 0-299-10904-6 paper

The maps are from Charles O. Paullin, *Atlas of the Historical
Geography of the United States,* edited by John K. Wright
(Washington, D.C.: Carnegie Institution of Washington and
New York: American Geographical Society of New York, 1932).

*For Carol, Bill, Dave†, Margot, and Mary*

# Contents

# Illustrations

# Preface

During America's transition from a colonial to a national status, those who paid the closest attention to demographic matters tended to be statesmen and other governmental and civic leaders. The writings on these topics by such men as Franklin and Stiles, Jefferson and Morse, Madison and Adams, have subsequently become well known to historians. During the early nineteenth century, as the nation's affairs became more complex, demographic studies, like other topics, increasingly became the province of scholars in special fields. The most prominent of these scholars were individuals who approached the subject as political economists, commentators ranging from Tench Coxe, Adam Seybert, and George Tucker, to Matthew and Henry Carey, J. D. B. DeBow, and others. Subsequently, economic historians dealing with such men have illuminated in considerable detail those parts of American demographic history that had to do with the labor supply, Malthusian theories, and other aspects of the "dismal" science. Until very recently, historians have understandably paid much less attention to the scattered demographic concerns of diverse individuals from the nineteenth-century religious and social-reform communities. But it is a cause for some surprise that they have devoted few of their studies to the extensive demographic contributions of medical men, a far larger and more homogeneous group.

Early nineteenth-century American physicians were, as a group, as concerned as the political economists with the country's fundamental demographic phenomena, though frequently for different reasons. They were often perceptive observers of the broad, general effects of demographic change upon their communities, but they were also analysts of its profound immediate influence upon medical institutions, medical practice, and public health. They published a large proportion of the demographic literature of the period. And they played significant roles in the establishment and working of many of the nation's mechanisms for collecting and processing demographic data.

This work examines all of these matters. It also considers the historical expansion of nineteenth-century American medicine itself as a demographic phenomenon within the framework of population movement, regional development, disease incidence, and social change. It is not, however, a study in historical demography as that term is usually used; I have not attempted to analyze statistically the demographic data of the past. Rather, I have simply aimed at identifying and providing a narrative account of those nineteenth-century demographic concerns that were also medical concerns. And, as part of this, I have tried to demonstrate that the rich themes of demography belong to medical history fully as much as to economic, sociological, or political history.

I have written this volume as a sequel to my *Demography in Early America* (1969). It is also very closely related to my *American Medicine and Statistical Thinking, 1800–1860* (1984). The latter work deliberately omits considerations of demographic matters per se. Nevertheless, its extended treatment of early nineteenth-century epidemics, urban public health measures, medical institutional growth, and vital-statistics registration activities does incorporate a great deal of detail about the medical-demographic configuration of the nation's older communities, principally those along the eastern seaboard.

The present work does not duplicate that treatment. Rather, it extends my study geographically to the remainder of the United States by portraying the medical-demographic development of the Midwest, Far West, and southern regions. It also goes on to consider the medical aspects of a number of major demographic changes, events, or problems which concerned several or all parts of the growing country. Throughout, the work is intended to depict the slow but steady processes of creating, accumulating, and improving demographic knowledge and data-collecting mechanisms, however flawed or elementary they may seem to be by late twentieth-century standards.

I am grateful to a succession of officials at the National Library of Medicine for having made it possible for me to devote extended periods of time to researching and writing this book and for providing substantial material support. I have also had generous assistance—tangible and intangible, large and small—from my colleagues in the library's History of Medicine Division.

Several members of the scholarly community—Drs. John B. Blake, Gert Brieger, Robert C. Davis, and Ronald L. Numbers—were each kind enough to read the entire manuscript and give me their suggestions and encouragement. The late Professor David V. Glass commented on early versions of two chapters. I thank all of them.

The material in Chapter 8 was presented in slightly different form at an American Academy of Arts and Sciences conference on "The Scientific Study of Fertility in the United States," held in Boston in May 1978, but has not been previously published. Small portions of the material in Chapter 4 pertaining to the history of medical journals and to the illnesses of migration have been used in previous publications. See my article, "The Flourishing and Character of Early American Journalism, 1797–1860," *Journal of the History of Medicine and Allied Sciences,* 38 (1983), pp. 135–150; and my chapter, "Why Self-Help? Americans Alone with their Diseases 1800–1850," in Guenter B. Risse, Ronald L. Numbers, Judith W. Leavitt, Eds., *Medicine Without Doctors: Home Health Care in American History* (New York: Science History Publications, 1977), pp. 31–48.

*Medicine
and
American Growth,
1800-1860*

# 1

## Seeds of a Demographic Science

Demography—the enumeration, description, and quantitative study of human populations and of the vital events occurring among them—was nowhere thought of as a separate scholarly specialty in 1800. Outside of Paris, perhaps, it hardly had any such status even as late as 1860. In fact, the term itself was not coined until almost the end of this period.[1]

However, ever since the Renaissance, demographic concerns had been looming progressively larger in magnitude and significance throughout the Western world. And leaders, decision-makers, and scholars were making ever greater demands for concrete information about these matters. The needs for demographic information were satisfied to some extent during the seventeenth and eighteenth centuries by the descriptive factual accounts of governments and societies that were compiled by a succession of German scholars from Hermann Conring to Gottfried Achenwall. However, rather more specificity of information was supplied, at least in Great Britain, by the intellectual heirs of Francis Bacon, John Graunt, and William Petty, by individuals who stressed the importance of systematic data accumulation and numerical analysis in the tradition of "political arithmetic."

These and other intellectual currents came together, just as the nineteenth century opened, under the name of *statistics*. Progressively numerical and quantitative in its outlook and methodology, statistics quickly gained acceptance as a central organizing element in every phase of material life—in government, commerce, social reform, finance, science, and other activities. For demography it proved to be, very simply, an indispensable ingredient. In fact, whatever progress demography subsequently made during the nineteenth century toward achieving the status of a science can be traced directly to the enhancement of this statistical ingredient—to the gradual introduction of effective data-collection mechanisms, along with the progressive adoption of statistical methods for studying the meaning of the data. In America as in Europe, no one group was more responsible for these innovations than the medical profession.

## American Population, the Census, and the Rise of Statistics

Colonial America's demographic events had been perceived and dealt with mainly within a framework of mercantilist regulations, ecclesiastical ambitions, and epidemic alarms. In all of these areas, colonials showed a general awareness of the principles of "political arithmetic," some appreciation of the use of accumulated facts, sometimes numerically expressed, in analyzing not only population matters but other concerns of the state and of society.[2] With Independence, however, a wealth of new kinds of governmental functions and social inquiries placed a greatly magnified premium upon factual treatment and numerical application. Demographic studies, for their part, expanded far beyond all previous bounds after the launching of the federal government's national census in 1790.

The decennial census provided for by the United States Constitution was an innovation which no European country prior to 1800 could yet match. The abundant supply of population data provided by the successive enumerations assured nineteenth-century Americans of an exceptionally full numerical foundation for demographic study. To be sure, the early censuses were restricted to only a few kinds of basic population information: in 1790, to data on heads of families, free white males aged 16 and over, free white males under 16, free white females, all other free persons (except untaxed Indians), and slaves. However, these kinds of inquiries were gradually refined and extended in later censuses. From 1820 onward, censuses included data on numbers of foreigners and on the occupational distribution of the population. Later came provisions for enumeration of disease and other medical events: of the deaf, dumb, and blind in 1830; of the insane and idiots in 1840; of mortality and its manifold causes in 1850.[3]

While the stated use of the census population data was to provide a precise basis for apportioning seats in the House of Representatives,

Map 1. Density of Population, 1800. From Charles O. Paullin, *Atlas of the Historical Geography of the United States,* plate 76.

other uses were quickly found by reformers, businessmen, scientists, physicians, and others. In fact, almost every flag-waving patriot was anxious to know the country's progressive size in numbers of people. In 1790, it was no secret to any one that the infant nation was economically weak, loosely organized, and poorly defended. And it was clear that the combined population of the 13 states was small and widely scattered. Adverse demographic factors—great epidemics, low immigration, declining fertility, a chronically insalubrious environment—if they came about, could easily diminish the population still further, leaving the nation or some segment of it fair game for any ambitious European power. Favorable trends or events, however, could be expected to tip the existing precarious demographic scale and ensure rapid achievement of the glorious national destiny that patriots at least since 1776 had been talking about.

The study of population in the new republic thus had a good deal of urgency attached to it. In turn, the various demographic pressures and concerns played a considerable role in increasing the new nation's preoccupation with numerical matters. In fact, on all sides, people seemed to be thinking increasingly in numerical terms, and in so doing were expanding the political arithmetic tradition of numerical analysis to new levels of importance and precision in this country. In the decades after Independence, Americans quietly shed their earlier intense preoccupation with the theoretical and began to take on an equally intense concern for the factual.[4] In the framework of representative government and republican ideologies, Benthamite objectives of the greatest good for the greatest number were taking root. In the hectic and rapidly expanding realms of commercial life, quantification and calculation were rapidly accepted as essential tools. In the growing fields of science, agriculture, and medicine, the well-established Baconian ideals of counting, weighing, and measurement were taking on new vitality. And, in the world of political economy, those who were accustomed to gather information about the state in the descriptive German tradition of *Staatskunde* gradually changed to increasingly numerical compilations of quantitative data, though the new mode retained the name of the old, statistics.

Most turn-of-the-century Americans seem to have taken the word *statistics* from the Scot, Sir John Sinclair. And, for several decades, some of the most conspicuous American statistical publications were works modelled more or less after Sinclair's enormous *Statistical Account of Scotland*. Starting with an 1806 work by Samuel Blodget, these publications were frequently labelled simply as "statistical manuals," or "statistical accounts," compilations of frequently miscellaneous facts and figures that, to some extent, took the place of earlier generations of gazetteers, local histories, and handbooks.[5] And, in most of them, along with the information pertaining to commerce, government, agriculture, and manufactures, population data and analysis figured prominently.

The general statistical manuals had no exclusive hold on the use of the term *statistics*. On the contrary, from such works the term was easily and quickly transferred for use in almanacs, government reports, periodicals, and other media of publication, eventually including those relating to every special field of material activity or inquiry. Conspicuous among these was the field of medicine.

### Physicians as Demographers

The remarkable implantation of the numerical outlook and of statistical methods in the United States at the beginning of the century was paralleled very closely by the coming into existence and rapid growth of an organized indigenous medical establishment. This included, among other things, the creation of medical societies, schools, and journals, particularly in the larger cities. Such bodies, in turn, became the sources of a steadily increasing cadre of trained practitioners. These were medical professionals who had built-in concerns for such demographic matters as the fertility, longevity, and mortality of the population, along with the specialized knowledge for studying them effectively. Large numbers of physicians played active and essential roles in society as observers and recorders of demographic data. And some of them produced extensive and sometimes penetrating analyses of the century's demographic events.

American medical men first applied the term *medical statistics* to local bills of mortality and figures pertaining to certain other vital events. The expression was soon extended to data compiled by hospital and medical school administrators, and ultimately to numerical data amassed by medical investigators at the bedside, in operating rooms, or in the field.[6] Long before the first American statistical societies were formed, American physicians in large numbers had not only endorsed the statistical enthusiasms around them but energetically furthered them with increasingly numerical medical compilations and analyses of their own. Not many of these individuals could be said to have originally been at all refined or critical in their uses of statistics. However, these uses of medical numbers were subjected during these decades to increasingly penetrating scrutiny. This process left pre–Civil War physicians as a group better qualified than most of their contemporaries to conduct statistical analyses and hence to deal with demographic matters.

Whatever their statistical competence, those physicians who were interested were ideally situated, in that prespecialized era, to become the nation's demographers. In fact, simply by virtue of their everyday medical activities, physicians were already very literally the midwives of many aspects of demographic change. They presided over the intimate events of birth, sickness, and death, and presumably affected the outcomes. In their professional visits to hospitals, dispensaries, asylums, and prisons, and their civic participation in temperance, missionary, immigrant aid, and other do-good societies, they came to know better than anyone else the human composition of their communities, as well as the various comings, goings, and dislocations of the people. Moreover, by building up their own network of medical societies, schools, and journals, they made certain that the medical aspects of demography would be thoroughly discussed and publicized, not only in local but in national contexts.

### Medical Concerns for Population in the Malthusian Era

When the first edition of Thomas Malthus's *Essay on the Principles of Population* appeared in 1798, the American medical establishment was just beginning to take on shape and substance. As various editions of the work appeared, physicians and others were impressed by, among other things, its extensive statistical compilations. Not a few were led to reflect on the possible relevance of Malthus's substantive views for the United States. However, the subject as a whole was not particularly new to very many; the medical community had an interest in population that long predated Malthus. In any case, few if any of its members made his views as such a major preoccupation prior to the Civil War.

As soon as the first national census enumerations were published, a few American physicians began linking the population data with information gleaned from local bills of mortality and drawing medically significant inferences from the data. Editors of the *Medical Repository,* for instance, noted from the 1800 census that more male children than female were born in the United States by a ratio of about 17 to 16, but also that somewhat more of the males died between the ages of 10 and 26. They went on to attribute this latter fact vaguely "to accidents incidental to the male sex, to maritime, military, and other exposures, and to youthful indiscretion and intemperance." Offsetting this, however, they noticed a considerably "increased extinction of female life after 26," which they found logical to blame on "pregnancy, child-birth, and diseases peculiar to the softer sex." The editors also drew attention to a developing geriatric problem in New England, where "owing to the emigration of the men from fulness of population, there is a considerable majority of elderly women." On a related matter, other observers pointed out the pitfalls of taking at face value census data which indicated greater average longevity in New England and other long-settled states than in the newer states. It seemed clear "that the cause of the difference is the emigration of the young and active to the latter, leaving behind the old."[7]

While the initial sparsity of America's population was currently a major concern, most citizens were apparently confident that this would not remain a problem for long. It seemed clear that ultimately, as soon as European nations overthrew their tyrannical governments, ceased their eternal wars, and permitted freedom of the seas, their peoples were certain to rush in ever larger numbers to the land of freedom and opportunity. However, for the time being, the most important factor in America's population growth was the continuation of the prolific native birth rate. While no large community yet kept accurate birth records, the successive censuses did provide good clues to trends in the birth rate.[8] In fact, the data made it clear that overall the country's population was doubling by natural increase approximately every 23 years, a rate which differed little from the late colonial estimates of Benjamin Franklin and Ezra Stiles.[9] Physicians were able to show that particular localities were doing even better than that. David Ramsay found in 1809 that, in some areas of rural South Carolina, the whites, following a pattern of early marriages, "steady industry," and wholesome diet, were more than doubling from natural increase every 10 years, while the slaves were almost trebling. In Ohio, Daniel Drake found that "from the abundance of subsistence, the preventive checks to population do not operate, and marriages are both early and productive." And Louisville, Kentucky, was thought about this time to be trebling its gross population in less than 10 years.[10]

Few Americans of this period publicly questioned the desirability of having large numbers of children. Moreover, few doubted that their peculiar national circumstances were favorable to this. Patriots, physicians among them, suggested that, contrary to some European reports, fecundity was materially stimulated by New World climate and other conditions. Some were sure that the republican political system itself provided one of the great stimuli. Thomas Hersey, for one, maintained that the circumstances of civil liberty in the United States not only encouraged earlier marriages than in Europe but generally served to "arouse the energies of nature, and elicit sexual emotions" to a greater degree.[11]

Benjamin Rush was another medical man who, before Malthus, strongly advocated a steady growth of the population in order to ensure the nation's prosperity. One means toward this end, he thought, was to encourage the westward migration of a certain proportion of the settled populace, but particularly "the idle and extravagant." "Their removal," he concluded, "by increasing the facility of subsistence to the frugal and industrious who remain behind, naturally increases the number of people, just as the cutting off the suckers of an apple-tree increases the size of the tree, and the quantity of fruit."[12]

Malthus's ideas, numerically expressed to a large extent, thus fell among members of an American intellectual and medical community that was already making empirical observations about the relationships of population growth to the fertility of the land. Prepared as they were, Americans reacted variously to the ideas. Most could agree in principle with Malthus's reading of history, that population tended to increase faster than the food supply, to the detriment of society, but few thought that this part of the doctrine had any special validity for the United States at that stage of its national existence. Jefferson, finding in Malthus support for his own desire to keep America essentially rural, thought in 1804 that the potential food surpluses which America's agrarian yeomen would raise could serve to feed "the now perishing births of Europe, who in turn would manufacture and send us in exchange our clothes and other comforts."[13] John Adams embraced Malthus essentially because the latter's conservative social outlook and antipathy to the perfectionism of Godwin, Paine, and Condorcet matched his own.

America's political economists ultimately incorporated the Malthusian doctrines into American collegiate courses and texts, where they left their imprint both on subsequent economic thinking and on American attitudes toward the poor. As a rallying point for those who opposed Enlightenment presumptions of social perfectibility, the doctrines eventually became serious deterrents to public health progress. Up to the 1820s, however, they were little more than a momentary source of pessimism for a few thoughtful persons. For the most part, as they watched their country grow in size and wealth, white Americans had too many blessings to be consistently pessimistic. As George Tucker put it, "The people are in the full enjoyment of all the arts of civilization, while they are unrestricted in their means of subsistence and consequently in their power of multiplication." Not even the economists or the statisticians could see any end to it. In fact, Adam Seybert reported, "No one has ventured to predict when our population will be at the maximum to be checked for the want of subsistence."[14]

The futility of even attempting such a prediction at this point in American history was underscored by travellers to the trans-Appalachian states and territories. One of them, the Reverend Timothy Flint, could not recall seeing "such hosts of children" anywhere else, and the explanation seemed obvious.

> The process of doubling population, without Malthus, and without theory, without artificial or natural wants, goes on, I am sure, on the banks of the Ohio as rapidly as anywhere in the world. Why should it not? The climate is mild, the cattle need little care or housing, and multiply rapidly. Grain requires little labour in the cultivation, and the children only need a *pone* of corn bread, and a bowl of milk.[15]

American physicians were probably no less interested in Malthus's social views than other intellectuals were, though relatively few had anything to say in print about such subjects. Those who did were mostly approving. Benjamin Rush long held the view that the high infant mortality of his day was really a blessing by reducing the amount of starvation in the world. However, he thought that, because of the abundance of the American environment, physicians here would not for some time to come have to cope medically with the implications of Malthusian realities.

> Here no part of the talents of a physician have ever been called upon to ascertain the smallest portion of food, fuel, light and clothing upon which man can subsist, nor to damp the ardour of inquiry into the means of preventing the ravages of death by pestilential diseases, least [i.e., lest] the means of supporting life should not keep pace with the increase of the number of the human species.[16]

A more specific medical endorsement of Malthus came from Samuel Latham Mitchill, who acknowledged that he had received "pleasure and instruction" from Malthus's book. In 1810, in fact, Mitchill sent Malthus an account of cannibalism in the South Seas as it had been reported by sandalwood traders from New York. The main cause of the practice, he concluded, was "the scarcity of food, produced by a too numerous population." Meanwhile, Mitchill's *Medical Repository* had already carried a review of the second edition of the *Essay on Population*. While the anonymous reviewer ventured few value judgments on this "laborious and learned" work, he did seem to approve of the way the book "exposes the error of foundling hospitals, poor-rates, and a considerable number of what are called charitable and benevolent establishments, in very strong terms."[17]

The naval surgeon Thomas Ewell also generally concurred with Malthus's view of overpopulation as a curse in many countries. But Ewell felt that the laws against early marriage which were often adopted were totally useless given man's sexual urge. He felt Malthus's call for moral restraint to be equally impractical. The solution, Ewell thought, lay in the use of physical means to prevent conception.

> The sexes will connect as every one of observation must admit. . . . If they cannot maintain children; if their children are to be brought up in every scene of temptation, to villany [sic], it is best not to have these children. To prevent their conception, by preventing copulation, is out of the question.

Ewell's views were unusual if not unique in the United States during his generation. However, he made them known only to his medical colleagues. Whether it was the kind of advice that should be passed on to the public, he was not sure. As it turned out, not only his generation but most nineteenth-century American physicians felt that it was not.[18]

Possibly the most "strenuous disciple of Malthus" among American physicians before 1815 was John Crawford of Baltimore. Crawford's articles of 1807 and 1808, addressed to both the laity and the medical profession of Baltimore, were mainly aimed at proving his conviction—highly unusual in the United States at that time—that invisible animalcules rather than either contagion or miasmatic effluvia were really the causes of epidemic diseases. Development of this view, however, was accompanied by his belief "that war and epidemic diseases are among the necessary means by which the excessive multiplication of mankind is to be kept within bounds, and their numbers reduced to the limit which is consistent with the health and peace of society." To illustrate this view, Crawford drew a vivid picture of the relentless struggles for subsistence and survival in the animal and vegetable worlds and the way they held back the multiplication of species, a picture which approached Darwin's later concept about as closely as did that of Malthus.[19] However, it is unlikely that even Crawford viewed early nineteenth-century America as a place where population pressures actually required the restraint of periodic epidemics. Virtually everyone of his generation saw the country's terrifying onslaughts of yellow fever, typho-malarial fevers, smallpox, and other plagues as devastating setbacks to those steady increases and free movements of the indigenous white population that they took for granted as being desirable.

Some physicians contemporary with Crawford were aware that medical practices then in vogue might well themselves be included in any list of the factors which held down population. Among them, William Currie wrote in 1815 that, "if Mr. Malthus . . . had been acquainted with the hopeful doctrines and random practice of physicians . . . , I fancy he would not have considered the introduction of the smallpox into Europe, war, famine, pestilence, and typhus fever, as the only instruments in the appointments of Providence for preventing the population of the world from becoming too great for the means of subsistence."[20] At the same time, however, none of the factors which had such detrimental effects upon the European population were seen to be operating with anything approaching the same severity in early nineteenth-century America. Seybert summed up this favorable situation. Not only was food highly abundant, but "few of our citizens are concerned in unhealthy occupations; our towns and cities are not yet so large as to endanger the health of their inhabitants; [and] fatal epidemics have not been very prevalent."[21] In short, barring unforeseen or outside circumstances, the nation's demographic prospect was a bright one.

# *2*

# Demographic Aspects of Early National Expansionism

Far from having to worry about Malthusian food shortages and population pressures, early nineteenth-century white Americans, by and large, were concerned with quite the opposite sorts of questions: how to expand the population, how and where to peddle their food surpluses, what to make of their vast territories. In fact, willy nilly, the United States as a nation was unequivocally expansionist—demographically, economically, and politically. Its families were moving west and south in search of more and better farmland; its ships were fanning out over the seven seas in pursuit of markets; its explorers were mapping the riches of the new territories. Pursuit of these expansionist interests and activities involved outside dangers or challenges, including the threat of war and the perils of disease. Expansionism thus directly stimulated the development of several special kinds of medical-care arrangements as well as mechanisms for measuring the health perils and demographic character of the various movements.

### Medicine in Foreign Trade and Military Preparedness

While the pressures for American expansionism were considerable, the mechanisms of the federal government for guiding and protecting this growth were feeble indeed during most of the time from 1789 up through 1812. This was conspicuously true of the expanding foreign trade. The ministers and consuls who were sent out to foreign countries were few in number, had few resources, and were too far from home to be of much

14

help. However, their reports, along with those of an occasional ship's surgeon, sometimes did provide an inkling of the grave medical problems frequently encountered by American ships at sea and in foreign ports.

The United States consul in Havana, Henry Hill, prepared a list of some 85 American seamen who died in that port of yellow fever between June 1805 and January 1806, and he thought that returns still to come from a few delinquent shipmasters would raise the figure to about 100. That represented, by his estimate, about 1/30th of the American seamen who had visited the port during that period. Attempting to account for this mortality in his report to the Department of State, Hill outlined Havana's environmental circumstances in some detail—its weather, climate, soil, and prevailing diseases—together with the vital statistics of the local population.[1]

Around this same time, in July 1805, William Baldwin arrived at Wampoa, China, as surgeon of the merchant ship *New-Jersey*. There were then eight American ships in the harbor, most or all of which were beset to some extent by what Baldwin identified as remittent and typhus fevers. By September, when the number of ships at anchor had grown to over 20, a serious epidemic was in progress.

Although a number of ships besides the *New-Jersey* also had their own surgeons, these were a minority.[2] The usual practice on merchant ships, whalers, and even small naval vessels, in the event of illness, was for the ships' officers to provide whatever medical care they could, using drugs and equipment in the ships' medicine chests and the simple directions of one of the standard medical manuals for mariners.[3] Baldwin felt that American seamen deserved more than that.

It is to be regretted, that the merchant ships are not more generally furnished with Physicians, especially when it is considered how extensive the trade has become, and how profitable East-India voyages are. If the lives of our seamen are considered of any importance, either in a moral or commercial point of view, some regard ought surely to be extended toward the preservation of their lives, in those climates where diseases are rapid in their progress, and too generally fatal in their termination, without the prompt aid of the Physician.[4]

While this situation improved to some extent over the next several decades, many ships continued to be poorly protected medically. The amount and kind of medical care at sea remained largely a matter of choice for each individual ship. At home, however, there was considerable feeling that the federal government had a responsibility to provide for seamen who were permanently disabled by shipboard accidents or who returned to the United States with serious or persistent ailments. That sentiment crystallized in 1798 in the Act for the Relief of Sick and Disabled Seamen. Under this act, customs collectors at every port began collecting from shipmasters 20¢ for each month that a seaman served, and in 1799 they began collecting also for officers and sailors of the navy. Funds collected went to the Treasury Department, whose officials were made responsible for the medical or custodial care of sick seamen. Such care was provided at first in temporary or contract facilities at various ports, but eventually permanent hospitals were built or purchased at some places. By 1810, Secretary of the Treasury Albert Gallatin, in accounting for the money collected, reported that the government owned two hospitals of its own (Boston and Norfolk), that city hospitals were being utilized for seamen's care in New York, Philadelphia, and New Orleans, that such care was being given in almshouses in Newport and Alexandria, that contract care was provided by a private physician in Baltimore, that funds for care in Charleston were disbursed by city officials, and that in 11 cities sick seamen were boarded in private houses.[5]

Plans for a separate network of hospitals for naval personnel were delayed by the War of 1812. However, beginning in the 1820s and through the nineteenth century, additional government-owned marine and naval hospitals were gradually built in other ports. Some of these were among the largest and most imposing edifices of their communities, often designed and executed in variants of Greek-revival architecture by such architects as Robert Mills, Thomas Haviland, Stephen Long, and William Strickland. In these institutions, as in the gradually emerging civil hospitals, increasingly better records were kept of such things as admissions, maladies, medications, and deaths. Until establishment of central medical bureaus at a considerably later date, both for the naval and the marine hospitals, the full scientific and demographic potential of these medical data could not be tapped, though in a few cases individual surgeons did use the information in local studies.[6]

During the decade before 1812, very few of these facilities were yet available for use in any potential war with France or Great Britain. In fact, the nation was little if any stronger than it had been in 1775. Simply from the point of view of population it was in no condition for armed confrontation with either of these nations. Most Americans had to agree with "Parson" Weems' earthy opinion that the situation could only be bettered by a long-range demographic solution.

> I am very clear that our *Yankee heroes* are made of, at least, as good stuff as any the best of the beef or frog-eating gentry on t'other side of the water. But neither this, nor our fine speeches to our President, nor all his fine speeches to us again, will ever save us from the British gripe or Carmagnole hug, while they can outnumber us, *ten to one!* No, my friends, 'tis population, 'tis *population alone,* can save our bacon.
>
> > List then, ye Bach'lors, and ye Maidens fair
> > If truly you do love your country dear;
> > O' list with rapture to the great decree,
> > Which thus in Genesis you all may see:
> > *"Marry, and raise up soldiers, might and main,"*
> > Then laugh, you may, at England, France, and Spain.[7]

Like other areas of life, American medicine was noticeably affected by the European naval quarantines and impressments which so raised national tensions during these years. If a certain number of American medical students still managed to get to Edinburgh for study, the medical and cultural tours of the continent that had pleased some of their predecessors were now becoming increasingly difficult to arrange.[8] Likewise, just as the European wars and restrictive measures cut immigration to America down to a trickle, part of it composed of refugees, so they reduced the supplies of medical instruments and drugs that arrived.[9] Dr. Thomas Ewell of Washington, D.C., thought it was just as well anyway to reduce dependence on such imports, and he put up prizes amounting to "thirty acres of good land" for suggestions to this end. He offered 10 for the best native substitute for foreign cathartics, and 20 for the best native means to give "tone or strength to debilitated persons without the aid of Peruvian bark, wine, or foreign medicine."[10]

Medical leaders also looked around for literature which could contribute to better preparedness in the profession. Benjamin Rush, whose own 1777 pamphlet, *Directions for Preserving the Health of Soldiers,* was reissued in 1808, thought that Americans could hardly do better than follow the advice in John Pringle's classic work, *Observations on the Diseases of the Army.* Accordingly, he prepared an annotated American edition of that work, which came out just at the beginning of the War of 1812.

Of much more practical utility to Americans just at this time, however, was the volume of *Observations on the Means of Preserving the Health of Soldiers and Sailors,* which was published in 1808 by the naval surgeon Edward Cutbush. In this work, Cutbush provided administrative guidelines for both army and navy medical officers. While he drew to some extent from European works on the handling of diseases by military men, his work in reality was an original manual on the organization and mechanics of running a military medical establishment in the American context. As such, it codified the procedures that had already been instituted in the fledgling American military establishment, but it also suggested a considerable number of additional procedures.

The turn-of-the-century armed forces for which Cutbush wrote this manual were unbelievably small for a country with so much vulnerable land frontier and coastline. The army consisted of a few regiments mustered off and on against the Indians, plus a cluster of tiny garrisons guarding the chief ports. The navy had but a handful of fighting ships and men. The medical personnel who served these forces were so few in number that no special central offices or bureaus were yet deemed necessary to coordinate their activities. However, when the military establishment grew, both the army and navy sought to provide greater uniformity in their medical services and procedures, including their record-keeping and reporting mechanisms. In the post-1800 navy, for instance, when medical personnel were being allocated to the larger fighting ships—frigates of 32 guns or more—the regulations specified that such individuals should keep certain basic medical records and from them compile reports for "the navy-office at the end of every voyage."[11] To facilitate his personal performance of these duties, Surgeon William P. C. Barton introduced the use of printed sick report forms on an 1809 cruise of the frigate *United States.* He also began the practice of submitting semiannual sickness and health reports, feeling that such data were too important to leave unreported until the end of a cruise.[12]

Cutbush's manual aimed at standardizing and expanding such local or individual procedures as these among all medical personnel of the armed forces. Cutbush himself had seen some medical service in both the army and navy, but particularly as chief of the American naval hospital at Syracuse, Sicily, between 1804 and 1806 when that installation was serving this country's Mediterranean squadron. His book thus reflected not a little of the highly developed ideal of hospital orderliness of his French contemporary Philippe Pinel. Cutbush carefully defined the duties of medical personnel at every level so as to enable each "to conduct his business with method and regularity." This meant, among other things, maintaining records and issuing both narrative and statistical reports. In the case of stewards, hospital assistants, apothecaries, and other lower echelons, this included keeping accounts of hospital stores, registers of patients, logs of employees, and the like. In the case of medical officers, it meant supervising this administrative record-keeping, but it also meant keeping clinical data on patients, preparing daily and monthly returns of sickness and mortality, and observing the weather on a regular basis. In the conviction that military surgeons should contribute to the scientific side of medicine as well as the purely clinical, Cutbush proposed that they should be equipped with such instruments as thermometers, pocket compasses, and portable chemical apparatus. Observations made with such equipment, together with the accumulations of clinical and administrative statistics, were expected to make possible valuable medical-topographical and other statistical reports, particularly when numbers of such reports could be correlated in the higher echelons, say, by regimental surgeons or fleet surgeons.[13]

Cutbush's work was well-received by the American medical press. The reviewer in the *Medical Repository* was specifically impressed by Cutbush's proposal to make statistical reporting a normal part of the military surgeon's routine, in other words, to mold the latter in the image or "idea of the man of business." It was particularly gratifying, the reviewer went on, "to see the regular forms of reports and returns, all prepared for the use of beginners in their several stations."[14]

In short, Cutbush provided a detailed blueprint for the orderly conduct of military medical activities, including the carrying on of statistical investigations both in peacetime and in time of war. However, implementation of such a scheme required time, money, and competent personnel. When war finally broke out with England in 1812, only some of its suggestions had yet been adopted, and little money or leisure could be found for the pursuit of others. Moreover, there was as yet only a tiny cadre of regular medical officers that had had any substantial experience in the military medical establishment or any appreciation for its existing record-keeping and reporting requirements.

### Medical Statistics in the War of 1812

For these and other reasons, the medical record of the War of 1812 turned out to be far from complete. Both in hospitals and in the field, reporting of wounds, diseases, and even deaths proved to be a spotty process, whether in the actual heat of battle or in its hectic aftermath. Militia forces were notoriously difficult to control anyway, and many of them failed to appreciate the need of commanders for concrete medical data. At least some seasoned medical regulars, however, did make the effort to supply such information, though many had to fall back upon impressionistic reports.[15] Their meager and scattered accounts were more often summaries of individual episodes than of the collective experience of the military. But they did reflect conditions on various fronts of the war as well as something of the civilian situation.

The outbreak of war found James Tilton, who had been a surgeon during the Revolution, enjoying a placid retirement on his farm near Wilmington, Delaware. In the fall of 1812 he went up to Philadelphia to deliver a paper to the Agricultural Society. Noting the unfortunate reliance of many Americans of his day upon foreign goods and foods, Tilton advocated a return to a simpler way of life, a reliance on purely domestic produce. From a reading of Virgil, he concluded that such a change could be a big step for the nation toward "real independence." And he almost welcomed the effect that war would have in accomplishing this.

> Providence may in compassion to our weakness, by cutting us off from foreign luxuries, oblige us to eat our own better victuals. All good men, like Virgil, will be forward and early in promoting a reformation, equally important in private economy and public policy.[16]

At about that same time, Tilton was preparing advice for his countrymen about their military establishment. In a work which appeared early in 1813, he suggested that certain aspects of military medicine, like American consumer habits, needed simplifying. Some of the medical provisions which had been developed during the Revolution were no longer appropriate, in his estimation. Most conspicuous of these were the great general hospitals, which, by massing large numbers of patients together, seemed rather to breed than to cure disease. In their place, Tilton urged a Spartan regime of hygiene and camp sanitation, with as few general hospitals as possible and with a reliance mainly upon small, well-ventilated regimental infirmaries. He also recommended that authorities take steps throughout the war to gather statistics about all phases of hospital operation and experience. From these he hoped that after the war a scientific analysis of the data could be made to provide later generations with sound recommendations for the most hygienic type of hospital and for the one best adapted to the American environment.[17]

Tilton further recommended that army surgeons simplify their therapeutic procedures by using only such standard medicines as calomel, opium, the bark, wine, and various salts and blisters. Like many of his contemporaries, he personally relied heavily upon calomel (mercury). This drug, he felt, "has the power of subduing all manner of contagion or infection that we are yet acquainted with," and should be indispensible to every military surgeon. But Tilton failed to mention that the drug also had its bad side, one which became evident when it was prescribed with too much enthusiasm and little scientific precision. Even as he wrote, Jabez Heustis was observing one such experience with calomel in Louisiana.

> At New-Orleans, in the year 1812 . . . three companies of the 1st Regiment of Artillery were than stationed at the barracks in that city, of whom a great portion died with the yellow fever, and from the effects of mercury. . . . This *Sampson of the Materia Medica* was not prescribed by the weight and measurement of grains; that would have been feeble and insignificant. . . . It was given to the patient in a cup; and he was directed to eat it by the spoonful, like so much sugar. A fatal surfeit! [Only] a few survived to tell the mournful story.[18]

Shortly after publication of his book, Tilton was chosen surgeon-general of the army. During the war he made some limited attempts to apply his ideas on hospital construction. He also tried to stimulate the collection of hospital and other medical statistics, though he had little leverage to press very hard for such information. Besides, few hospital surgeons were in a position to comply.

James Mann reported that, in most places along the active New York State front at least, medical personnel were kept so busy just taking care of patients "that little time was allowed to record . . . the diseases and medical transactions of the army, as they occurred." Surgeons in Mann's area were swamped by successive epidemics of dysentery and various fevers. These took a heavy toll among their troops, but the surgeons could not often say just how heavy—only that the mortality from these diseases was even worse among the nearby civil population. In the Niagara area Mann found no regular records at all, and even at the large Burlington General Hospital no sick records were kept until the winter of

1813–1814. Subsequently, Mann was able to initiate thorough record-keeping at Burlington as well as at some other posts where he served. He felt that such procedures were essential to the establishment of method and order in military hospitals, though he saw that they would not become very widespread in the American army "until the surgeons feel that a neglect is an abandonment of duty."[19]

In certain commands, where there was little or no action, surgeons had more leisure to collect medical data. The regimental surgeons who served in the harbor defenses of New York were particularly thorough. Their regular reports between April 1813 and June 1815 revealed that there had been 825 admissions to the general hospital and 55 deaths, but that only two amputations had been performed and little other surgery had been needed. Samuel Akerly, who later analyzed the reports, divided the 11,955 cases of sickness which had been reported into six main categories:[20]

| | | | |
|---|---|---|---|
| Intermittent fever | 625 | Dysentery | 1,269 |
| Remittent fever | 1,256 | Diarrhea | 1,945 |
| Typhus fever | 551 | Other diseases | 6,309 |

Naval surgeons as a whole were probably no more consistent in their wartime record-keeping than their army counterparts, and relatively few efforts along this line seem to have been made. In any case, Usher Parsons was able, after the naval Battle of Lake Erie on September 13, 1813, to pull together a rather complete medical report on the entire American squadron of nine vessels and their 600 odd officers and men. On Commodore Perry's flagship, the *Lawrence,* out of 100 men who had reported fit for duty on the morning of that day, 21 were killed in the fierce fighting and 63 were wounded. After the battle, Parsons, the only available surgeon, spent what was left of the first day tying up severed arteries and then managed to administer opiates to all the wounded before dark fell. The next morning beginning at daybreak he performed amputations on the *Lawrence* until about 11:00 A.M., and then, working until midnight, he operated on the other wounds in descending order of their severity. The following day he took care of the wounded from the rest of the ships. When things settled down, in a few days, Parsons jotted down the figures for the whole squadron:[21]

| | | | |
|---|---|---|---|
| Compound fractures | 25 | Concussions of brain | 2 |
| Simple fractures | 4 | Concussions of chest | 3 |

| | | | |
|---|---|---|---|
| Grape shot wounds | 3 | Concussions of pelvis | 2 |
| Cannister wounds | 4 | Contusions | 10 |
| Splinter and lacerated wounds | 37 | Sprains | 6 |

A different order of war experience was reflected in the records of the naval surgeon William Baldwin. At his post in St. Mary's, Georgia, Baldwin for over two years treated the diseases and repaired the wounds of personnel of the small flotilla which operated along the southern coast. As part of his work routine, Baldwin made a point of faithfully maintaining a register of weather observations and one of the incidence of diseases. He even found time to make an occasional trip up the St. Mary's river in search of botanical specimens. Then, between sick calls, tropical storms, and enemy alarms, he classified the specimens he had gathered and bundled them into packets for his Pennsylvania correspondent, the botanist Henry Muhlenberg. Throughout the war, despite the uncertainties of mail sent by sea on coastal schooners and the equal uncertainties of receiving anything sent by stage, Baldwin and Muhlenberg continued a warm and mutually useful correspondence, each man making a conscious effort to keep the spirit of scientific inquiry alive in the midst of the difficult times.[22]

The American medical profession paused momentarily, early in the war, to pay its last respects to Benjamin Rush. Its nonmilitary members then hurried back to join their neighbors in the digging of local defenses or in treating civilian diseases. In the winter of 1812–1813, physicians in the northern states were beleaguered by a severe pneumonia epidemic which spread both among civilians and soldiers. Samuel Latham Mitchill, laboring to keep the *Medical Repository* going during wartime, obtained and published accounts of the epidemic from medical men in many communities, especially the hard-hit areas of upstate New York.[23] Mitchill also kept active during the war with his service in Congress, by work on a commission to develop a steam warship and by occasional sanitary inspections of camps. Late in the war, with something of the same historical approach to war that characterized Tilton, he wrote to James Monroe, then secretary of war, recommending that the latter read a seventeenth-century work on military medicine by the Italian Luca Porzio.[24]

In Baltimore, *Niles' Register* published weekly lists of the prizes captured by United States ships. It also reported on blacks who had been stolen by marauding British troops and sent by ship to the West Indies or elsewhere. Of an early batch sent to Halifax, 30 out of 300 blacks were said to have died en route, while the remainder arrived ill and in poor physical condition.

Some writers in this periodical were concerned with the failure of New England to support the war, though particularly with extremists of that region who were advocating armed resistance to the war or political secession. One correspondent thought that such seditious proposals could perhaps be handled by exposing the disloyal to one or another of man's most loathsome diseases. "Frenzy to the brain that shall plot to dismember, and leprosy to the arm that will not draw to defend, the union."[25] There was no doubt, as Benjamin Waterhouse discovered, that as a body New England physicians, as well as their patients, felt little taste for the war. At the same time, like doctors from other sections of the country, they resented the condescension toward things American which British writers often continued to display. Even in 1812, New England hackles were being raised by the allegation of the *London Medical Review* that America generally, and Massachusetts specifically, "seems to be the country of epidemics, as much as it is of swamps, woods, and savannahs." One physician felt it necessary to reply in kind, that England "seems to be the country of scrophula and consumption, as much as it is of fogs and vapours." He went on to marshal two pages of statistics to prove that America had a healthier climate and had fewer diseases than not only Great Britain but any European country.[26]

This moderate protest was aimed against the indiscretions of an individual Englishman. Other statistics, had they been compiled, would doubtless have revealed that throughout the conflict, by and large, New Englanders remained sympathetic to Great Britain—certainly those who were proved to be so vocal as to make life uncomfortable for supporters of the war, so much so that not a few were forced to leave the region. The editor of *Niles' Register* noted that the establishment of the New England Emigration Society just at the end of the war, to promote settlement in the West, was one of the bitter reactions to this oppressive Anglophilia which pervaded Boston.

> In the language of Jonathan Russell, "It is the pestilential atmosphere of British influence from which they flee." And may they, in their new habitations, find that perfect ease, freedom, and real independence which was denied them in the places of their nativity.[27]

The end of hostilities released this and a great many other demographic energies. It triggered a new burst of native enterprise, commerce, and manufactures. It reopened American ports to European immigration. It brought the inhabitants of all eastern states a new freedom to migrate to the West. And it liberated white Americans to resume the process of exploiting the vast continent, a process in which the native Indian population was painfully involved.

## The Demography of the Vanishing Red Man

While many early nineteenth-century whites, especially those along the frontier, frankly subscribed to the view that "the only good Indian is a dead one," others, particularly if they lived safely back of the frontier, held more tolerant and humane attitudes about the Indians' existence. Both kinds of whites contributed to nineteenth-century society's store of data pertaining to the Indian population. And all could agree that this was a race that had been overtaken by demographic catastrophe. The exact, far-reaching nature of some of the most fundamental causes of this catastrophe were not yet understood—particularly the insidious spread of pathogenic organisms, brought from the Old World and distributed among nonimmune populations. However, the broad outlines of what was happening were all too evident.[28]

It had become clear to American whites long before 1800 that the Indians around them were declining in devastatingly large numbers. Throughout the eighteenth century, observers often considered the decline, from a religious perspective, as a literal instance of the "perishing heathen." As late as 1792, in fact, Jedidiah Morse thought he detected "the hand of Providence . . . in these surprising instances of mortality, among the Indians, to make way for the English. Comparatively few have perished by wars. They waste and moulder away—they, in a manner unaccountable, disappear."[29] During the nineteenth century, whatever the role of providence, the process continued, most probably at an accelerated rate. However, even if the pace of the decline was no greater than it had been before, it at least seemed so, because more people paid systematic attention to the phenomenon.

After 1800, more observers were also becoming aware that the decline was directly related to the whites' relentless grab for land. And they knew that the Indians' losses in battle were only parts of the story. Even more significant were the population pressures which followed the battles, pressures so prompt and so intense as literally to squeeze out the various Indian tribes from their lands. The French traveller Alexis de Tocqueville concisely summed up the current common perception of what was going on. ''Not only have these wild tribes receded, but they are destroyed; and as they give way or perish, an immense and increasing people fill their place. There is no instance upon record of so prodigious a growth or so rapid a destruction.''[30]

The Indians' plight, of course, stimulated much romantic sympathy, some curiosity among intellectuals and scientists, and some largely ineffective efforts among politicians and church groups at reversing the tide of history. From all this a good many inquiries into Indian life and culture resulted. In the process, a considerable mass of statistical data documenting the Indians' decline accumulated, including some on the diseases which substantially caused and hastened the decline.

By 1800, except for an occasional depraved individual living in poverty on the edge of the white man's towns, the northeastern Indians had all died off, been killed, or been removed to a few small reservations.[31] During the next few decades most of the other tribes east of the Mississippi, most of which were in the South, went through similar experiences, including that of removal. Wherever they occurred, removals were brutal and tragic occurrences which directly affected the mortality and decline of specific tribes.

Both east and west of the Mississippi, the nineteenth-century aspects of decline were observed and frequently recorded by traders, government agents, army physicians, and missionaries, as well as by a sprinkling of explorers, scientists, and miscellaneous travellers who roamed across the opening territories. The painter George Catlin spent eight years among the Indians of the upper Missouri and Rockies area in order to prepare a pictorial record of the dying race. James Fenimore Cooper drew up a very similar record in literary form. Army surgeon Edwin James participated in the effort at civilizing the Indians by translating the Bible and writing grammars and spelling books for them. And the Indian agent and scientist Henry R. Schoolcraft began systematic attempts not only to preserve the legends, manners, languages, and history of the Indians, but to accumulate detailed statistics of their current state.

Not a few Americans felt, during the 1820s, at least before accounts came back of some of the disastrous removals, that the federal government's plan to remove eastern tribes to permanent western lands was not only rational but humane and favorable to the Indians. Cooper, for one, thought that if the plan were successful, ''there is reason to think that the constant diminution in the numbers of the Indians will be checked, and that a race, about whom there is so much that is poetic and fine in recollection, will be preserved.''[32] However, the clergymen Jedidiah Morse and Timothy Dwight thought that the removal process could not ensure the Indians with a promising future unless it included adequate funding and other provisions for fully civilizing them. In fact, Morse felt that a biological step would also be necessary.

> Let the Indians . . . be taught all branches of knowledge pertaining to civilized man; *then* let intermarriage with them become general, and the end which the Government has in view will be completely attained. They would then be literally of one blood with us, be merged in the nation, and saved from extinction.[33]

Charles Caldwell, a physician who considered that most attempts to civilize the Indian were only making his plight worse, thought there was some merit in Morse's proposal. But extensive racial intermarriage was no more realistic a proposal in 1830 than it had been in the colonial era, when suggestions to this effect had been advanced by such prominent spokesmen as Robert Beverly and William Byrd. Tocqueville contrasted the French of North America, who ''were not slow in connecting with the daughters of the natives,'' with the Englishman, who had ''avoided with care the union of his race'' with the Indians. White Americans seemed to have retained much of the aversion of their British forebears in this respect.[34]

Observers who lived in America's frontier areas acquired considerable insight into the disease conditions which were contributing both to the Indians' immediate misery and mortality and to their long-term demographic plight. Only a scattered few of their observations, however, made their way into either the general or the medical press. The Moravian missionary John Heckewelder, mapper of the Western Reserve and informant of Benjamin Barton as to the habits of the Indian, noted that Indians of the Midwest did not always suffer from epidemics which decimated nearby white settlements, and that they never seemed to be bothered by the ''itch.'' But other diseases, such as whooping cough, which were not usually serious for whites, were frequently ''destructive'' to Indians, particularly the children. At Onondaga, New York, the early settler and salt merchant James Geddes noticed that the local Indians decreased from 133 to 105 between 1795 and 1798, and he attributed most of their deaths to ''phthisis pulmonalis.''[35] Chief Joseph Brant told the Baptist missionary Elkanah Holmes that what he called yellow fever had been one of the most deadly diseases for the Iroquois around the turn of the century.[36]

No malady seemed to contribute more directly to the decline of the Indian than smallpox. Colonel William A. Trimble, in a report to Secretary of War John C. Calhoun, related that the Comanches had lost 4,000 from this disease in 1816 alone, and he urged Calhoun to introduce vaccination among them, a course he felt to be "dictated by humanity." Some straggling tribes that Trimble found along the Red River were already "nearly extinct," apparently from the same cause.[37] Comparable mortality from smallpox occurred among other tribes during these decades. Dr. John Barnes of St. Louis summarized the results of a particularly devastating onslaught in 1837 and 1838 throughout the upper Mississippi and Missouri basins. "The Pawnees lost about one-half of their nation. The Ponchas lost two-thirds, and the Omahas, Ottoes, Missourias and Kansas lost at least half of their people. The disease raged with the most desolating effects amongst the Assineboines, the Blackfeet and other tribes," while the Mandan tribe of over 2,000 died almost to a man.[38]

Such epidemic figures, as well as much other information about the Indian population, were mostly based on the wildest sorts of estimates. Like their colonial forefathers, nineteenth-century Americans rarely had anything more than a vague impression of just how many Indians there were at any point in time. Government agents could and sometimes did make rather accurate enumerations of Indians in or around given reservations, and army officers occasionally did the same at posts where tribes congregated. But it was difficult to determine anything very concrete about the strength of the nomadic tribes who remained separate from whites. Since the federal census specifically excluded Indians "not taxed" from its enumerations, statistical compilers like Adam Seybert had to rely on the often impressionistic published reports of explorers, missionaries, and travellers. This resulted in some wide differences in the overall estimates of Indian population. Volney thought in 1798 that there were around 39,000 Indians left east of the Mississippi and perhaps 600,000 more in the rest of North America. In 1836, Albert Gallatin estimated a total of 345,000 for the United States and Canada, including Eskimos, but Cooper felt there could not be over 120,000 within the boundaries of the United States. At about this same time, however, George Catlin plucked the grand figure of 1,400,000 from somewhere.[39]

It was generally conceded that since 1600 smallpox had accounted for roughly half of the total Indian deaths and was the chief factor in their numerical decline. No attempts seem to have been made to estimate the deaths from other diseases which had originally been European or African. Analysts simply tended to agree with Catlin that "the sword, the bayonet, and whiskey" had been responsible for most of the remaining half of the decline, though not everyone listed these agents in the same order of importance.[40] In any case, few humane observers of the nineteenth century could see any real prospect of reversing the devastating mortality trend. Any shift of national policy which might effectively insulate the Indian from the whites and ensure large areas of hunting lands to the former in perpetuity was clearly chimerical. And relatively few thought that the Protestant missions to the various tribes could either civilize the Indians or shelter them enough to prevent their eventual extinction.[41]

## Army Medical Officers as Demographic Monitors beyond the Frontier

Second to none in their observations of the Indians' rapid decline as a race were the army medical officers. In fact, these physicians were uniquely placed to observe and specially qualified to record virtually all of the varied kinds of human events which occurred outside of the moving boundaries of the white man's civilization.

Despite the obvious importance of ensuring proper medical care, the early nineteenth-century army for a considerable time lacked the number of medical officers it needed, even for the expeditions which set out to explore the trans-Mississippi West. Neither the Lewis and Clark nor the Pike expeditions, for instance, made provision for physicians among their complements, though a St. Louis doctor went along on Pike's second expedition as a volunteer. In the case of the former, both Lewis and Clark were sufficiently trained in practical medicine to treat most of the needs of their personnel. They had, moreover, been well briefed by Benjamin Rush in the types of medical information to look out for, while Jefferson himself specified other kinds of data that he wanted. It is true that, had the expedition included a physician, its reports might well have been fuller in demographic and medical-topographical details. Still, even as it was, the two leaders did bring back important facts about the population and health of given Indian tribes, together with some information about aboriginal diseases and remedies.[42] The reviewer in the *Medical Repository* found that Pike's reports were similarly valuable for their enumerations of Indian tribes and for illumination of the physical geography of Louisiana. But he was disappointed in the paucity of their information about the area's natural history.[43]

An example of the medical-demographic role that an energetic and curious army physician could play was furnished, early in the century, by Jabez Heustis. During extended military service in lower Louisiana, Heustis seems to have been faithful in keeping the required official medical reports for his detachment. In addition, however, he gathered information on the topography, population, botany, agriculture, and other aspects of the region, information he assumed might have some relation to the incidence of disease. When, in 1817, he published an account of this Louisiana service, Heustis found it necessary to sound a warning to would-be settlers and travellers as to the heroic diseases and terrible mortality they could expect to encounter throughout the lower Mississippi basin. He also advised American physicians not to rely on British accounts for authoritative medical information about this area, since the latter tended to be based on medical experiences in other countries. In fact, making one's own original medical and scientific observations constituted a superb opportunity for the American doctor to assert his independence from Europe. Besides, the United States provided unexcelled opportunities for such observations.

> It is here that he will find a greater variety of disorders, with their characteristic features more strongly marked, than in any other country. . . . Truth tells us, in spite of our forbearance [i.e., deference to Europe], that there is greater originality of genius, a more ample scope for observation, and a more extensive and better field for improvement in the United States, than in any other portion of the world.[44]

Within a year or so of this publication, steps were initiated which aimed at producing more army medical observers in the mold of Heustis. These steps represented, at long last, the realization of various of the recommendations of Cutbush and Tilton for better army medical administration. When the army was reorganized in 1818, a permanent central medical department was established and placed under Surgeon-General Joseph Lovell. Lovell standardized the varied medical record-keeping functions and arranged for field medical officers to send detailed sickness, mortality, and other reports to Washington on a regular basis.

Thus centralized, the statistics of the army's medical experience could eventually be effectively studied for scientific and administrative purposes.[45] This is not to say that all of the army's surgeons automatically became good record-keepers. Tobias Watkins, an inspector of this period, concluded that some individuals seemed to be constitutionally negligent of such matters, while others lacked the training to appreciate the need for statistical reports. Even so, he thought that a majority seemed to be maintaining reasonably good sick registers and other records.[46]

From 1820 on, most of the military medical officers were widely dispersed in a far-from-stationary necklace of tiny garrisons which stretched around the periphery of the United States. Starting at the Atlantic seaboard, the posts circled the shores of the Great Lakes, extended out into the prairies, and looped back along the Gulf of Mexico and to the southeast. At these posts, the medical officers administered to the sick and wounded at small infirmaries or hospitals and, in areas where there were hostilities, they sometimes accompanied the troops out on field expeditions. Along with their periodic reports, they sometimes sent accounts of their more interesting medical cases and therapies back to Washington. Few of these accounts proved to be as scientifically significant as Surgeon William Beaumont's observations beginning in the 1820s on the digestive system of Alexis St. Martin. But some others, such as J. H. Bill's midcentury analysis of the incidence, effects, and care of arrow wounds, had much practical interest at the time.[47]

Some army medical officers occupied their free time with scientific pursuits, notably the making of botanical, ornithological, or geological collections, which ultimately often went to the Smithsonian Institution or to such scientists as Agassiz and Ehrenberg. In addition, however, all of the physicians were requested to make as careful and extensive observations as possible of the geography, resources, and surroundings of their posts and to report upon them periodically. The accounts which went to Washington thus often included firsthand observations of the Indians, their customs, diseases, and rapidly declining numbers. Some included comments on the condition of the scattered Mexican populations of the southwestern territories. Many noted the instreaming whites from the East: "adventurers" flocking into Lake Superior country in 1845 with the discovery of copper; a sprinkling of squatters near Astoria in 1852; trains of emigrants passing Forts Riley, Dodge, Kearney, and Laramie, often riddled with diarrheas, fevers, and suffering from exposure, if not also cholera.[48]

Assistant Surgeon Roberts Bartholow, accompanying the 10th Infantry out of Fort Leavenworth bound for Utah in 1857, watched his own force of 629 shrink by nearly 100 during the first week of marching, mainly because of the three D's—desertion, disease, and drunkenness. But, "when whiskey and civilization were left behind," the regiment quickly became a healthy and effective fighting force. Later, during a year spent in Utah Territory, Bartholow sent back reports about the half-wild mountain traders, the debased nomadic Indians, and especially the exotic Mormon colony, whose practices were proving so scandalous to other Americans.[49]

Among the western troops served by Bartholow and other medical officers, relatively little of the overall sickness and injury was incurred in actual combat against the Indians. Some resulted from long and fatiguing marches. Even more occurred during tedious periods of duty at garrisons which were often in insalubrious locations. Troops that were not sick seemed to be constantly digging drainage ditches, cutting trees, erecting barracks, and performing other laborious tasks associated with the establishment of posts that all too often were only temporary. Frequently, garrisons were occupied only a few months before they were abandoned and the troops sent farther west to start all over. Surgeon-General Lawson in 1850 noted this continuing process of relocation, one that was necessitated primarily by the rapid western thrust of population.

> A comparatively short period of time places the outpost in the midst of a population dense and far advanced in civilization, and its garrison is then removed to some other point where protection of frontier settlers is more imperatively required. Thus our posts have gradually moved further and further west.[50]

As the military garrisons moved steadily westward, their uneven line marked the ever-receding divide between white civilization and what that generation of whites regarded as barbarism. With every forward thrust of the trans-Mississippi frontier, the troops moved on ahead of settlement. Some safeguarded the population movements into the Southwest; Texas alone had large problems of surveillance after achieving statehood in 1845. Posts in Missouri, Kansas, and Nebraska, in turn, provided the policing of the trails to Oregon and California. And, with the discovery of gold at Sutter's Mill, these troops saw the westward emigrant stream become a flood.

# 3

---

# Medical Geography of a Growing Nation

The army's medical officers made their observations of population movements, as well as of the health of the troops in their garrisons, within the framework of a vast and overarching physical environment that could not be ignored. Sometimes they could perceive the promise of almost endless bounty and wealth in the environment; equally often they noted aspects that were harsh and menacing. In any case, all nineteenth-century Americans, military and civilian alike, who moved into and helped open up new lands went through more or less extensive and some-times harrowing periods of adjusting to, coping with, or defending themselves against that environment. Civilians had to go through these processes even as they were engaged in trying to establish the social, political, economic, cultural, and medical institutions of their new communities. Accordingly, they felt a very practical need, from an early stage, to find out all they could about the physical characteristics of the enormous territories into which they had moved. Fairly early in the nineteenth century, therefore, systematic scientific inquiries were started which aimed at filling out, confirming, or refuting the sketchy informa-tion contained in the reports of the original explorers on such matters as the nature and quality of the soil, the location and extent of mineral resources, the kinds and peculiarities of the local flora and fauna, the patterns of climate and weather.

One of the large and crucial matters that nineteenth-century people felt needed investigation was the influence of the physical environment upon the populations in it. Migrants invariably wanted to learn in advance all they could about the salubrity of the sites where they planned to settle.

And, as soon as they had settled in, each one began, consciously or unconsciously, to evaluate his new homesite in terms of its healthfulness. The historian may suppose that extended personal or family sickness in the first months after arrival in a given location, or a marked excess of disease among one's neighbors, led many a family to move on again quickly in hopes of finding a more healthful site elsewhere.

The conventional wisdom about "seasoning," of course, tended to regard it as useless to uproot oneself for such a reason, because, in its early period of coexistence with nature, almost any new settlement was thought likely to prove unhealthful. Yale's Timothy Dwight, after his tour across the wilderness of central New York State before the War of 1812, extended this common view into a three-stage theory of salubrity and settlement. "While the country is entirely forested, it is ordinarily healthy. While it is passing from this state into that of general cultivation, it is usually less healthy." Only with an eventual substantial advancement of agriculture, settlement, and civilization could any important return toward the original level of salubrity be expected.[1]

During the six or eight decades prior to the Civil War, a large portion of the area of the United States was in the process of being changed from the first and into the second, more or less unhealthful, stage. And, during this time, the medical profession acted upon the assumption that much of the ill health, particularly that arising from infectious diseases, was an expected result of the basic demographic-environmental interaction. In fact, throughout the period, in this country as well as in Europe, the premises of medical geography and topography were firmly entrenched in medical thinking and practice. A large proportion of the profession endorsed the neo-Hippocratic position that a close causal relationship existed between health and disease and the varied phenomena of the physical environment. But the details of this relationship were still obscure. It was accepted that a major collective effort was needed, on the part of physicians throughout the civilized world, before the peculiar characteristics of geography and topography, rocks and waters, climate and weather—characteristics that presumably contributed or gave rise to disease—could be ferreted out and understood.

Physicians who had the time and inclination thus considered it a natural part of their professional duties to make more or less extensive observations of these phenomena. Those who did so usually kept some records of the occurrences, and a fair number managed to compare the accumulated data with figures pertaining to the diseases they treated or with the vital statistics of the community. Well before the War of 1812, state medical societies in Massachusetts, South Carolina, and New York were encouraging their members and constituent societies to conduct such inquiries. And editors of the new medical journals devoted much space to the findings.[2] Subsequently, medical geography and topography acquired progressively greater status in an age when most of the therapeutic efforts of the medical profession were in disrepute.

Medical-environmental surveying thus became an important phase of a nationwide impulse to lay bare the rich and varied characteristics of the great land. Jacksonian America became, in fact, a veritable anthill of busy investigators criss-crossing the country in the conduct of their multitudinous surveys. Army explorers and mappers fanned out farther and farther to establish bases for new territorial claims. Canal and railroad surveyors probed valleys and mountain passes to determine routes for new lines. Botanists spread their nets even farther in their searches for specimens. Geological surveys, launched by a few states as early as the mid-1820s, were eventually undertaken in other places. Surveys of agriculture were about as numerous. By the late 1830s, the New York State legislature was supporting a comprehensive survey of the state's natural history, including zoology, mineralogy, geology, agriculture, and botany.

The nineteenth-century physicians who conducted medical-topographical inquiries were aided considerably by some of these other surveys. They were also beneficiaries of progressively more sophisticated information on environmental subjects that was appearing in European scholarly publications. At the same time, occasional visits to America by European geographers, climatologists, and other scientists—notably the great Humboldt—stimulated much enthusiasm on this side of the Atlantic. Meanwhile, improved scientific tools steadily became available for sorting out and measuring the various environmental factors. With such developments came a demand for greater systematization of information about environmental matters, including broadening and coordinating the network of inquiries devoted to obtaining that information. Accordingly, as medical-topographical studies incorporated increasing amounts of the new scientific findings, especially the improved data of geology and meteorology, they were regarded as increasingly valuable sources of health information.

## Rocks, Soils, and Diseases

Early nineteenth-century physicians readily agreed with Daniel Drake that "the medical history* of a country can never be properly written before its geological constitution is known."[3] However, concrete facts about the health role of America's geological and topographical features were hard to obtain. Charles Caldwell felt in 1801 that there was "perhaps no subject, on which medical records are so completely barren as that of the topography of large cities."[4]

In 1797 Samuel Latham Mitchill, in the course of surveying the geology and mineral resources of New York State, hypothesized that there was some sort of relationship between the different kinds of soils or rock strata of a region and the "septic exhalations" which he supposed were the causes of fevers and epidemic diseases. Mitchill did not offer any specifics; in fact, he really did not go beyond the conventional European wisdom of the day.[5] Nevertheless, his assumptions were readily taken over by many of the next generation of American physicians.[6]

Actually, Mitchill's ideas about geology and health seemed to be borne out by numerous simple empirical observations. A number of observers pointed out the value of digging drainage ditches deep enough to allow surface water to percolate through various soil and rock strata as a measure to reduce malaria and other "country" fevers. J. B. Hiester was positive that in Pennsylvania certain epidemics, such as dysentery, "were defined with great sharpness by the different strata." And a midwestern doctor concluded from talking with a few farmers that the black slate of Kentucky was "the favorite abode" of fever and ague.[7] Hiester also thought that long residence in dwellings located over certain geological formations might affect longevity of the occupants to the degree that their bodies absorbed certain inorganic substances or failed to take in others. In turn, Edmund Ravenel of Charleston suggested the operation of a vague "radiation" from rock strata which allegedly affected the disease miasmata in the atmosphere.[8]

More specific and much more extensive was a study of calculous diseases in Ohio. In 1850, a medical committee noted that the state was almost equally divided between limestone areas in the west and sandstone or coal areas in the east. On the basis of reports on about half of the state's population, the committee found a "striking preponderance of

---

* The term *medical history,* as Drake used it here, meant "medical profile," or "medical characteristics."

calculous diseases in the limestone region," that is, an incidence of 1 in 60,000 persons there compared with 1 in 238,000 in the eastern region.[9]

Not a few physicians, of whom Charles T. Jackson was one of the best known, were convinced that cholera was both more prevalent and more virulent where limestone was the surface rock than where granite or other rocks predominated. Jackson, armed with only a mortality report from Sandusky, Ohio, as evidence, tried to get the 1849 meeting of the American Association for the Advancement of Science to endorse this view. But Louis Agassiz refused to get into a debate over it, and John C. Warren dryly pointed out that verification of such a hypothesis "required a great number of facts carefully observed and clearly expressed."[10]

To obtain such facts, many looked to coordinated state medical-topographical surveys. It was appreciated, however, that to be useful such surveys would not only have to be performed well in all areas but also be carried out periodically, say every 10 years. In 1830 the Medical Society of the State of New York asked all county medical societies to update their old surveys. Its circular that year, in addition to quantitative questions as to diseases, therapies, diet, native plants, education, and the like, called for expanded data on such matters as geographical boundaries, latitude and longitude, rivers and mountains, agricultural characteristics, rock formations, the nature of the soil, weather, and climate.[11] Going further, the state medical society of Pennsylvania in 1851 urged county societies to consult the results of geological surveys before proceeding with their overall topographical surveys. However, few of those bodies went very far along this line.[12]

From time to time, the rural diseases that were associated with topographical features prompted some kind of control efforts. Physicians in coastal regions of Georgia, alarmed by fevers which went along with rice cultivation, tried in vain to get planters to switch to corn and similar grains that did not require swampy fields. In Saratoga County, New York, when certain highly malignant fevers were traced to newly constructed mill dams, court actions of private citizens "finally induced the owners to open their dams and draw off the water during the sickly months." Everywhere, land drainage was pushed as a practical step toward better community health.[13]

Urban health reformers of this period considered it essential to make themselves knowledgeable about the geological peculiarities of their communities. One of their worries was the unhealthful saturation of the soil within cities, brought about by concentrations of liquid filth from outhouses, cesspools, and kitchens. Sanitary inspectors were increasingly utilized to map the offending conditions in tenement districts and other areas of cities, and to note their proximity to sources of drinking water. Health officers, in turn, attempted to improve their ability to account for the excesses of epidemic disease by identifying the peculiar underlying rock formations which could assist or hinder the dispersal of liquid filth and the presumed spread of miasma. Such information formed a direct basis for cleanup activities and other sanitary action.

City cleanups, rural drainage projects, and other internal improvements were eventually launched at least partly on the strength of disease patterns revealed or confirmed by local bills of mortality. Fully as much as local physicians and officials, the architects and engineers who often directed these projects—men such as Thomas Bulfinch, Benjamin Latrobe, and Robert Mills—keenly appreciated the statistical equation between their improvements and the good health of the respective communities. Mills, who subsequently compiled a general statistical survey of the state of South Carolina, emphasized that systematic drainage, by improving health and opening more land to cultivation at the same time, would help the state to "realize immense wealth and prosperity."[14]

Those attempting to measure the effects of such enterprises on health, however, by and large had to rely on rule-of-thumb methods and spotty data. Not that people did not know better. Throughout the period, informed individuals had recognized that such measurement could be carried out only by a continuing process of gathering vital statistics, medical figures, *and* environmental data year after year in regular form. Only in this methodical way, concluded the geographer Jedidiah Morse, as early as 1798, could one expect to obtain an accurate view of "the natural increase of inhabitants, the comparative healthfulness of the several towns and larger districts . . . and, in general, the probability of the continuance of life in the several states."[15] Still, it was long after the Civil War before some of these kinds of data, particularly the vital statistics, became full or accurate enough in most communities to help such studies along very much. And by then most physicians had long since grown skeptical of there being any very close etiological relationship between environment and disease.

For want of this sort of coordinated data-gathering, America's quantitative studies of the hygienic aspects of geological phenomena remained few and superficial at midcentury. This was also true in most other countries. In fact, the fruitful pursuit of environmental studies depended not only upon comprehensive field observations and statistics, but also on laboratory work in medical chemistry, physiology, mineralogy, and other areas. In Bavaria, Max von Pettenkofer's many-faceted studies along such lines were just beginning and had little if any effect in the United States until after the Civil War. Here, university departments, laboratories, or institutes where environmental elements in hygiene could be examined in this systematic way were several decades away. In the meantime, Americans could devote their energies to studying other aspects of the medical environment for which they were better equipped.

### Meteorological Facts and Medical Ideas

Of these, few offered such hopeful prospects of yielding medically useful results as did inquiries into the weather, climate, and atmospheric conditions. Early nineteenth-century physicians, scientists, and other observers almost universally believed that these conditions had very significant effects on health; it only remained for the secret workings of these relationships to be discovered.[16] Moreover, the pursuit of such inquiries appeared to be eminently feasible in terms of the current state of American technology, education, and science.

In impressive numbers, post-Revolutionary naturalists, preachers, teachers, and others kept personal weather records on a more or less regular basis, and increasingly they began to use instruments. Physicians were particularly active in carrying on such activities. Observers noticed that one of the first things many a physician did upon moving to a new town during these years was to start a weather register.[17] In Harrisburg, Pennsylvania, these earliest fragmentary weather records of doctors were earnestly compared with mortuary records for evidence that the town was a salubrious and desirable site for the state capital.[18] Normally, such a physician would take thermometric readings twice during the day and once at night, sometimes using both indoor and outdoor instruments. Along with these he generally also made a note of wind direction, cloud conditions, and precipitation.

At first, few observers of this period had any instruments beyond their thermometers and pencils. In fact, in 1814, when Surgeon-General Tilton decided to have meteorological records kept throughout the army, many of his medical officers had not yet been supplied even with thermometers.[19] Well before this, however, some fortunate observers had barometers, hygrometers, pluviometers, and eudiometers. A few, such as Garrett Pendergrast and John Shecut, used these or other devices in modest experiments on the health effects of atmospheric conditions.[20]

Since actual meteorological experimentation of any kind was still so scant in this country, editors of early medical, agricultural, and other journals were usually satisfied just to publish the simple weather diaries sent in by their readers. Yet, most were well aware that the medical and scientific value of the diaries was enhanced whenever the raw data were presented in a more or less systematic manner. Felix Pascalis of Philadelphia pointed out that environmental causes of yellow fever and other diseases could be effectively demonstrated by preparing "atmizological" tables—numerical tables of exhalations or other causes of prevalent septic gases—"as we do for the common meteorological observations." But Pascalis himself could not resolve the problem of determining gradations of the exhalations, since "the results of the hygrometer cannot be applied to these observations."[21] Moreover, few if any Americans before the 1820s actually went to any statistical lengths with such data. An exception was John Redman Coxe, editor of the *Philadelphia Medical Museum,* who in 1804 prepared his own thermometric and barometric observations in tables "formed, with considerable trouble, on the plan of the ingenious Professor Playfair."[22]

The keeping of meteorological observations may well have outdistanced the maintenance of either private or public mortality registers throughout the period. Sometimes meteorological data were published alongside the bills of mortality in medical publications and sometimes separately in the daily press or in scientific or commercial journals. Occasionally the same individuals who kept weather registers also gathered the mortality data of their communities.

In any case, physicians, scientists, and others of this prebacteriological period increasingly looked to the cumulations of both vital and meteorological data for their insight into the salubrity of any given place. By the 1840s it had become a prime objective of a variety of groups to improve the mechanisms for registering both kinds of data. Franklin Tuthill of New York, explaining the medical view, observed that together these observations "will enable the sanitary philosopher to learn the law that governs the waste of human life, perhaps arm him to drag to light the hidden causes of the mortality of our cities, and to some extent to stay the fearful progress of our epidemics." Thorough vital-statistics registration would provide "a map of the fatal diseases" of the community, while meteorological data would furnish "a map of the atmospheric phenomena" accompanying the diseases. Using these two sources of data together, the health officer would be better enabled to forecast disease and pinpoint with some precision the unhealthy areas of his community.[23]

Daniel Drake thought that the country's climate and atmospheric influences would be revealed in short order if all of its medical students could be marshalled to perform meteorological observations in their spare time. Science, of course, would be greatly advanced thereby. But in addition, such observations could have a beneficial effect on the professional formation of such students. Meteorology leads them, Drake asserted, "to notice the beautiful phenomena of the atmosphere, and to remark upon the influence of the various atmospheric changes on health; it promotes habits of observation, incites to punctuality, and last, though not least, makes them early risers."[24]

No concerted gatherings of meteorological observations by medical students materialized; in fact, medical schools did not provide formal instruction on the subject.[25] Nevertheless, meteorology became ever more conspicuous as an adjunct of medicine. Medical societies continued to encourage systematic observation of the weather, while by the 1840s medical staff members were making such observation a regular part of the routine activity in hospitals and health offices. Censuses and city health reports increasingly included analyses of meteorological data for the various seasons along with those of mortality data.[26] The better-read of the physician-observers, men who were influenced by the scientific language and method of Humboldt, were also beginning to draw tentative isothermal and isotheral lines across the map of the United States; to calculate the arithmetic means of temperature, wind, or rainfall for given localities; and especially, from their mortality registers and case records, to plot the statistical incidence of diseases in their geographic and climatic settings.[27]

One such attempt to test the weather-disease connection on a limited scale took place in St. Louis, where the naturalist-physician George Engelmann had begun keeping regular meteorological observations in 1836, soon after his arrival in this country. Within a few years, like observers everywhere, Engelmann was publishing his observations in local newspapers and medical journals. And in 1853 he made a systematic examination of 17 years of data in their relation to the amount of sickness he had treated during those years.

Engelmann's purpose at this time was a simple one, to test statistically some of the common rural and folk beliefs about the relations of weather and sickness. To do this he vowed to abandon the "winding and flowery pathway of theory" and confine himself to a tabular arrangement of facts which he felt would lead to "unavoidable deductions." When he interpreted his collected data on the sickness he had treated in the summer months, a number of popular maxims did indeed seem to be substantiated. Among these were:

> A wet summer is a healthy summer.
> A wet fall is a healthy fall.
> A dry and hot summer is a sickly summer.
> A dry fall, whether warm or cool, is a sickly fall.
> A wet summer and dry fall combined make the most sickly fall.

Englemann recognized that there was a risk in generalizing from a single physician's observations. Nevertheless, he was convinced that, even if his figures "do not give the exact mathematical truth, they come sufficiently near it to make them proper elements in this investigation."[28]

A different kind of individual study of meteorological influences was made by Benjamin Joslin, then a practicing physician and Union College professor. In the hope of determining whether atmospheric conditions had any measureable influence on the occurrence of spontaneous hemorrhage, Joslin examined his private case records for a three-year period in the mid-1830s when he had made particularly extensive personal meteorological observations. He found that 54 of his cases had been properly recorded by date and half of these as to the hour of attack. His analysis led to the conclusion that "atmospheric condition of the period preceding a storm is more conducive to hemorrhage than that which immediately succeeds one." Acknowledging a lack of correlation in some particular cases, he observed that the important thing for the scientific physician was that "atmospheric agencies . . . still manifest themselves in the average results."[29]

While Joslin and Engelmann reached limited conclusions from limited observations, other observers drew wide-ranging conclusions from the data at their disposal. Especially ambitious in his generalizing was Edward H. Barton of New Orleans. Barton, one of his city's leading physicians, had, like most of his contemporaries North and South, decisively rejected contagionist or animalcular views of disease etiology in favor of a strongly environmental rationale. In fact, by 1850 he was asserting that "the various proportions of heat and moisture . . . explain almost everything in relation to health—excepting man's personal habits and constitution." For Barton, as for others, meteorology provided the much-needed scientific explanation of the vague influence that men had long termed miasma. As he saw it, at least in the context of New Orleans' yellow fever, the principle causes of insalubrity were "great elevation of temperature, [poor] ventilation, undue moisture and filth." The presence of filth alone, the "terrene" cause, was like having only one blade of shears; it could not cause yellow fever by itself. But, "couple these 'terrene' causes with meteorological conditions—with a high saturation and a high temperature—and 'the shears are complete.' "[30]

Since Barton's particular focus was upon dampness or dryness, the rise and fall of the dew point, he urged that every sanitarian have a hygrometer in order to be able to measure this condition. While not the first American to stress the role of humidity in disease, his prominent use of hygrometric data in the New Orleans sanitary survey of 1854 popularized such measurements in public health circles.[31] With no false modesty, Barton likened his uses of the hygrometer to Humphry Davy's safety lantern as a contribution to scientific clarity.

Not a few northern sanitarians and editors concurred that Barton had indeed provided the key element needed to go with vital and sanitary statistics in order to make public health studies truly scientific. They agreed with his proposed role for the hygrometer, and they repeated his analogy of the two blades of shears. Many concurred with him that "a large proportion" of the diseases of man resulted from meteorological conditions. As Sanford Hunt of Buffalo concluded, "The investigations of modern meteorology have settled the whole question of miasm."[32]

Actually, even among anticontagionists, there were many differences as to the overall relationship of climate and disease. There was endless wrangling about the relative influence of heat, moisture, wind, electrical current, and other elements. Moreover, some voices were skeptical of the whole thing. Josiah Nott of Mobile, who by 1847 had come to believe in an animalcular hypothesis of the causation of the South's great epidemic disease, concluded that "appreciable changes in our summer weather have about as little to do with yellow fever as they have with small pox or measles."

In New Orleans during the 1850s, physicians who agreed with Nott pounced on Barton's extreme position on meteorological influences to help discredit the latter's proposals for public health reform. Bennet Dowler observed that "too much is taken for granted in meteorology," and that much more research in chemistry and physiology was needed before it could be intelligently applied in public health and medicine.[33] Morton Dowler, in turn, found it a total "absurdity" to attempt to relate either yellow fever or cholera to the weather and climatic conditions of New Orleans. It was ridiculous to rest a theory of disease on "a little 'meteorology,' a little 'medical topography,' a little 'geology.' " In 1854, he rightly observed, meteorology was still "a science which had shed but a feeble and unsatisfactory light on the aetiology of epidemics generally." Just as vital statistics would never become respectable until the causes of death in registers were determined uniformly by experts, so meteorology and its data could not provide reliable bases for sanitary action until people knew more about the science.[34]

## The Federalizing of Medical Meteorology

Medicine and meteorology were complex enough as separate sciences, and each had huge, still-uncharted areas. The questions about their interrelationships presented great additional difficulties and great challenges to mid-nineteenth-century investigators. Dowler's point was that many enthusiasts did not realize the difficulties. In any case, the field of inquiry was in a state that was fragmentary at best. Individual scientists working alone could not hope to contribute more than tiny new fragments of information to it. And in some parts of the country relatively few individuals had yet started keeping systematic weather observations.[35]

However, at least some steps had been taken well before the 1840s to undertake collaborative searches, efforts to obtain larger amounts of relevant data through the establishment of networks of meteorological observers. In New York State, observers at state-supported colleges and academies had since 1825 been furnishing records of their readings to the regents of the state university. The Pennsylvania legislature in 1836 provided for each county to send monthly meteorological reports to the Franklin Institute, and in 1842 Ohio attempted to organize a similar system. But the longest-established American network, and one with specific medical objectives, was that conducted by the Medical Department of the United States Army.

Upon the modernization of that department in 1818, Surgeon-General Lovell ordered that surgeons of every hospital and regiment should "keep a diary of the weather, and to note everything of importance relating to the medical topography of his station [and of] the climate," and send quarterly abstracts to Washington.[36] Despite the uncertainties of communication and the occasional breaks in observations when posts

were abandoned or being moved, this system proved workable and produced a remarkably steady flow of data from the military outposts
scattered around the nation's periphery.[37] Lovell thought that sufficient
cumulations of such data, when studied, could help resolve controversies
over the relationship of climate to population increase and the
cultivation of the soil.[38] But, their main long-term use was to be in
conjunction with the medical records of sickness and mortality that were
accumulating in the same Washington office. Lovell accepted totally the
prevailing wisdom, that weather and climate had important effects upon
diseases, and he saw that the accumulating data would eventually
provide someone with an unprecedented opportunity to illuminate the
nature and extent of that influence.

Such an opportunity arose in the late 1830s when Lovell's successor,
Thomas Lawson, made arrangements for the abstracting and publication
of the large mass of reports which had accumulated since 1819. Lawson's
assignment of the young Assistant Surgeon Samuel Forry to do the
abstracting and analysis proved to be an inspired choice. Forry, who had
a University of Pennsylvania medical degree, had been with the army in
Florida between 1836 and 1838. Now, in the surgeon-general's office, he
turned out to be a prodigious worker whose intense belief in the importance of medical meteorology was matched only by his total conviction
of the key role to be played by statistics in medicine and society. The
results of his labor included an abstract volume of the army's meteorological readings for about 11 years, together with a massive statistical
summary of and commentary on the sickness and mortality throughout
the army over the 20-year period 1819–1839. The latter volume also
included extracts from the narrative reports of individual medical
officers concerning the topographical features at army posts all over the
country.[39] Taken together, the two volumes included a great fund of
hitherto unavailable raw materials on the human experience in the
topographical and climatological setting of the United States. Forry
thought that, in the aggregate, they furnished the means "not only to
investigate morbid action by the numerical method, but to show its
relation with climate. As these diversified facts admit of classification
according to certain geographical limits, the results, it is hoped, will
furnish some general laws towards the basis of a system of *medical
geography.*"[40]

In 1841 Forry left the army to devote himself more fully to making just
such a synthesis. Parts of the resulting analysis appeared shortly in
several long journal articles, while his book, *The Climate of the United*

*States and Its Endemic Influences,* appeared in 1842. Forry's 1842 book was the first extensive study of the American climate since a turn-of-the-century work by the French observer Constantin Volney.[41] Forry devoted much of this volume to summarizing the known climatic features, classifying them by geographical area, and generalizing about them. This done, he attempted, in a self-conscious "application of the Baconian philosophy to medicine," to relate the army's sickness and mortality to the climate of the various areas. Forry recognized the difficulty inherent in trying to calculate the various pathological and therapeutic variables for such correlations in every specific disease. But he thought that enough was known to allow valid generalizations about broad classes of disease. Accordingly, for these classes he discussed in turn the influence of climatic factors on causation, therapeutics, and prevention. And using the recent reports of Alexander Tulloch, he was able to compare parts of this American military medical experience with that of British troops over a comparable span of years.[42]

Forry's synthesis had its weak points. Some readers pointed out that disease in the scattered geographical areas covered by the army data represented only a tiny part of the overall American experience. Some questioned the accuracy of the army's meteorological readings. And others suggested that until at least 1830, army medical officers had been so dissipated in their habits as to reduce the value of their early vital statistics reports.[43] A few, moreover, including one of Forry's former army colleagues, noted that the data sample was for an unrepresentative part of the population. These were "statistics of picked men. From them are excluded the old, the young females, and invalids."[44]

Such criticism aside, most of Forry's medical contemporaries recognized the volume as an original contribution of the first order, as the most extensive American contribution to date both in medical statistics and medical geography. Charles Caldwell called it "the book of books," one marked by the excellence of its arrangement, the grandeur of its purpose, the elegance of its style, and "the masculine spirit and love of philosophy which pervade it," along with the originality and significance of its content. Caldwell's assessment was widely shared. There was, therefore, real shock in the medical community when Forry died in the fall of 1844 at the age of 33. Medical eulogists could recall few Americans who had done so much by a comparably early age. To be sure, he was no Humboldt. Still, at least one observer ranked him with a celebrated young French physician. "If France mourned over the gifted Bichat, America will long remember the young climatologist."[45]

The army medical officers whose garrison and field observations formed the basis of Forry's principal publications usually had the help of an enlisted man who acted as clerk. The equipment for their reporting duties normally consisted of only a few bare essentials. For the reporting of diseases, deaths, and topographical information, of course, the principal tools were pens and paper, one or more permanent journals, eventually a nosological list, and a few standard forms. Instruments provided for meteorological observations were limited during the first few years to thermometers and wind vanes, though rain gauges were added at many posts in 1836. Only in 1843 were barometers and other instruments provided to significantly increase the scope and value of the army observations. Around the beginning of that year some of the larger posts were thus taking readings four times daily on "the barometer, the thermometer attached and the thermometer detached, the pluviometer, Daniell's hygrometer, the wet bulb, the observations upon the clouds, the clearness of the sky, and the force and direction of the winds." Steps were also taken, on advice of Alexander D. Bache, James P. Espy, and other outside experts, to standardize procedures from one post to another and to ensure uniformity of the instruments used. These and the other improvements during the decade or so after 1840 made the army's subsequent compilations of meteorological, topographical, and mortality data increasingly valuable and sophisticated.[46] Even such a critic of meteorology as Morton Dowler found the reports scientifically important, especially by "furnishing the world with reliable data on which duly to appreciate the *aetiological fictions* which have been associated with yellow fever and cholera, and which have been authoritatively palmed on the credulity of the public and the profession."[47]

The advances in the army system reflected both a steady improvement in American meteorological practices generally and a continuing overall expansion in the numbers of observations. By the 1840s, self-respecting individual observers were no longer satisfied with just having a thermometer. And coincidentally, changing economic and technological conditions were making it possible for larger numbers of observers to satisfy their desires for more instruments. A key factor was the appearance of better qualified native American instrument-makers than previously and the emergence of a capacity on their part to supply good instruments at lower costs than foreign makers.

In 1843, for example, the hygrometers and barometers used in the army medical network were European imports. But patriots could take pride in the fact that the thermometers were American products, "made to order by Mr. George Tagliabue, philosophical instrument maker, New York, after standard No. 6 of the National Observatory." By 1850, most of the other standard instruments being introduced into the various American meteorological systems were also native products. In that year, barometers and thermometers were by James Green, while rain gauges and wind vanes were by Pike and Son, both firms of New York City.[48]

With more and better instruments now easily available, Americans expanded their meteorological networks and began to talk about coordinating them. Because of the lack of such coordination until this time, American learned societies had had little choice but to decline formal participation in a number of international meteorological projects. Specifically, during the late 1830s and early 1840s, British as well as Belgian scientists proposed large schemes for the observation of the weather and other periodical phenomena, including demographic and biological, but all were premature so far as the United States was concerned.[49]

By the late 1840s, considerable progress had been made in tying together the American meteorological networks. The key step during the period was the involvement of the new Smithsonian Institution in this area of science, and its decision in 1849 to organize a truly nationwide meteorological system. This involved enlisting many new observers, whose observations were to be coordinated with those from the existing systems of New York, Pennsylvania, and the army. An enthusiastic response from colleges, natural history societies, physicians, and others in every state ensured the rapid success of the network; by 1851, some 155 observers were regularly sending data to the Smithsonian offices.[50]

Thanks to the expanded number of observers, the acquisition of new instruments, and the general improvement in meteorological data, midcentury physicians and scientists were persuaded that the task of plumbing the links between environment and disease would now be carried on with increased precision. Professor Elias Loomis of New York was hopeful about the outcome. "That it is possible to discover such a connection, if it really exists, cannot admit of a reasonable doubt." But discovery of the cause of disease would be only the first medical gain; for this, in turn, would be a step toward the cure of disease. "And it is by no means chimerical," he concluded, "to suppose that a complete system of meteorological observations throughout the United States might be the means of extending the duration of human life."[51]

However, all of this pulling together of meteorological data could serve but little medical or public health purpose unless corresponding amounts of regularly collected and accurate vital statistics were also assured. Recognizing in 1850 that few state registration systems were as yet providing such data, Secretary Joseph Henry suggested that the Smithsonian Institution might cooperate in an alternate scheme if the American Medical Association were willing to play a major role. Under this, the Smithsonian would furnish appropriate forms and receive vital-statistics returns from the field, provided the AMA could take care of distributing the forms to its members and analyzing the data sent in.

This proposal proved to be much more than the infant society was prepared to cope with. The best it could do was to refer the project to the state medical societies in the hope that they would be successful in getting individual physicians to make regular death returns. Not unexpectedly, nothing came of this. Nor was there apparently any substantial result from an 1859 AMA committee report which urged every county medical society to create the office of registrar, to be filled by physicians who would make regular meteorological observations as well as reports on medical topography and vital statistics.[52]

Accordingly, the first substantial analysis of data from the Smithsonian system was published in 1857 by Lorin Blodget in his work on the *Climatology of the United States.* In contrast to Forry, Blodget, who was not a physician, devoted only a single chapter of his book to the relations of climate and disease. He did not attempt a systematic original analysis of the meteorological data in their relation to mortality data. Rather he satisfied himself with summarizing the statistics of other investigators with respect to the varying relationships of climatological conditions to yellow fever, cholera, malarial fevers, and other diseases.[53]

Although this particular work happened to be by a layman, that did not mean any diminishing of medical enthusiasm for meteorology during the antebellum period. In fact, this enthusiasm manifested itself in ever-increasing ways. Private practitioners scrutinized the weather reports of faraway places on behalf of invalid patients who planned to travel for their health.[54] Medical school professors kept weather observations along with their collections of fossils, butterflies, and birds nests.[55] Editors and reviewers widely agreed "that atmospheric causes, the state of the dew-point, and every hygrometric condition, have a powerful effect upon disease."[56] And men who were regarded as the "scientific" physicians of the day worked with great energy to confirm, strengthen, and apply this belief. It was no accident that these and other environmental concerns formed central aspects of one of the most original major medical works of antebellum America.

### Daniel Drake's Environmental View of Mid-American Disease

Daniel Drake's *Systematic Treatise* of 1850, on the diseases of the great Midwest, was, in fact, the supreme American attempt to use Baconian methods to fathom the natural environment for medical purposes.[57] At an early stage in his career, Drake had determined that "the first . . . business of philosophy is to observe and register [the facts of nature], the second to arrange them into natural orders, the third and highest to deduce from them the principles of science." He himself set out to examine natural phenomena in this way. For some years he limited his inquiries largely to the city of Cincinnati, but his scientific horizons subsequently expanded to encompass the entire central valley system of the United States. In 1822 Drake issued a first appeal to physicians of this area to send him data for a compendium on western diseases, a project he hoped to complete in about two years. This time schedule proved completely unrealistic, for little information was forthcoming during that time. Meanwhile, until he could produce such a volume, he advised physicians to rely on Noah Webster's "learned, but neglected work on epidemic diseases"; few other authors, he thought, had made such a comprehensive attempt to understand the environmental influences on disease.[58]

While Drake's information-gathering lagged somewhat during the 1830s, he encouraged other physicians and medical students to develop the sort of fact-finding habits that might eventually help him. He made a special point of urging young physicians to undertake observations in collateral sciences that had bearing on medical topography: geology, zoology, botany, geography, vital statistics, and meteorology. And he asked readers of his medical journal to send in material that would shed "light upon the diseases, climatorial temperament and geological constitution of the [Midwest]."

Ultimately, during the early 1840s, Drake was able to resume his original project in earnest. Feeling a need to know more of the central region personally, he set out on a series of travels during which he wandered extensively around the Great Lakes area, up and down the Mississippi and its larger tributaries, and along the shores of the Gulf of

Mexico. Over a three-year span, during long medical school vacations, he travelled an estimated 15,000 miles. Having done that, he then issued another call to physicians and scientists of the region for further data to supplement what he had gathered himself.[59]

The monumental *Systematic Treatise* was ultimately built only partly out of information from these varied personal sources. It was made feasible by the new accumulations made by others of relevant kinds of scientific data: the state geological surveys, Forry's army reports, medical and meteorological material from the various professional journals. Drake's work was the most extensive antebellum American effort to deduce disease etiology from such data and generally to sort out the medical significance of the environment. Drake's first section brought together comprehensive material on the region's geographical, hydrographical, and geological features, and somewhat less on the flora, fauna, and other resources. A second large section dealt with climate and meteorological conditions, while a shorter third section was devoted essentially to anthropological, social, and hygienic matters—including race, occupation, clothing, diet, and housing. Altogether, he devoted some 700 pages to delineating the many environmental factors before he got down to discussing their relations to specific diseases.

Drake's consideration of diseases was essentially in the form of a nosology arranged in five large classes: autumnal fevers, yellow fever, typhus fevers, eruptive fevers, and phlogistic fevers. Most were subdivided in turn into genera and species, sometimes on the authority of classical writers, sometimes on the basis of Drake's own experience. In varying degrees, for each disease there were discussions of distribution, diagnosis, treatment, and the various hypotheses regarding causation. Drake's discussions of the known pathological characteristics, placed within the vast framework of topographical details, led him in most cases to the conclusion that the environment played an immediately causal role. However, unlike most of his contemporaries, he visualized this causal relationship, at least for cholera and malaria, in terms of a concept of minute animalcules or germs that swarmed in the air and water and whose multiplication and spread were governed by the various topographical, hydrographical, and meteorological conditions.

Drake's work obtained quick recognition as an outstanding accomplishment, especially for the United States. One contemporary termed it "the most valuable and important original production, of a strictly professional character, that has yet appeared from the pen of any of our own physicians." Another saw in it the fulfillment of a "noble object."

And some seemed to feel it was a success simply because of its formidable size.[60]

Others realized that the size of the project was in fact a weakness, and that neither Drake nor any other single individual could possibly deal adequately with so many complex matters. At least some readers pointed to carelessness or superficiality in some parts of the work, the consequences of "desultory verbal statements, gathered during rapid journeys through 'the Valley.'" And Drake himself realized that his data were all too sparse, since there were not yet enough trained observers. One thin area was meteorology itself.

> Thus, with a few honorable exceptions, the results are but doubtful approximations to the truth. However all this may be regretted, we need not be astonished, for the Valley is too recently and sparsely settled, to have raised up a body of professed meteorologists, and practical physicians are, in general, too much occupied, and too often absent from home, to make and record regular observations.[61]

Two other contemporary criticisms of Drake's work deserve attention. The first of these, by Bennet Dowler and apparently but little shared, implicated the whole set of midcentury preconceptions about disease etiology held by the bulk of American physicians. Dowler agreed that Drake was a sincere man who had compiled an "elegant and learned" synopsis of the medical topography of the valley. But, given the current fragmentary state of knowledge about meteorology, geology, and other sciences, it seemed to him that Drake's views about disease etiology could only be regarded as hypothetical.

> The history of the diseases of the valley . . . is really the least valuable part of the work. The statesman, the geographer, the geologist, the civil historian, will dispute with the pathologist for the right to this work. . . . But [the author] leaves the great problem still to be solved, namely, the invariable connections between the physical agents, and the special diseases of localities. The great desideratum which connects, as cause and effect, the meteorology, the hydrography, and general topography of a delta, a basin, a plain, a lake, a river, a swamp, a mountain, and a country, with the maladies of the population, is still an open question.[62]

A second criticism, related to the first and almost equally serious in the antebellum view, focussed on the basic inadequacy of some of Drake's other statistics. Drake himself regretted that he had been unsuccessful in obtaining bills of mortality for most of the valley localities. He also conceded that much of the disease information supplied by his informants was fragmentary and subjective in nature. Recognizing such deficiencies in these data, he half-heartedly attempted to explain away his quantitative shortcomings.

> I cannot concede that observations not made on the numerical method are of no practical value. On the contrary, I attach importance to the conclusions, at which acute and observing men have arrived, under the daily and reiterated impressions made on their minds in the practice of their profession. Our diagnoses and therapeutics have been constructed of materials thus collected; and will continue to be improved and perfected in the same manner. The numerical method may throw its exacter contributions into the great volume of data, but will never exclude those collected in a different mode.[63]

D. Francis Condie of Philadelphia saw the weaknesses in Drake's compromise. Like most reviewers, Condie had nothing but praise for Drake's energy and perseverance. But the unevenness of the data generated for the study had to be recognized. Obviously, "loose general statements, imperfect records, and indirect sources of information" were not proper bases for broad generalizations. Drake had doubtless done all that anyone could have, given the imperfect statistical sources available at that time for mid-America.

> In the absence, however, of a correct series of medical statistics, with all his industry and research, our author's account of the comparative prevalence and mortality of different diseases, in the several portions of the valley, are deprived of that precision so essential to arriving at correct conclusions in regard to the etiological influence of locality and climate, while, for determining the influences of these upon the duration of life, we are left without any reliable data.[64]

Though Drake could not back his environmental hypotheses with enough figures to suit Dowler or Condie, not many of his generation were inclined to challenge his persuasive catalog of topographical, hydrographic, and meteorological influences on health. By and large they were well satisfied that environmental factors were, at the least, highly contributory to infectious disease, even if they could not be shown to be immediate, efficient causes. And a large proportion of physicians and laymen alike were persuaded that changing an individual's physical environment through travel was the most promising measure then available, either for improving one's general level of health or for dealing with certain specific diseases, notably tuberculosis.

## Americans Travelling for Health

Year in and year out, in the United States as well as in Europe, except for an occasional epidemic outbreak of some other disease, tuberculosis (commonly called consumption or phthisis) remained numerically first in the deaths reported on bills of mortality. True, there had been some decrease, attributed to better housing and other improvements in the standard of living.[65] Still, the continuing destructiveness of the disease called forth intense medical efforts to learn more about its causation, distribution, and behavior. The full panoply of numerical methodologies was enlisted, in studies drawing on clinical, topographical, pathological, meteorological, and other data, but little certain knowledge accumulated during this period, particularly as to etiology.[66]

Antebellum therapeutic efforts were almost equally futile. Of course, if symptoms of the disease were discovered in time, the early stages of tuberculosis were treatable. However, fully developed classical cases of the disease were, during those years, little affected by medical intervention, except some symptoms could be temporarily relieved. In fact, from the 1830s onward, a succession of such therapies for tuberculosis as "depletion, mercurialization, cathartics, emetics, counter-irritants, low diet, and confinement in an uniform temperature within doors" were all progressively abandoned in favor of a heavy reliance on simple hygiene. Adopting a regimen of plenty of rest, careful diet, sensible clothing, and suitable housing, but especially an abundance of fresh air and exercise in the outdoors, physicians discovered that "recovery from the disease is not infrequent, and its progress in fatal cases is far less rapid."[67]

Such a regimen was not always feasible in mid-nineteenth-century home environments, and particularly not for city-bound consumptives, though some of the latter could get healthful open-air exercise in the new rural cemeteries and public parks. However, the prevailing philosophy of therapy also suggested, where possible, a complete change of environment—climate, weather, living arrangements, and occupational surroundings. Travel in itself, either ocean voyages or inland trips, was thus urged, but also, when possible, travel to spend a season at some distant site or resort.[68]

Therapeutic travel, whether for consumption or some other condition, was obviously limited to those who could afford it. But the rapidly expanding facilities for transportation brought such travel within the reach of larger numbers of Americans every year. Travellers for health, particularly females, thus became about as conspicuous along the antebellum turnpikes, waterways, and railways as the wandering emigrants, drummers, reformers, lyceum lecturers, or assorted entertainers and con men of the age.[69] As a matter of fact, health became a justification for the travel of the healthy, as well as for that of the invalid. For the well person, travel was considered to be not only a matter of educational improvement but also a means of ensuring continued mental vigor and, through it, bodily health. Trips to admire the Catskills, Niagara Falls, the Great Plains, or the Rockies were sometimes about as much a part of preventive medicine as of entertainment. Meanwhile, the efficacy of travel for the not-so-healthy was demonstrated by the way it revived flagging members of the generation of intellectuals—the Danas, Parkmans, and Emersons—who had been allegedly enfeebled by too much study. And, where members of the laboring classes were found to have become enervated by their work inside unventilated factories or counting rooms, providing means for their travel was seen as a worthy new form of philanthropy.

> No charity would diffuse equal happiness, nor really prove more beneficial to thousands of feeble, pale, sickly young women, the victims of incessant toil with the needle, who have but a few luxuries and no privileges, than giving them the means of making excursions and breathing the fresh country air. We should be rejoiced to hear that some benevolent man, whom God has placed as steward over large possessions, had obeyed the command of loving his neighbor as himself in this respect.[70]

Early Americans of means had often sought restoration of their health abroad, along the shores of the Mediterranean, in Madeira, the Azores, or the West Indies. Some continued to go to such places, though Cuba, for one, lost some of its popularity when Americans began to find its political climate and customs objectionable. By the Jacksonian period, however, the middle classes were conspicuously patronizing sites within the United States, a phenomenon which in itself provided much impetus to permanent settlement.[71]

The country's steady growth into unoccupied territories greatly expanded the antebellum possibilities for therapeutic travel. In particular, the spread of steamship service and rail lines in these areas brought a host of attractive locales within easy reach. Hot springs or mineral waters that had been used by Indians and trappers were increasingly developed as resorts thanks to enterprising promoters. Mammoth Cave and other sites came to enjoy vogues as health resorts even when they lacked special waters. In all parts of the country, reports began to accumulate about those localities whose climatic features appeared to be particularly beneficial for invalids.[72]

Though far from universal, there developed a tendency for northern physicians to send their patients to southern resorts and southern physicians to do the opposite. In the early 1830s, "travellers for health and pleasure" from the Deep South divided themselves mainly between three areas: the famous springs of Virginia, the Great Lakes and Saratoga (where they made a "league between fashion and health"), and the seashore resorts of New England or the Middle Atlantic Coast.[73] The most popular of the Florida resorts up to that time were St. Augustine and some of the Keys. As hostile Indians were driven out of the state, invalids also began visiting Jacksonville, St. Mary's River sites, and other areas. New Orleans, despite a dubious reputation for salubrity, attracted some midwesterners in the winter seasons. Travellers and missionaries were recommending the Sandwich Islands to consumptives as early as the 1830s, and some tubercular patients had settled in southern California even before the gold rush. The development of Colorado as a center for the consumptive followed about a generation later.

The virtues of particular healthful sites were disseminated both orally and in print, sometimes by returned patients themselves or by the physicians who had suggested they travel. Accounts varied widely, but characteristically they included a considerable range of information. Prominent, of course, were more or less detailed observations about the prevailing winds, ranges of temperature, humidity, and other aspects of weather and climate. Meteorological readings and bills of mortality were included, where available, along with the number and composition of the population. Equally useful, some guidance was often provided as to local hotel or boarding accommodations, foods, churches, recreational facilities, and available modes of transportation.

Since no one site was strong in every feature, the patient had to choose from among conflicting advantages and disadvantages. Thus, in St. Augustine, unstable winter winds and damps were admittedly deleterious to the health, but the town's hotel accommodations were generally found to be the most comfortable in Florida. In Honolulu, doctors boasted about the incomparably soft climate, but they had to admit that the long hard voyage to get there put it out of reach of most consumptives.[74]

Most physicians found themselves deeply involved in the recommendation of travel therapy, even when they realized that some patients, particularly among the consumptives, could not benefit from any change, no matter how favorable the climate and other circumstances.[75] The chronic antebellum patient had come to view travel as his ultimate resort and to insist upon it as his right. Characteristically, he was *"sure that sea-voyaging, change of air, and avoidance of . . . inclement atmosphere will effect a cure, or at least prolong and alleviate existence."*[76] Since the patient relied heavily on his physician to choose between the various forms of travel, climates, and resorts, medical men in turn demanded statistical data which would help them arrive at intelligent selections.

It was obvious that most of the early reports about a given resort could not be taken at face value. Many of them, more often than not, were merely passing impressions hastily drawn up by inexperienced observers. But others, as the Massachusetts physician Luther Bell pointed out, were the productions of local entrepreneurs who all too often filled them with self-serving data rather than with objective information. Florida provided one of the early object lessons.

Within a few years of the American acquisition of East Florida in 1821, great efforts were made through puffing circulars, tracts, and newspaper articles, to lure northern invalids to St. Augustine, and with some success. During the winter of 1830 alone, 75 out of 100 invalids in the city were found to have come in response to such advertising. Unfortunately, in place of the attractive Eden of health which had been promised, the new arrivals found a rather run-down community which had few recreational advantages, little choice of food, poor facilities for transport, and virtually no luxuries of any kind. More serious, the weather proved more changeable and far less soothing than had been promised. Bell found that weather statistics cited in the advertising propaganda had been incomplete, improperly taken, or made with inadequate instruments. In fact, he concluded that at that point in time, St. Augustine had a "deficiency of everything which can amuse, improve or restore the invalid, and the presence of everything which can serve to irritate his feelings, impoverish his estate, and disappoint his hopes."[77]

The health buildup of a newly opening territory and of its climate did not necessarily include deliberate deception. Many of the reports about a given site came from perfectly well-meaning enthusiasts. But these, too, when inaccurate, were often the cause of dashed hopes among invalids who had travelled long distances at considerable cost in physical discomfort and monetary expense.[78] In any case, for any area, physicians faced the necessity of sorting out both the deceptions and the early enthusiastic impressions from the statistically verifiable facts. The California experience was a conspicuous case at hand.

Physicians who joined the gold rush to northern California in the late 1840s and early 1850s rapidly found that they as well as many health-seekers had been "grossly deceived" about the state's climate and healthfulness by earlier "highly gilded" reports. Accordingly, some came to regard it not so much as an abstract scientific mission as a duty to set the record straight for other eastern physicians and invalids who might be contemplating the journey west. Almost from their arrival in California, impressive numbers of physicians thus did proceed, like Thomas Logan, in an unmistakably Humboldtian manner, to examine and record the topographical and meteorological features of the state, and to try to relate them, often in considerable detail, to the fevers, mental disturbances, and other ailments of the forty-niners and their successors.[79] The recorded impact of malarial fevers and cholera was a source of great concern. Even more so was that of consumption.

Early spokesmen who hoped to build up the population and economy of California agreed on the importance of learning to what extent tuberculosis would thrive under the influence of the Pacific weather and climate; few other facts would do as much to shape the state's image as a refuge for the eastern invalid. During California's first decade as a state, however, the mortality statistics from consumption remained highly inaccurate, partly because of loose record-keeping and partly because of poor diagnosis. Understandably this made for wide differences of opinion as to the possible sources of the state's tuberculosis. F. W. Hatch had no doubt that the numerous cases were essentially local in origin. They resulted, he thought, at least in part from a widespread disregard of hygiene on the part of the forty-niners, and their misguided reliance "upon the supposed salubrious influences surrounding them." G. L. Simmons similarly concluded from statistics available to him that the California climate was as conducive to consumption as that of any other state.

By contrast, Charles D. Cleveland felt that the early tuberculosis mortality in California could not really be blamed on the state's climate. A more likely cause, he believed, was the existing condition of the individuals who came into the state, many of whom were in advanced stages of the disease. William H. Doughty could go along with that. In fact, in 1860 he found little doubt remaining that California met "most of the essential conditions of a climate for the consumptive, . . . a relatively high and uniform temperature, limited ranges of the thermometer, freedom from non-periodic extremes, a moderate dew-point, abundant facilities for exercise of the physical man and also diversions for the mind." The main things that were needed now, he thought, were vital statistics good enough to be able to test and compare the salubrity of individual localities of the state.[80]

This was equally true elsewhere in the United States. Despite all of the far-flung travelling, to California, Hawaii, Florida, and other sites, there were still few conclusive data available for determining which locales were the most favorable for the treatment and cure, whether of tuberculosis or of other diseases. Moreover, not a great deal could be done to speed the accumulation of such data. At the same time, the steady growth in the numbers of travellers and of migrants provided an ever-expanding base for potential medical observations in the new communities. There was also a steady influx of new physicians. This movement ensured both that many such observations would be made and that the desired vital-statistics registration systems would eventually be created to go along with the other institutions essential to the communities.

# 4

---

# Medicine and the Westward Movement

The organizational and observational talents of physicians often seemed to be about as much in demand, during the various stages of the settlement process, as their presumed therapeutic skills were. As waves of population burst, after the Revolution, into new territories west and south of the Appalachians, doctors or other individuals with medical knowledge were, of course, needed at every step to try to keep the migrants alive. But physicians also came into considerable demand, it turned out, as natural leaders and organizers of, and sometimes spokesmen for, the westward movement. As a group, they were as swept up in the mystique of the phenomenon as anyone, but they also had more practical awareness than most people of what the settlements and communities should be like. They often took the lead in shaping not only the medical institutions of the West,* but also its other institutions. When they were not treating diseases, many of them could be found presiding over the growth of these varied institutions, trying to measure the progress of their communities, and generally sorting out or even trying to guide the powerful demographic energies and components of the movement.

---

* Throughout this period the areas between the Appalachians and the Rocky Mountains, as well as the regions extending on to the Pacific, were thought of as part of America's *West*. Accordingly, I use the terms *West* and *western* in reference to both of these general geographical areas. However, I have also employed the modern terms *Midwest* and *midwestern* in a good many contexts, where appropriate.

## Medical Movement and Community-Building in Mid-America

Physicians in the older states were thoroughly conscious of the West. Like other citizens, they were constantly being exposed to general accounts of western travel and exploration. Eastern medical editors frequently published letters from doctors who had ventured across the Appalachians recently or who had grown up in the new areas. Some editorialized about national expansion. Most medical writers seemed to think that the western thrust was both inevitable and good. Some, like Walter Channing, who were social reformers even spoke of stimulating emigration of the poor to the new lands as a promising means of relieving the growing unemployment and misery of eastern cities.

Members of the eastern medical profession were also sensitive to the restlessness which affected many of their patients and neighbors in the post-Revolutionary decades and which caused some to pull up their roots. Benjamin Rush noted that, in Pennsylvania, these were typically men who had outlived their credit or fortune in the established areas of the state. Actually, he found a considerable core of men in the state who, almost exactly "in proportion as population increase[d] around" them, became uneasy and pushed on to still unspoiled areas. In fact, not a few were known to have moved and gone through the laborious settlement process as many as four times within the confines of Pennsylvania alone.[1] Physicians in New England, for their part, became aware that there were aesthetic as well as economic motivations guiding those individuals who were giving up their hard-scrabble farms to look for something better in the West.[2] In turn, practitioners in the Old South could understand the reasons why landowners packed their slaves off from the worked-out plantations for the long trek to fresh lands in new territories of the Deep South and Southwest.

North and South, the exodus left empty houses and often such a decrease in population as to adversely affect local business, at least temporarily. Physicians were among those affected, particularly those who were just starting out in practice or who had never built up more than small, marginal practices. Accordingly, not a few joined the great western migration themselves.

There were various possibilities for the westering physician. Some few, acting out of religious conviction, threw their lot in with one or another of the remote mission stations among the Indians. Others such as Edwin James signed on with federal expeditions or surveys. During the 1840s, increasing numbers attached themselves to organized emigrant trains or signed as ships' surgeons. Still others, loner physicians who were naturalists, of whom James Fenimore Cooper's Dr. Obed Bat was a caricature, pushed deep into the forests and along the river bottoms to look for specimens away from the main paths of migration.

Most physicians, however, looked for more stable places among other emigrants in one or another of the trans-Appalachian settlements. There, while trying to establish their practices, they labored along with their neighbors—the usual mixture of surveyors, farmers, lawyers, speculators, clergymen, artisans, merchants, teachers, and others—to pull their fledgling communities through the difficult early years. Some few fortunate doctors, like Edward Jarvis, were able to obtain prearranged practices among particular groups of new settlers. Jarvis in 1837 went to Louisville upon the specific invitation of a group of former New Englanders who "felt the want of a Yankee Doctor with whose habits and sympathies they were familiar."[3] Still, the bulk had to start out virtually from scratch with few if any such advantages.

Emigrating physicians naturally gravitated mainly to population centers that were already or presumably would be large enough to support decent practices—sites that included railroad junctions, county seats, and above all, the already well-established first generation of midwestern cities. Communities located along the busy emigrant routes, like Buffalo, Cincinnati, Louisville, or St. Louis, were particularly desirable. Doctors settling in such towns tended to locate their offices as near as possible to the stage stops, railroad stations, or steamboat landings in order to "catch the transient business."[4] To be sure, there was no assurance, even in large centers, of quickly building up a lucrative practice. Would-be practitioners in the Midwest were at an early date often discouraged by the extent of the competition around them and by other obstacles to success. In fact, large numbers of them tended to move on, after only a few months of practice in a community, to other localities that seemed to hold out greater promise. Daniel Drake deplored this "endless shifting of place which our western and southern profession displays." So far as he could see, the constant movement merely kept many physicians chronically unemployed and ruined more medical careers than it enhanced.[5]

Some of the less qualified among these practitioners turned into itinerants offering their services to the widely scattered farm and backwoods populations. Such itinerants—bloodletters, healers, bonesetters, dentists, and patent-medicine salesmen—along with the era's saddlebag preachers, drummers, mesmerists, daguerreotype-takers, tinkers, and confidence men, became part of a veritable army of individuals who wandered back and forth over nineteenth-century backcountry roads, trails, and waterways. While some of these individuals may have peddled a certain number of worthless portions along with the wooden nutmegs, the genre as a whole nonetheless played an essential role in bringing necessities and amenities to the remote areas of mid-America and making early life there supportable.

The physicians who remained in town often filled somewhat comparable roles. Many combined their careers in medicine with land speculation, business, banking, or farming. Some took on active roles as lobbyists to attract new settlers, and some worked to bring railroads to their communities. Not a few became involved on the side in the organization of lyceums, colleges, and libraries, or in nonmedical scientific pursuits. A great many naturally became involved with the problems of organizing and building up the medical institutions of the region.

In the newer midwestern communities, just as in the older eastern cities, medical-care institutions tended to multiply in a way that more or less directly reflected population growth. In the course of its development, any given city expected gradually to acquire its almshouse, a pesthouse or quarantine station, one or more private hospitals, varied clinics, asylums for the insane and other unfortunates, a public dispensary, and ultimately a philanthropically supported or city-run general hospital. In practice, this general pattern did prevail, though with local variations.

Some Mississippi Valley cities also, after the mid-1830s, became the sites of federal hospitals providing for the illnesses and injuries of mushrooming numbers of riverboat men and Great Lakes sailors.[6] Where there were no separate institutions the boatmen were cared for under contract, often at almshouses or private hospitals. Such patients, along with increasing concentrations of immigrants and other poor, forced some of the private hospitals to expand rapidly to considerable size. New Orleans' Charity Hospital was by far the largest in the region for much of this period. However, not only Charity Hospital, but the Catholic-run hospitals of Buffalo, St. Louis, and other cities remained for long periods the principal institutions serving the general public in those communities.

Ultimately, social, economic, and population pressures forced governments and philanthropies to provide further facilities. In 1844, for instance, Mobile was reported to have both a city hospital and a marine hospital, but it was still trying to obtain an insane asylum and institutions

Fig. 1. Marine Hospital at St. Louis, Missouri. Courtesy of the National Library of Medicine.

for the blind and deaf. Buffalo citizens in 1848 were petitioning the state legislature for $40,000 to help build a new hospital which would permit it to cope more adequately with the vast numbers of recently landed sick immigrants who were passing through that city. St. Louis, with a population approaching 150,000 at midcentury, provided 750 beds in its three hospitals, and also had the services of several public dispensaries and clinics; but no one pretended that these facilities fully met the needs of the community. Almost everywhere, such institutions followed the needs, rather than anticipating them. However, as they rose, they became convenient symbols, both of the community's presumed well-being and of its desirability as a center for medical practice and learning.[7]

Another aspect of the nineteenth century's dynamic medical expansion was the proliferation of professional bodies. This included the buildup of an orthodox medical establishment from a mere handful of scattered medical societies, journals, and schools in 1800 to a highly impressive number in 1860. But it also included, after around 1830, the parallel emergence of similar institutions sponsored by some of the new therapeutic sects. As with the medical-care institutions, this professional growth roughly reflected the growth of the population itself and the creation of new communities, and it more or less kept pace with those phenomena. However, as Daniel Drake observed, under America's federal system, it was often the ambitions and jealousies of the various regions and states, as much as their actual needs, which lay behind the demands for professional medical institutions. In any case, creation of such bodies was part of the institutional growth that was necessary to any city that hoped to be able to compete with other communities.[8]

Once in operation, the professional institutions, and notably the numerous state, county, and city medical societies, did what they could to protect and further the interests of their own membership or clientele—not that they were actually very effective in this much of the time. The societies, for instance, in many places progressively lost their influence over the outcome of antebellum medical-licensing legislation. Still, they did continue to serve their particular constituencies as a kind of cement which gave individual practitioners at least some sense of professional belonging and worth. They also provided varying opportunities for scientific discussion. Moreover, as they grew, the changing numbers of these and other professional institutions in themselves provided superficial measures of the progress and strength of nineteenth-century medicine.

## The Multiplication of Medical Journals

Prominent among the indicators of growth were figures reflecting the rise and remarkable spread of native medical journalism. Medical journals began to come into being in given American communities following the accumulation there of a substantial number of doctors, and usually after the latter had made progress in organizing medical societies and medical schools. The pioneering *Medical Repository* of 1797 was followed during the six or seven decades after 1800 by a flood of emulators or competitors, and these organs became conspicuous and essential parts of the medical establishment. According to one calculation, 7 journals were founded by medical "regulars" between 1797 and 1810, 10 more from 1810 to 1820, 28 in the next decade, 29 in the next, and 44 from 1840 to 1850, and in the next quarter-century an additional 133 came into existence. While the early medical journals grew up exclusively in urban centers along the eastern seaboard, after 1820 others began to appear steadily along the Ohio and Mississippi rivers, around the Great Lakes, and in the South.[9]

As the sects grew, journals sprang up to promote their distinctive therapeutic views. This growth, which occurred mainly after 1830, quickly became fully as remarkable as that of the regulars' journals. Over a 20-year span, some 27 botanical and 35 eclectic journals were launched, and, between 1835 and 1860, some 40 different homeopathic periodicals.[10]

Observers or regional boosters like Daniel Drake considered it a sign of social and medical maturity when the Midwest proved able, in 1842, to support as many as three regular medical journals at the same time. Within half a dozen years, however, the region had eight such periodicals and just as many sectarian publications.[11] In the two decades before the Civil War, more than 15 separate regular journals came into existence in Kentucky alone, while St. Louis readers during that same period had their choice of 4 regular medical journals, 1 dental journal, and 10 sectarian journals.[12]

This teeming of medical journals seems to have been largely an American phenomenon, one whose scale was not approached in Europe. Contemporaries noted, in fact, that as early as 1845 the United States was "in a fair way to exceed, not only any but all other nations put together" in the numbers of such periodicals.[13] In 1850 the United States had roughly twice the 15 regular medical journals then published in Great Britain, or one such periodical for every 715,000 people.

The publication of medical journals during these decades, like other types of periodicals, was greatly advanced by innovations in printing, while their distribution was enormously expedited by the advent of the steamship, the railroad, and the telegraph. Even across the great American distances, distribution time was reduced between 1830 and 1850 from a matter of months to one of weeks or days. As a result, by the latter date, according to Drake, "even the village surgeon now cuts according to the newest fashion of some great transatlantic operator; and when two country physicians meet for consultation in the log cabin of a backwoodsman, they discuss the propriety of a practice, which, but thirty days before, had been professed by a Professor in . . . Europe."[14]

Nevertheless, these new organs were fragile creations; large numbers failed to survive more than a single issue or two, even when they enjoyed the sponsorship of medical schools. The typical regular journal was a small, mainly local operation, run on a shoestring and rarely having more than 500 or 600 subscribers. The regulars could never understand where the support came from that sustained the even feebler irregular medical journals. The regulars did perceive, however, that Jacksonian democracy demanded an outlet for every theory, however far-fetched. As one of them put it, "When each man and woman has a Journal to be the exclusive organ of their individual opinions on medicine, the millennium will be near at hand."[15]

## A Spawning of Medical Schools, a Surplus of Doctors

Of a parcel with the increase of journals, but with far more sweeping effects as an aspect of medical demography, was the rapid proliferation of medical schools. In fact, largely because of this growth, in hardly half a century the new United States went through a remarkable medical transformation, from a land with a grave scarcity of trained physicians to one with an equally serious apparent surplus. It was and is an open question whether the alleged new abundance was really a benefit to the population. There is little doubt, however, that the mechanisms which governed the supply did distort the normal development of medical education in this country.

During most of the eighteenth century, the large bulk of America's practitioners received their training from preceptors; only a handful of physicians had European medical degrees. Moreover, the five tiny native medical schools which were founded between 1765 and 1800 produced between them fewer than 250 physicians during that entire period. With the nineteenth century, a steady increase in the number and output of the schools changed these figures radically. The handful of institutions of 1800 grew to 22 in 1830, and the latter figure more than doubled by 1860, a growth paralleling the rise of population from the roughly 5 million of 1800 to over 31 million in 1860. During the decade of the 1830s alone, these orthodox institutions produced an estimated 6,800 graduates, while two decades later the number was nearly 18,000.[16]

This multiplication of medical schools was in part a normal result of society's effort to provide medical care for its increasing numbers of people. In early nineteenth-century America, however, medical education also became a manifestation of laissez-faire economics. Among the regulars, since the M.D. degree gradually replaced the license as the principal criterion for judging medical competence, degrees were increasingly sought after. Posts on medical faculties thus took on ever greater power and influence in the medical community. As proprietary faculties gradually took over administrative control of most medical schools, the economic temptation to produce degree-holders in large numbers steadily subverted the desire to impart quality medical knowledge. In virtually every state, as the century progressed, rival groups of regular physicians vied with each other to obtain the necessary charters for medical schools. On the road to getting established, the schools' officials scoured local communities for grants of land or for city, state, and private funds to help them erect their buildings. By the 1830s numerous such edifices, some of them sumptuously designed in Greek, Gothic, or other styles by well-known architects, had sprung up in many corners of the United States, and in them raged a fierce competition to produce medical students.

Charles Caldwell in 1834 thought that the situation had degenerated into a "medical school mania." It had already created over 20 medical schools where less than half a dozen had existed in 1800 and where 4, he thought, would still suffice. In his view, one school should normally be enough to serve as many as 4 or 5 million people. Up to 1820, Caldwell's own school, Transylvania, had had a monopoly in the West. But since then schools had been formed in Cincinnati and Louisville to compete for the vast mid-American reservoir of potential students. By Caldwell's figures, the United States as a whole now had one medical school for approximately every 750,000 inhabitants, "and still a fiery thirst for more."[17] And over the next several decades as the proliferation continued unabated all over the country, establishment physicians by the dozens—men like Caldwell who had financial stakes in some medical school or other—went into print to protest the appearance of allegedly needless new schools, competitors all.

For a variety of reasons, medical-school creation did not become nearly as prominent a feature of sectarian expansionism as of the regulars' growth. Some sects, notably the Thomsonians, originally were actively hostile to formally trained physicians and deliberately fostered the idea of every person acting as his own physician. Others, such as the eclectics and homeopaths, drew many of their practitioners from among already trained native regulars or sometimes, in the case of homeopathy, from the ranks of German immigrants.[18] Nevertheless, as Waite discovered, the homeopaths did organize some half dozen schools before 1860, while the eclectics and botanical factions together formed 21 chartered colleges, along with some unchartered institutions during the same 30-odd years.[19]

Overall, the multiplication of medical schools became a matter of no little chauvinistic pride. In the 1830s and 1840s, in fact, some commentators boasted that the United States now had more such schools in proportion to its population than England, France, or any other European country. Other analysts, however, argued that this was not the case at all and challenged the statistics which supported such an assertion.[20]

There was also much uncertainty about the disposition and future of the new graduates. As early as the 1830s, many observers had the impression that the numerous American schools were producing more physicians than could be absorbed. Much like the legal profession, it seemed, medicine had become so "crowded with candidates" that many were abandoning the field almost as soon as they had taken their degrees. Those that stuck it out had to face greatly reduced practices and increasingly precarious incomes. One editor, only half in jest, wondered if the army could not hire more full-time medical officers. "If it could be contrived so that a thousand or two expectants [i.e., new doctors] could be put upon regular pay and rations, it would encourage them, relieve their friends, and open a market for a multitude of rival medical schools!"[21]

In order to determine the magnitude of the problem, some medical leaders started collecting enrollment data of the various regular schools.[22] Others tried sorting the numbers of existing practitioners according to their medical allegiances.[23] One editor in 1845 counted 78 physicians in Buffalo's population of 30,000—or a ratio of 1 to 400, which was recognized as being mathematically far too great to permit all to gain a living in medicine. Roughly half of that total was thought to be composed of irregulars, many of whom practiced among the large

German population. The St. Louis profession had grown by then to an estimated 100 regulars plus unknown numbers of irregulars. A Cincinnati medical count of 1850 showed a similarly overcrowded profession; out of 179 practitioners there were 127 regulars, 8 botanics, 17 eclectics, 10 homeopaths, 1 Indian doctor, and 16 unknown.[24]

Discouraging as these figures of overcrowding were for urban physicians, they showed only one side of the supply picture. Those who looked beyond the cities saw that nationally the problem was one of maldistribution. For in the backcountry of most states, but conspicuously in the new territories beyond the Mississippi, there were desperate shortages of physicians. Charles A. Lee, noting the 40,000 or so regular physicians enumerated in the 1850 census, challenged the conventional wisdom of a national surplus, and noted the urgent needs of the sparsely populated areas. John K. Mitchell of Philadelphia went somewhat further than this with his 1850 estimate that "scarcely half" the physicians that were needed around the country were being produced. The Virginia economist George Tucker, in turn, calculated that the annual supply was no more than 20–35 percent of the demand, a shortage which guaranteed the continued presence of uneducated practitioners on the fringes of the profession.[25]

By midcentury, several eastern medical editors were suggesting that the new medical graduates seriously consider careers outside the heavily populated areas, and specifically in the trans-Mississippi areas. Such a course would presumably ease the fierce competitive struggle faced by the graduates while also reducing the surplus of urban doctors. An 1848 editorial pointed out that there were "fine openings for the benevolent exertions of young physicians, in the Indian regions of the West." But most of the long-range medical opportunities, of course, seemed to be in the rapidly sprouting new white communities.

> Why not strike manfully into the virgin regions of the West, and grow up with society [there], into wealth, usefulness and distinction? . . . Wherever there are human beings, there the advice of the physician is required; and as population increases, so does the odor of his good name. In short, prosperity and usefulness will in most cases be the reward of those who leave the old hive, to act their parts and gather and get gain in the unoccupied localities of Oregon, Nebraska, and Kansas.[26]

Large numbers of physicians obviously did follow this advice. They, in turn, were eventually followed by later waves of doctors who went on to yet newer territories. Settling in towns that were progressively farther west, each wave repeated the patterns of medical organization and civic involvement of its predecessors, including the establishment of new medical schools. By 1849 such a school had already sprung up in remote Iowa City, "in a region which was in the undisputed possession of Sioux Indians but a few years ago."[27]

Contemporaries recognized that the "mighty tide of emigration" would continue to spawn medical schools in the Midwest and West to meet the needs for physicians. They could only hope that the new institutions would be solid enough medically to provide quality education. The prospectuses which announced the start of some of these were far from auspicious, filled as they often were with extravagant promises more in keeping with business hucksterism than with science. In fact, none of the promotional literature of the competitive new midwestern cities was more florid than these medical school blurbs.[28] Physicians who were trying to break in on the profits of the proprietary system sought to outdo each other in the visions of future greatness they foresaw in their projected medical schools. Some assured would-be students that the blue-printed institutions not only would be easy to reach but were also certain to become scientific meccas because of their proximity to recently completed railroads. Others, "looking through the glorification spectacles," assured readers that their institutions would become the crowning jewels in the cultural and scientific development of the respective cities.[29]

Not a few physicians deplored the optimistic exaggeration and outrageous puffery in this promotional material. Yet such an approach to medical growth was not really out of place in a region which placed such great stock in the tall tales of its Paul Bunyans, Mike Finks, and Davy Crocketts. Moreover, the great valley was already proving its immense wealth of land and other resources. Accordingly, orthodox and irregular medical spokesmen alike were as persuaded as laymen of the tremendous prospects of the region. Indeed, as one of them proclaimed, it really seemed to be "the garden of the world, reserved by the wise Disposer of human events for the scene of the finishing glory of human attainment."[30]

By 1850, expressions of the vision of midwestern and western growth had been reduced to clichés by energetic publicists and political orators. In fact, the ultimate demographic fulfillment of the areas beyond the Appalachians already seemed only a relatively brief matter of time, given the vigor of America's materialistic pursuit of land and commerce.

Edward Everett, in one short burst of rhetoric, outlined what still had to be done.

> Let these fertile wastes be filled up with swarming millions; let this tide of immigration from Europe go on; let the steamer, the canal, the railway . . . subdue these mighty distances and bring this vast extension into a span. Let us pay back the ingots of California gold with bars of Atlantic iron. Let agriculture clothe our vast wastes with waving plenty. Let the industrial and mechanic arts erect their peaceful fortresses at the waterfalls. And then sir, in the train of this growing population, let the printing office, the lecture-room, the village schoolhouse, and the village church be scattered over the country.[31]

And physicians, under the spell of the same vision, had not the slightest doubt that the spread of medical schools and medical-care institutions would continue to be an essential factor in consolidating such growth, in determining whether the future of mid-America and the West would indeed be great and glorious.

### Migrating Americans and Their Illnesses

The medical efforts of midwestern and western physicians were directed primarily toward the more or less permanent inhabitants of the growing communities and toward disease conditions which were often measureable. But a very large and not always measureable segment of the western population was a perpetually moving one. It was often a matter of great difficulty for physicians even to reach such persons to administer medical treatment. Individuals were inaccessible enough when they settled down for a time in isolated cabins or farmhouses miles out of the orbit of law, schools, or regular medical care. But many such persons never stayed in one place for very long. In the Midwest just as they had earlier back East, they soon became restless and gave in to the urge to move onward. As one medical editor observed in 1833, the New Englander who had gone on to Ohio or Indiana tended to move on to Iowa, Kansas, or the Michigan Territory, while the Virginian, far from being content with his move to Kentucky, "now makes it, half the time, a mere reconnoitering ground, from which he takes a fresh departure for Missouri, Alabama, or Louisiana."[32]

As a result, the medical and demographic events of such individuals' lives frequently failed, for long periods, to show up in anyone's records

Fig. 2. The Country Doctor. From *Harper's Weekly* vol. 13, March 6, 1869, p. 145.

as statistics. However, only let the wanderers settle down for any length of time and let a town spring up nearby, and the numbering processes soon came into play, propelled by social, medical, political, or economic demands. The families then rapidly turned up on a variety of rolls and registers, thanks to the provisions of local lawmakers and the energies of assorted surveyors, editors, marshals, clergymen, clerks, philanthropists, and physicians.

Meanwhile, the New Englanders and Carolinians, Irish and Germans, rich and poor, who swarmed by the hundreds of thousands along the antebellum emigration routes, were confronted by manifold difficulties and problems, including medical hazards. Migrants sometimes had the benefit, from letters, newspaper accounts, or emigrant guides, of at least some general advance information about the weather, climate, diseases, and other conditions along the routes. But there was rarely enough information to allow them to prepare adequately. At best, therefore, the long trips by canal barge, steamboat, stagecoach, pack animal, or eventually train were merely uncomfortable and fatiguing, with modest lodging and not always palatable food. All too often, however, the trips were nightmares.

The opportunities for injury or disease were so omnipresent that persons setting out were advised to prepare for any eventuality. Well-off travellers thus often organized in bands and engaged physicians to accompany them. Numerous others equipped themselves with handbooks on domestic medicine and medicine chests. But many emigrants had started out from home on the narrowest of financial margins. These individuals had no physicians at hand, tended to be wretchedly clothed and equipped, and carried few if any medicines, let alone medical manuals or rudimentary comforts. Some could hardly afford Sappington's pills, a popular form of quinine, which almost by itself made the processes of western settlement and exploitation feasible in the face of the ubiquitous remitting fevers.[33] Often undernourished and exposed to harsh weather conditions, such unfortunates frequently were badly hit by illness before ever reaching their destinations.

Whatever their preparations, every group could expect at least some illness during a trip that lasted anywhere from one to six months. By far the worst experiences, as a rule, were with malaria and other seasonal fevers, with diarrheas or dysentery, and with cholera. On the Indiana prairies in 1838, emigrants died in large numbers of malarial fevers, a mortality that the medical profession thought could have been held down if there had been enough physicians and enough quinine.[34] Farther west, seriously sick emigrants who dragged themselves to one or another of the tiny scattered military posts were out of luck when the detachment and its medical officer were away fighting Indians. And when illness occurred along the trails beyond the outposts of civilization, such as the Overland route through South Pass, there was no possibility of obtaining local care or relief.

One widespread condition was not an immediate cause of death but was highly demoralizing for a great many of the migrants and new settlers and proved generally beyond the competence of physicians to do much about. This was the dark depression of homesickness that often settled in, a severe despondency over having uprooted themselves from familiar surroundings and homes in exchange for a difficult if not hostile environment. The clergyman Timothy Flint during the 1820s told of frequently encountering intense and immobilizing feelings of regret among New Englanders who had moved into the Ohio and Mississippi valleys. As he thought about the problem, he wished that it were possible to devise a statistical measure of the happiness of such individuals to be applied before and after emigration. Such a calculation, he suggested, could be invaluable in helping others to make up their minds about whether to emigrate.[35]

The depression of the recent migrants was heightened in many instances by the attitudes of those who had preceded them. In the cities and villages along the emigration routes, physicians, midwives, public officials, volunteer groups, and others originally did their best to make newcomers welcome or care for them when necessary. However, as the westward movement gathered momentum, the volume of travellers simply became greater than people in the valley towns could cope with. As a result, local populations gradually hardened to the human needs of the migrants. As early as the 1820s, Flint reported that the "scenes of suffering had become so frequent and familiar, as to have lost their natural tendency to produce sympathy and commiseration." In Cincinnati, Flint found large numbers of sick and dying New Englanders huddling in miserable hovels, friendless, without money for food, medication, or doctor, and with the local charities dried up. Similarly, a few years later, he found "multitudes" of poor Irish immigrants helpless, ill, and dying "unnoticed and unrecorded" in New Orleans. While lacking exact figures for any city, he gloomily concluded that the romantic processes of settling the West could not be separated from "numberless accompaniments of wretchedness like this."[36]

Subsequent observers in other cities—notably editors and health officials in such places as Montreal, Buffalo, Chicago, and Louisville—amply confirmed Flint's impressions. And, where any sort of counts could be made, these observers took great pains to point out that the diseases and deaths of the travellers should not be calculated as normal debits in the cities' vital-statistics reports. St. Louis, for one, did not want its normal salubrity judged by the impoverished and disease-stricken emigrants who passed through the city in the late 1840s. On the eve of the gold rush, on the outskirts of St. Louis, one could see large numbers of such travellers encamped for months at a time in the utmost misery, "sheltered only by boards temporarily thrown together, . . . badly provided with the necessaries of life, . . . [and] inattentive to the means of preserving health."[37] Some perished in these camps. Others recovered and managed eventually to push farther on to Fort Leavenworth, South Pass, or other points west, perhaps only to succumb later from some ailment or other. In 1850, among the estimated 50,000 persons who travelled the Overland route to California, huge numbers suffered from diarrheas and other diseases. One observer counted 600 graves in the fall of that year along the south side of the Platte River between the Missouri and Fort Kearney. Along the alternate north-side route, however, he found but three graves, though just as many persons had passed along it. He attributed the large difference in mortality chiefly to the fact that the south side had been used mainly by small, largely unorganized groups, while the north side of the river was generally used by the larger organized emigrant parties, many or most of which were accompanied by physicians.[38]

It was bad luck for many that the discovery of gold in California came in the midst of the nation's second great outbreak of cholera. As with other illnesses, many of the cholera cases along the trails occurred outside the notice of compilers of bills of mortality. But the rough estimates of mortality that trickled back East were enough to seriously alarm the travellers who came afterward. By the mid-1850s, it was common knowledge that "the routes to California, through vast prairies, arid deserts, and mountain regions, are strewed with the bones of emigrants who perished from this disease a thousand miles from houses, homes and crowded, filthy cities."[39]

Of course, there were some fortunate migrants who had relatively few medical problems. This was illustrated by the medical experience of the Ithaca and California Mining Company's 1849 trek, although having four physicians along, as this expedition did, was probably exceptional. In any case, during its arduous five-month journey between Ithaca, New York, and Salt Lake City, the group had no fatalities at all. During the early months, there was an assortment of diseases—many serious cases of diarrhea, two cases of cholera, several rheumatic affections, two of typhoid fever, several of "mountain fever," and many of *Rhus* poisoning, but all were kept under control. By the time the band reached the Rocky Mountains, its members were in excellent physical condition and virtually free from serious disease, though how much of this was due to the four physicians is an open question. One of the accompanying physicians, Dr. I. S. Briggs, attributed this largely to the constant physical exercise of walking and to the adoption of simple habits of living. When he heard some of the group singing as they crossed the mountains, Briggs marvelled at the way obesity, indolence, ennui, hypochondria, and other diseases of civilization had been left far behind. His letters, like those of the missionary physician Marcus Whitman, assured easterners that there could be medical advantages of going west.[40]

Whatever the medical problems that people encountered along their ways west, they were rarely as serious as the ones they encountered at the sites of their ultimate settlement. Invariably the greatest need for the wisdom of the medical handbook and the few carefully selected remedies came during the first few months or years of settlement. This was the time of "seasoning," the trying period that dampened the optimism of the strongest of the new settlers. Operation of the seasoning process could be observed in almost every inhabited area after every forward thrust of the frontier. It was a particularly direct form of natural selection which took both stamina and luck to survive.[41]

### Disease and Medical Growth in Gold Rush California

Nowhere in nineteenth-century America were the processes of physical adjustment or seasoning more severe than in California. Whether they arrived by sea or by land, the forty-niners soon found that there was fully as much disease as gold in California. In San Francisco, the thousands who paused on shipboard or in tents while buying mining equipment found the climate damp and unpleasant. They also suffered heavily from diarrheas, dysentery, and pulmonary disorders.[42] Later, out of San Francisco, up along the Sacramento and other rivers, they encountered large amounts of remittent, intermittent, and congestive fevers. Once in the mining districts, there were all of the above diseases and many more: frequent cases of scurvy; a great deal of exposure, rheumatism, poison-oak, and fatigue; occasional typhoid; and a multitude of accidents. Cholera went through the unsanitary mining towns in 1850 with terrible mortality. And, as the state grew in population, physicians had to cope with increasing amounts of smallpox, tuberculosis, measles, erysipelas, and insanity.

Much of the disease and suffering occurred simply because so many people arrived before the basic facilities had been provided to accommodate them. A shortage of proper food led to malnutrition and scurvy; a shortage of building materials kept many persons exposed to the elements in primitive shelters. Dr. J. D. B. Stillman described the miseries and disorder of the thousands who camped along the river near Sacramento during the winter of 1849–1850.

> With no covering but their tents, or beds but their blankets, barely raised from the wet earth, clothing filthy and covered with vermin, their condition when sick was wretched in the extreme. The immigrants were exposed to all the hardships of a camp without the discipline of any army, and the comforts or conveniences which . . . a quartermaster provides, or the intelligence and care of a medical staff. Although they started from home with partial organization, very few of them held together after touching the auriferous earth. Each man was thrown upon his own resources, ignorant of the dangers by which he was surrounded, and insufficiently provided to meet them.[43]

Demands for medical care were obviously very considerable, but only some of these could be satisfied. The migration into California included, as it happened, an unusually large number of medical men of all types, men who were as badly infected with gold fever as anyone. As early as June 1849, San Franciscans could consult "any quantity of doctors and apothecaries." By the time of the 1850 census, the state as a whole, with 626 regular physicians, was reported as having more practitioners than any other part of the United States, or one for every 147 inhabitants, plus almost innumerable sectarians, quacks, and pretenders to medical skills. Some of the physicians quickly constructed small private hospitals, while San Franciscans raised enough money by subscription in 1849 to build a public hospital. Private hospitals sprang up almost as early in Benicia, Marysville, and Sacramento, closer to the gold fields. In addition, a federal marine hospital was quickly established in San Francisco, a state hospital in Sacramento, and a mental hospital in Stockton. Within a surprisingly few years, with the organization of a society, a journal, and a medical school, California physicians acquired virtually all of the trappings of professional organization that their eastern colleagues had long had.[44]

Despite the early existence of such institutions in California, and an apparent abundance of physicians to serve them, the obtaining of quality medical care remained a problem for some time. Most hospitals were poorly equipped and had badly trained attendants. Medicines were often in short supply, while doctors' fees were exorbitant. The official 1850 fee bill adopted by the Medical Society of San Francisco turned out to be a monstrosity; contemporaries believed it had the highest fees ever adopted in any civilized country. Even Californians quickly came to view it as one of the all-time "curiosities of medicine." Meanwhile, "medical rapacity" so often "drained the poor miner of all his hard-earned dust" as to create intense public hostility toward the medical profession as a whole. In this situation, Thomas Logan reported that "many a worthy [i.e., reputable] physician studiously conceals his title," and never enters into medical practice at all. Not a few went directly to the gold fields. He came across others working as ox drivers, laborers, or in jobs "at barrooms, monte tables, boarding houses, etc."[45]

In short, the California environment greatly intensified those problems of physician supply and distribution which were bad enough elsewhere. It also tended, for all but the most dedicated, to further diminish the attraction of certain medical pursuits which even back East did not yet appeal very widely to the ordinary physician.


### Numerical Enthusiasms and Frustrations in the West

Despite the many distractions of life in midcentury California, as well as in many other areas west of the Appalachians, some of those physicians who remained in medical practice managed to find some time for the pursuit of medical studies, albeit only the modest inquiries usual at that point in history. In the Midwest and Far West as well as in the East, the most widespread mode of medical inquiry before the Civil War was through the use of numerical analysis. However, the special circumstances of western demography, prevailing social and medical attitudes, and institutional development created obstacles which made the pursuit of such studies in the region a frequently frustrating affair.

In the East, by the 1840s, the Baconian and statistical approaches were beginning to permeate almost every area of medical activity, administrative, professional, and scientific. Compilations and analyses were being made of hospital populations and other kinds of institutional data. Laborious clinical studies of disease were being undertaken using the numerical method of Pierre Louis. In almost every state, movements were being started to improve public mortality registers and generally to obtain better vital data. And, being launched with them were quantitative studies of the relations of such factors as poverty, urban life, and the physical environment to health and disease.[46]

Among those eastern physicians who migrated west, not a few were thoroughly inoculated with these quantitative enthusiasms. To them, it seemed only natural that the Baconian outlook, as well as the statistical methodologies and agencies, should be taken along as part of their baggage and implanted in the new western communities. And, to some extent, this transfer was made. However, the process was slow and the results spotty, and nowhere more so than in the spread of numerical method in clinical medicine.

When a physician was sufficiently motivated, he could study one or another aspect of his private practice with little reference to other physicians or local medical institutions. And some western physicians did just that, by themselves gathering numerical information about their obstetrical cases; analyzing the quantitative incidence of goiter, the stone, or cancer; studying their experiences with quinine or some other therapy. However, these studies were usually of limited value, since among other reasons, they tended to be based on small numbers of cases. As in the East, circumstances did not become favorable for really substantial clinical studies until well after the Civil War. The gathering of substantial patient populations in hospitals, asylums, and other medical-care institutions was an important step toward such research. However, even with the gradual appearance of such institutions in Cincinnati, St. Louis, Chicago, and other midwestern cities, only a small amount of serious clinical investigation seems to have gone on in them before the Civil War. The numerical studies carried out in the Buffalo almshouse and other institutions of that city by Austin Flint and Frank Hastings Hamilton were exceptions seldom matched elsewhere in the Midwest or West (and matched in the Deep South only in New Orleans).

The fact was that, for the majority of western physicians, medical investigation was regarded with a mixture of indifference and near-hostility. Such an attitude was, of course, still widespread among eastern physicians of this period as well, but everyone agreed that it was far more pervasive and deep-seated in the West. Edward Jarvis, visiting in Cincinnati on his way from Massachusetts to Louisville, found as late as 1837 that even among the local medical school faculty there was virtually no appreciation or use of Louis's numerical method of studying disease.[47] And outside such institutions as that there was even less interest in medical inquiry, whether by statistics or other modes.

There were several sources of this negative attitude, but none more direct than the concepts of Benjamin Rush. Rush, during most of the three immediate post-Revolutionary decades, was easily the most influential professor at the University of Pennsylvania's medical school. Through his lectures, he helped indoctrinate hundreds of students in a highly dogmatic generalized approach to medicine, one which assumed that there was really only one disease and, therefore, that only a single basic treatment was ever necessary—a combination of vigorous purging and strenuous bloodletting. Large numbers of these disciples emigrated to the West, where they tended to practice Rush's heroic therapy with great enthusiasm, and were able with little difficulty to perpetuate the dogma among their own students, because it was so simple and uncomplicated to apply. Naturally, physicians who were wholehearted believers in such a theory saw no need whatsoever of keeping numerical clinical records for the study of disease.

Rush's heroic therapy seemed to be tailor-made for a region that not only had out-sized folk heroes but also was supposed to have truly gargantuan diseases. Dealing with the latter clearly suggested forceful and out-sized therapies. At the same time, the region's doctors came to assume that there could be no real understanding of how to approach these diseases except by those with long personal familiarity with them.

Though suggested somewhat earlier, the simplistic concept of a peculiarly "western" medicine achieved particular strength and popularity during the 1840s. Many a physician contributed to its outlines. Samuel Cartwright asserted that the high mortality west of the Appalachians proved the justification for a distinct western medicine, one "independent of hyperborean Europe" as well as of the eastern United States.[48] A. B. Shipman went on to declare that western diseases were so universally "of a malarious origin, in the shape of fevers, or so modified by malaria" as to stagger the newly arrived eastern physician and render useless most of his training. Daniel Stahl, in turn, considered the eastern and European medical schools suitable only for instruction in the sciences. In other respects they were next to useless from his viewpoint, for they "cannot teach their pupils the symptomatology, aetiology, course and treatment of our western diseases." Similarly, many westerners regarded the standard texts by eastern medical authors as being largely unsuitable for the use of western physicians and medical students. Joseph Gallup's treatment of therapeutics, for instance, in his *Outlines of the Institutes of Medicine,* was dismissed as applicable only to the diseases and climate of New England, and was thus "inadmissable in the treatment of our western diseases."[49]

Eastern editors, along with those westerners who had no particular axes to grind, early viewed the claims of a distinctive western medicine for what they really were, "shallow sophistry," devoid of any basis in observational or experimental science.[50] Moreover, they recognized that the energetic promotion of such claims was principally made "by those interested in, or connected with, medical schools, and from considerations purely selfish." The critics conceded readily enough that there were differences in the type and character of various diseases from one section to another. But they found it absurd to pretend that such differences would be "stumbling blocks to a *thoroughly* educated physician." Such an idea seemed unworthy of the legitimate medical profession and "degrading to science."[51]

While the case for a peculiar "western" therapy was ridiculed by some within the region as well as by outsiders, few residents questioned the view that westerners themselves ought to go out of their way to support their indigenous medical institutions. Particularly persuasive in arguing this case was Cincinnati's Daniel Drake. In doing this, Drake avoided the most extreme chauvinism of some advocates of regional medicine. However, he was consistent, throughout a long career, in urging western medical students to patronize local medical schools. As an avowed supported of Henry Clay's "American system," he saw the need to protect and encourage the region's infant medical enterprises. At the same time, he was an enthusiast with a genuine conviction of the medical advantages existing in his "great and glorious valley," the Ohio-Mississippi basin. Drake pointed out that, by attending a local school, the medical student would not only be spared a long and expensive trip, but would also, by being able to make a close early study of western diseases, be qualified upon graduation to go quickly into practice in the region. Moreover, the new medical graduate who wanted to broaden himself scientifically before settling into practice could accomplish as much toward that end by staying close to home as by going to Europe. Somewhat in the mold of Thoreau, who studied the infinite by "travelling widely in Concord," Drake urged the young western physician to fill out his training by travel and careful observation of natural history, geology, anthropology, and disease, all while remaining within the confines of his own native valley.

Drake was convinced that two years spent by the fledgling physician making such kinds of Baconian observations "would do more to develop his character, and fit him for every day usefulness, than even the boasted European voyage." The successful pursuit of such an undertaking, of course, would require adopting orderly work habits, a real challenge in an area where disarray and disorder in physicians' offices seemed to be the rule. It demanded care in making observations, in marked contrast to the usual haphazard practice of western physicians, "whose habits of observation are extremely imperfect." And it meant keeping careful records of the scientific, medical, and demographic phenomena that were observed.[52]

The principal kind of demographic data-gathering in which the medical profession was involved had to do with the statistics of deaths and births. These were events that were supposed to be reported by individual physicians, sextons, and midwives, to be collected centrally wherever official provisions had been made. Here the East was admittedly more advanced. By fairly early in the nineteenth century, most large eastern cities had made provisions for the regular gathering of mortality data; in 1855, it was reported that 10 of them had even been collating and publishing such data in periodic bills of mortality, "some for many years." Some western cities also took steps as soon as possible to provide for clerks to gather comparable information. But enforcement of such data-gathering provisions was notoriously difficult in the early years of any community. As a result, the records were so spotty that no city in the region had started publishing its bills prior to 1855.[53] However, in certain communities, individual physicians, perhaps acting for medical societies or boards of health, occasionally dug out, analyzed, and published such data.[54]

During the 1840s and 1850s, the campaign to obtain effective public registration of vital statistics resulted in the establishment of registration systems in nine eastern states and in three western states—Kentucky, Ohio, and California—prior to the Civil War.[55] Everywhere—East as well as West, North as well as South—these state efforts were tedious and slow. But the new, and still largely rural, western states had particularly severe obstacles in the way of passing such legislation. The experience of California provides an example.

Numerous observers confirmed that for some time after the gold rush, the "chaotic state" of California's society remained "very unfavorable for statistical information." However, a few individual physicians had begun to work for public vital-statistics registration in the state almost as soon as churches, saloons, theaters, and other public facilities were erected. Pending such registers, of course, various attempts were made to determine the general extent of the diseases and mortality. Very rough ideas could be obtained from early coroners' and undertakers' records. But it probably was easier simply to glance at the potter's fields which sprang up on the edge of towns. J. D. B. Stillman counted close to 1,000 graves near Sacramento alone as early as April 1850. From them, he inferred that in the entire state fully a fifth of the forty-niners, or roughly 18,000, had died within a few months of their arrival.[56]

In late 1849, at a time when it could not really do much more for its people than furnish them with coffins and bury them as necessary, the provisional government in Sacramento did make an attempt to keep a record of the deaths. However, in the general disorder, this proved decidedly premature and useless. In San Francisco, an official death register was begun in 1855. This was composed essentially of data obtained from the sextons, but causes of death were sometimes confirmed by physicians.

As conditions around California began to stabilize during the decade of the 1850s, medical leaders and health officials finally persuaded the state lawmakers in 1858 to enact vital-statistics legislation. The provisions of this registration act were fairly advanced for that period and even included compulsory medical certification of the causes of death. However, inclusion of such provisions ended by making the law unworkable, since California physicians themselves failed to comply with them.[57] Large numbers of doctors, it seems, under the distractions of the "hot and entrancing pursuit" of gold, conspicuously gave up any pretense of scientific precision, fell into unsystematic habits, and generally failed to cooperate with any kind of authority.[58] Ultimately, moreover, society as a whole was far from ready. The law quickly had to contend with "an insurmountable prejudice against its provisions on the part of the people," and accordingly was repealed in 1860.[59]

Such "prejudices" against or hostilities toward vital-statistics registration were certainly not peculiar to Californians but were almost equally present elsewhere in the antebellum West. They arose partly out of ignorance, partly out of the age's resistance to physicians and to medical authority, partly out of a preoccupation with business affairs that left little room or patience for learning, science, or social organization. But they also had their roots in the population distribution of every western state, in the large predominance of rural over urban inhabitants. The demand for registration systems normally arose out of urgent public health problems encountered by urban physicians. Rural legislators, with scattered populations and less dramatic public health problems in their districts, could see little practical need for statewide registration. Furthermore, registration was workable only where populations were compact. This demographic factor was readily apparent even to an eastern commentator in 1850. "In a state possessing but one large city, and in which the country districts are . . . far from being densely populated, many years will probably elapse before the State Legislature shall be ready to organize a general and complete system of registration."[60] And indeed, it proved to be well into the twentieth century before many of the western states were able to have workable and effective registration systems.[61]

## Demography in Utopia

Western society was clearly not yet ready to push full speed ahead toward the mid-nineteenth-century ideal of a "republic of facts," to a community guided by statisticians who "take the observations, make the calculations, issue the orders, and guide the destinies."[62] But easterners were so taken with this ideal that it could hardly have been a surprise if some impatient enthusiast had attempted to launch, somewhere in the West, a utopian community specifically dedicated to and organized on statistical principles and practices. This did not actually occur. However, as it happened, many of the religious and secular communities that were actually founded did share to some extent in the statistical enthusiasms of the general society, though their uses of numbers in demographic and medical contexts varied widely.

Even certain of the century's religious communities which basically put little store in worldly affairs found some uses for numbering and record-keeping. But these did not usually include the collection and study of population data. The Shakers at New Lebanon, New York, for instance, paid close attention to keeping records of their herbal medicine enterprises in order to be able to meet business competition.[63] Yet, with their celibate life and lack of ambition for the quantitative growth of their community, the Shakers found no great need to study its demographic trends.

Similarly, the Rappites of the Harmony Society were the most thrifty, industrious, and orderly of people, whose prosperity owed much to the systematic records they kept of their agricultural, commercial, and other enterprises. However, as millenarians who believed that the second coming was close at hand, they were basically concerned with improving their present individual relationships with God rather than ensuring the future of the community on earth by having large families. The spiritual quality of their lives did not depend on gathering an ever-increasing quantity of people into the community. Fully satisfied with their present numbers, they prepared for the approaching millennium by their intense devotions in church and their playing of instrumental music as they labored in the fields. Similarly, it would have been a waste of time to undertake statistical studies which might reveal the demographic direction their group was taking.[64]

The Owenite experiment which, in the mid-1820s, followed on the same Indiana site, at New Harmony, might well have been expected to put a high premium on statistics and demographic analysis. After all, as one of the founder's biographers has remarked, Robert Owen himself "was never seen to read anything but statistics." Owen founded New Harmony out of a concern for the present world, not a future one. And he peopled it with an abundance of curious and intellectual individuals, some of whom were already experienced in collecting, classifying, and analyzing various kinds of data. However, lacking organization and direction, New Harmony disintegrated before its scholars could do much if anything along statistical lines under community auspices, and also before very substantial demographic statistics of the experiment could accumulate for study.[65]

Another experiment, Icaria, had it ever flourished, had been specifically intended to rely heavily on statistics. Its founder, Etienne Cabet, originally visualized using statistics to help organize and shed light on commerce, agriculture, government, education, population, and almost every aspect of communal life—"sur tout." In fact, separate buildings were set aside in the plans for keeping the records and making the necessary numerical studies.[66] Like New Harmony, however, the Icarian communities that were actually launched—in Texas, Nauvoo, and elsewhere—proved far too weak and transitory to create and sustain any significant mechanisms of that sort.

The statistical and demographic history of the early nineteenth-century Mormon community is of an entirely different order. For one thing, in sharp contrast to New Harmony and Icaria, it had staying power. Equally important, unlike the Rappites, its leaders had powerful ambitions for the earthly as well as the heavenly development of their community, ambitions which clearly involved numerical expansion. A church community with the unique doctrines of Mormonism required statistics to justify itself before the rest of society and to sell itself to potential members. And, when its concept of eligible members extended backward through all of recorded time, as did that of the Church of Jesus Christ of

Latter-Day Saints, its demands for vital population records became well-nigh insatiable.

From the outset, then, comprehensive record-keeping became almost as much a badge of Mormonism as polygyny did. Individual Mormons early developed the genealogy syndrome, with all it implied of ferreting out ancestral documents as well as carefully preserving contemporary family records. And, in the community as a whole, establishment of the offices of church recorder and church historian were among the first concrete steps taken upon formal organization of the church in 1830. In their various ledgers, these officials recorded such things as baptisms, current membership, sealings of both the living and the dead, and so on. Registration of vital events continued until civil offices were established. Meanwhile, in Liverpool and various continental cities, agents of the church kept records of the emigrants who were taking passage to join the Mormon community in America.[67]

Mormons embraced the Biblical injunction "to increase and multiply" even more enthusiastically than did the general populace, if that was possible, and even before the practice of polygyny became public. Their effort to build a strong church made large families desirable as a matter of course. Mormon newspapers occasionally carried items referring to the preventive checks of Malthusianism, but church leaders were even less interested in such restrictive demographic concepts than most persons in general society were. In fact, virtually the only prominent Mormon to go into population matters during the church's first half century was the mathematically minded but largely self-taught apostle Orson Pratt. And Pratt's concern was really limited to a series of abstruse attempts to calculate such things as the heavenly demography of the number of spirits in the preexistence.[68]

Outsiders were, of course, more interested in the worldly than the spiritual demography of the Mormons. The community's growing population was a matter of alarm to some. But far more noteworthy was the practice of polygyny, though the information that reached the public about the extent of the practice was mostly a prurient compound of rumor and imagination. A number of physicians addressed some of the medical aspects of polygyny during the 1840s, though mainly to relate the practice to life in a brothel, to note vaguely that few children are ever born in brothels, and to assert from uncertain statistical authority that "children diminish in proportion to the number of husbands."[69]

Much more specific, and equally titillating though little more based on actual statistics, were published comments on the medical and genetic effects of a generation or so of polygyny. A number of such accounts were given in the late 1850s and 1860s by army medical officers assigned to duty in Utah. Assistant Surgeon Roberts Bartholow in 1857 found that orthodox medical learning was in disrepute among the Mormons because of their preference for faith healing, particularly the laying on of hands to try to cure diseases or heal wounds. However, he found the climate of Utah remarkably healthful, with the only serious disease being "mountain fever," possibly typhus. At the same time, Bartholow, from his conventional Protestant viewpoint, took a hostile view of polygyny. He claimed he could see evidence that the practice, based on the "eager reach for young virgins," was already beginning to change its adherents biologically into a new and distinct race. The outward features of the new race were "the yellow, sunken, cadaverous visage; the greenish-colored eyes; the thick protuberant lips; the low forehead." Other observers eventually associated these traits more plausibly with malaria, but Bartholow chose to connect them to what he regarded as a fundamental immorality of the Mormons, one "compounded of sensuality, cunning, suspicion, and a smirking self-conceit." He also thought that the Mormon practices were resulting in increased sexual debility, in a preponderance of female births, and in a high infant mortality.[70]

Assistant Surgeon Charles H. Furley struck the same themes after a 1863 visit to Salt Lake City. The faces of virtually the entire Mormon populace, he concluded, were "stamped with a mingled air of imbecility and brutal ferocity," clear evidence of their sensuality and moral degradation. There was also a "feebleness and emaciation" in the bodily physique of individuals of "every class, age, and sex," which he felt proved their physiological inferiority to Gentiles. Furley remarked on the fact that although Mormon couples cohabited "only at such periods as are most favorable to impregnation," the fecundity of the women was still remarkable. On the other hand, he found that the polygynic children born of these unions "were puny and of a scorbutic tendency" and with such a noticeable disposition to tuberculosis that many of them were "doomed to an early death." Though he produced no statistics on the subject, he readily concluded that this infant mortality was so "much greater than in monogamous society, [that], were it not for the European immigration, the increase of inhabitants would be actually less than in gentile communities."[71]

Another community that had to face great outside hostility because of its sexual practices was that of the Perfectionists, centered at Oneida, in rural upstate New York. Unlike the Mormons, the numerical size of the tiny Perfectionist groups was never a source of great alarm to neighbors or other outsiders; at its peak in the 1860s and 1870s, it barely reached a membership of 300, all told. Despite the small numbers, however, the body placed even more emphasis on record-keeping, statistical methodology, and demographic analysis than did the Mormons. As such, it came closer than any other mid-nineteenth-century utopian community to becoming a full-fledged "republic of facts."

Perfectionist social and religious ideals, along with the cult's early economic difficulties, made for a unique demographic outlook, one involving a high degree of social discipline and strict limits on population. The group's leaders had nothing against the ultimate quantitative growth of the community. But they were strongly against indiscriminate growth or any expansion which might adversely affect the quality of life.[72]

A numerical watch over population thus became a central feature of the methodical ordering processes that the patriarch John Humphrey Noyes imposed at Oneida. Noyes had no doubt that science could be a "true handmaid" of his Perfectionist faith, and he embraced it wholeheartedly for its potential contributions to order. In his view, science was essentially a matter of pursuing such Baconian elements as measuring, weighing, and counting, and then analyzing the resulting statistics. Noyes thus made sure that careful records were kept of all of the community's activities, and he designated one of the community's members as its resident "statistician." True, since all property was held in common by the group, no interior accounts between members were found necessary. As one member observed, "Communism saves a deal of figuring." However, the community's fruit-preserving, thread, trap, silverware, and other enterprises that involved the outside world, needed careful business record-keeping in numerous ledgers and journals.

The planning and management of the community's human affairs required equally extensive record-keeping of demographic, medical, and sociological data. These records had far more than an archival or antiquarian interest. Community leaders were forever scrutinizing the ledgers which contained them, tabulating the data, searching for whatever meaning the figures might hold as to the success and progress of Perfectionism. How many new members were there? How many secessions? What were their states or countries of origin? What were the proportions of males and females in the membership? The age distribution? What were the sickness rates in the Children's House? At the drop of a hat, someone could produce figures on the oldest person in the community, on the heaviest, tallest, and shortest, and on the averages of such individuals. In fact, the membership as a whole seemed to have a voracious "appetite for statistics," one which was often put into play in discussions at the evening general assemblies of the members.

In the 1850s, Noyes instituted a numerical methodology, which he termed mathematical criticism, as one of the key elements in maintaining control in the community. This consisted of public criticism sessions, in which observations on the behavior or attitudes of given individuals were made by panels of peers. At the end of a given session—which was often a highly traumatic experience—the person involved was rated on a scale of one to six. As the *Oneida Circular* explained it, after the interrogators made their separate ratings, "the sum of estimates against [the] particular [individual] was taken and divided by the number of critics, which gave precisely the average of the opinions of the whole on each case."

Statistics were equally crucial in the administration of the Oneida community's peculiar social practices. Perfectionist belief centered on a notion of universal earthly love, which adherents went to great lengths to distinguish from "free love," and which they called Bible communism, or complex marriage. The system also included, from the late 1840s, the concept of scientific breeding, or stirpiculture.[73] However, the application of this latter concept—the selective propagation of Perfectionist babies—had to be postponed for nearly 20 years because of the group's extreme poverty. During those years (i.e., from about 1848 to 1868) virtually all conception under this nonexclusive marriage system was successfully avoided by the Spartan practice of "male continence." And subsequently, after the stirpiculture experiment had actually started, the same practice prevented the random and unrestrained procreation which Noyes hated so much, which he passionately felt was the basic cause of the poverty, the ruined women, the neglected children, and various other miseries of general society.

During its early years, in anticipation of the ultimate day when some conceptions could be permitted, and as an essential preliminary to scientific breeding, the community devoted great attention to building up the health and vigor of its members—hence, the close track they kept of such matters as height, weight, and sexual development. They worried lest their women grow delicate and frail, for, as their spokesmen pointed out, "maternity requires rugged health. If our female branch is sickly, propagation that is worth anything is out of the question."

Records of disease and mortality in the community were thus carefully maintained and earnestly studied. When smallpox threatened, most individuals were quick to have themselves and their children vaccinated. In other disease outbreaks, the community placed but little reliance on conventional medicine, and they used their accumulated figures to prove themselves right. Statistics of a diphtheria outbreak at Oneida in 1864 thus showed that two out of every three individuals who had been treated by regular physicians succumbed to the disease, along with two out of nine who had received standard medications without the attendance of physicians. However, no fatalities at all were reported to have occurred among 59 affected persons who had been treated by the leadership's own empirical measures. These measures included the liberal use of ice in the throat, applied along with energetic efforts to bolster the patient's religious faith and courage through the process of Criticism. Twenty-two of the 59 testified that they were substantially cured by Criticism alone.

To ward off sickness as much as possible, the members of the community again relied heavily upon faith, but also upon careful diet, fresh air, and attention to other aspects of hygiene. This stress on prevention seems to have paid gratifying dividends in reducing child mortality, at least by the community's own calculations. In 1860, they pointed out, 45 percent of the total mortality in Philadelphia was of children 15 years and younger, while in rural New England and New York, the figure was 40 percent. In Oneida, however, child mortality had been reduced to less than 25 percent of the total.

A decade later Theodore R. Noyes compared the overall mortality of the community during its first 21 years with the national experience. The Oneida population admittedly constituted a very small sample, but Noyes thought the general mortality patterns shown by the figures reliable. Actually, despite its preventive efforts, the community's death rate from diseases of the digestive, urinary, generative, and respiratory systems, as well as from accidents, exceeded that of the United States as a whole as reported in the 1860 census. On the other hand, Oneida's record was far better than the national figure in the case of zymotic diseases and slightly better for circulatory diseases.

Members of the American medical profession were especially interested in the community's statistics of mental and nervous disorders because of the light they might shed on the effects of complex marriage on the participants. John Humphrey Noyes and other community leaders had readily admitted that considerable nervous tension, both among males and females, accompanied the effort to control the sexual impulse in the course of male continence. However, an analysis made by Dr. Theodore Noyes, son of the patriarch, seemed to show that only where overindulgence or other sexual excesses occurred was there any unusual occurrence of mental or nervous disorders. Properly practiced in the community, the younger Noyes wrote, the combination of complex marriage and male continence resulted in an "exceptionally small" amount of serious nervous disease in comparison with the general population.[74]

The records of the stirpiculture experiment were not entrusted to the community statistician but were kept by the elder Noyes himself. Couples desiring to participate in the stirpiculture experiment made their wishes known to a testing committee or to the community's central council. But the authority to decide who should be allowed to mate always remained with the patriarch. Noyes made his decisions in these cases scientific as far as he was able, decisions based upon his accumulations over the years of medical, genealogical, and sociological data on the various individuals in the community. "Accurate pedigree accounts," he maintained, were essential to a program of eugenic propagation. Science, for him, constituted a far more compelling motive for keeping pedigree records than the property interests or family pride which impelled most people. *"Their* records, compared with those which scientific propagation necessitates, are mere 'chalk marks.' They will answer well enough for 'mongrel' society; but are wholly unsuitable to the approaching era of stirpiculture."[75]

Actually, accounts of the sexual history of every individual were being maintained well before the launching of the main phase of the stirpiculture experiment. At least those sexual solicitations which males made within the agreed-on system became part of an official record, as did any denials by the leaders of requested matings, or formal rejections by the females. The stirpiculture decade of 1869–1879 in itself was not long enough to produce a very large volume of statistics. The key figures were the 51 applications considered from couples desiring to become parents, 42 of which were approved. The resulting unions brought forth 58 living children, 9 of whom had been sired by the community's patriarch, Noyes.

Noyes considered it to be the business of any communistic society to pay close attention to such data and, through statistical analysis, to determine and apply the laws of scientific breeding. In his own community, he attempted to weigh some of the variables which indicated a superior breed of woman: her longevity, her state of health after successive pregnancies, her mental and spiritual qualities, the character of her offspring, and so on. Noyes recognized that he could not go far toward determining general laws with only the limited population of Oneida to work on, and he urged like-minded individuals of the 1870s—

phrenologists, popular physiologists, and Darwinists—to join him in the further collecting of the statistics of parentage which were needed.

Throughout the years of its existence, Oneida's leaders were continually publishing quantitative information to justify the experiment in the eyes of the hostile outside world. Almost any issue of the *Oneida Circular* was filled with figures and explanations to dispute some assertion or other about the community's practices. An article in 1869 presented statistics aimed at refuting the allegation that complex marriage was stunting the growth of the community's women; "systematic measurements," the author declared, demonstrated that "more than three-fourths of our young women were taller than their mothers." The following year, Theodore Noyes reported on sperm tests which were conducted to disprove the frequently made suggestions that the long practice of male continence had left Oneida's men impotent. Equally persuasive were statistics presented to the medical community showing that the practice had not left the women sterile; when the stirpiculture era finally got under way in 1868, 16 out of 24 women were successfully impregnated in the very first two and a half years of the experiment.

A major use of statistics at Oneida was in defending the community against charges of licentiousness. In the Perfectionist view, their practice of "separating the social from the propagative in the sexual relation" was the very opposite of licentiousness. This was proven, they argued, by the community's dramatic success, between 1848 and 1868, in limiting conception, and also by the record of its members' good health. Spokesmen loved to point out, in those Spartan early years, that the community's entire natural increase of population, by birth, was actually "considerably less than the progeny of Queen Victoria alone. So much for the outcry of licentiousness."

Numbers thus became Oneida's main bulwark of defense. As a spokesman concluded: "We gave our enemies physical facts—statistics— 'figures that cannot lie.' The syllogism we present is this: Licentiousness inevitably leads to disease and illegitimate propagation; but there is no disease or illegitimate propagation among us; *ergo,* we cannot be licentious."

The defensive statistics of the experimental communities were as understandable as the exaggerated data produced by many of the West's other new communities. Moreover, they were not dissimilar in some ways to the figures emanating at this same time from the South. However, in magnitude and complexity, the realities of southern regional demography were a far cry from those of these tiny societies.

# 5

# The Medical Arithmetic of
# Southern Regional Development

The social, demographic, and medical expansion of the antebellum South was hardly less dynamic than that of the West. As the South exploded beyond its eighteenth-century numerical and territorial limits, its leaders and spokesmen sometimes seemed about as concerned with changes in population and the rise of cities and towns as with the prices of tobacco, cotton, and slaves. As population moved into the Deep South, a substantial buildup of medical personnel and institutions accompanied the multiplication of other institutions—social, political, and scientific. Here as elsewhere, physicians were uniquely situated to observe and comment on demographic matters as well as upon such strictly medical matters as the incidence and treatment of disease. In this part of the country, however, the health-related statistics which were produced were often profoundly shaped by the special circumstances and ideologies of southern regionalism and slavery.

The central demographic and social fact in the South throughout this period was the uneasy coexistence of its two principal populations, of whites and blacks "fastened to each other," as Tocqueville observed, "unable to separate entirely or to combine."[1] Consistently, from 1790 to 1860, well over one-third of the officially enumerated population of the region was composed of blacks, and all but a small fraction of those were slaves.[2] (In certain states, of course, the blacks greatly outnumbered the whites.) In addition, there were fairly substantial numbers of Indians. Although the Indians were almost certainly far fewer than the blacks in 1790, the exact numbers were not known, since the tribes were not enumerated in the various censuses. During the next 70 years, however,

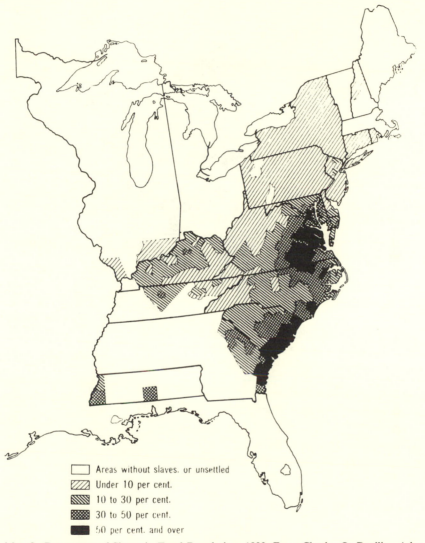

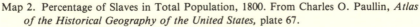

☐ Areas without slaves. or unsettled
▨ Under 10 per cent.
▩ 10 to 30 per cent.
▦ 30 to 50 per cent.
■ 50 per cent. and over

Map 2. Percentage of Slaves in Total Population, 1800. From Charles O. Paullin, *Atlas of the Historical Geography of the United States,* plate 67.

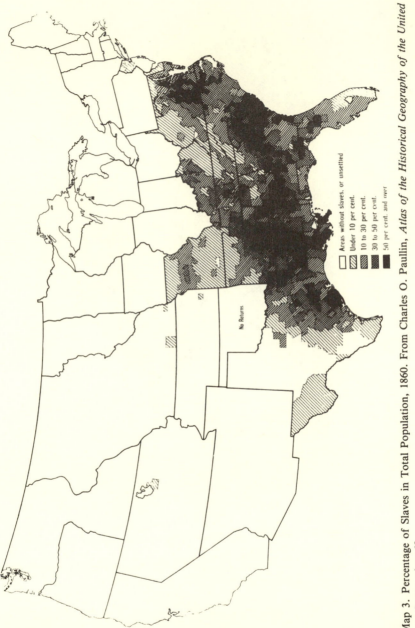

Map 3. Percentage of Slaves in Total Population, 1860. From Charles O. Paulin, *Atlas of the Historical Geography of the United States*, plate 68.

Areas without slaves, or unsettled
Under 10 per cent.
10 to 30 per cent.
30 to 50 per cent.
50 per cent. and over

No Returns

it is well known that these numbers dwindled to no more than a few thousand, in part because of the relentless effects of wars and removals, but principally, perhaps, because of the impact of the whites' and blacks' diseases.[3]

By contrast, both the blacks and the whites continued to increase, partly by augmentation from outside sources and partly naturally. In the case of the outside increase, however, there were certain restricting factors. The white population continued to have limited infusions of migrating northerners and of European immigrants. But, by early in the nineteenth century, far more of both groups were deliberately rejecting the idea of going to the South. Eventually it became a truism that "the emigrants shun the slave states, where labor is degraded," in favor of the North and West. By midcentury this could be documented; a British commentary reported that "six of the border free states had, in 1850, a population of 1,403,629 foreigners, while the six adjacent slave states . . . had not above 190,138, less than one-seventh of the other."[4] The black population, for its part, continued to be built up by continuing shipments of slaves, either directly from Africa or by way of Caribbean ports. However, after the slave trade was made illegal, in 1808, this traffic seems, despite continuing illicit shipment, to have greatly reduced.[5] Certainly, as the century progressed, natural increase accounted for progressively greater proportions of the increase of both the whites and the blacks.

Expansion of population made for more and sometimes larger plantations, towns, and cities in some of the older areas of the South. At the same time, stimulated by such factors as the opening of the former Indian territories and the exhaustion of land in the older South, very large numbers of both whites and blacks removed from those eastern areas to new lands, new plantations, and new communities in the Deep South and Southwest. In these new areas as well as in the old, no topics stirred up greater demographic interest among southern whites than those dealing with the black population, its possible disposition, and its vital events.

## Early White Perceptions of Black Demography

By 1800 many whites, South as well as North, had come to regard the institution of slavery as a malignant tumor on the body of American society, and fervently looked for some way to end this acknowledged evil. In fact, an emancipation movement had gathered considerable momentum. In 1810, Timothy Dwight and others thought that this presaged the imminent freedom of all of the blacks.[6] By the 1820s, however, the movement to obtain emancipation laws in the individual states had virtually ended. Northern states had indeed effectively abolished the institution, but southern slavery remained relatively little affected.

In both sections of the country the emancipation laws, along with voluntary manumission, created significant and steadily growing populations of free blacks.[7] As they considered these new populations, some observers in both regions saw that emancipation, given the current social attitudes of the dominant whites, was not always a favor to the blacks, at least in a demographic sense. In fact, in many places, notably the large cities, the economic and social condition of the free blacks was such as to rapidly make them appear as members of yet another badly degraded and declining race that could not compete with the dominant whites. Commentators such as Tocqueville noted obvious parallels between their deplorable condition and the plight of the Indians.

> They remain half civilized and deprived of their rights in the midst of a population that is far superior to them in wealth and knowledge, where they are exposed to the tyranny of the laws and the intolerance of the people. On some accounts they are still more to be pitied than the Indians, since they are haunted by the reminiscence of slavery, and they cannot claim possession of any part of the soil. Many of them perish miserably, and the rest congregate in the great towns, where they perform the meanest offices and lead a wretched and precarious existence.[8]

These generalizations seemed to be strongly supported by the records that were accumulating in New York and Philadelphia. The former, between 1820 and 1826, was reported to have an average death ratio of 1 in 40.17 among whites and 1 in 19.01 among blacks. Very similarly, Philadelphia, through the decade of the 1820s, had ratios of 1 in 42.3 among whites and 1 in 21.7 among blacks. And in both places, observers had no doubt that the preponderance of deaths among the blacks was "owing to the effects of poverty upon that degraded race."[9]

In Philadelphia, the dispensary physician, Gouverneur Emerson, noted by 1820 that the poverty of the blacks was among the worst of any group in the city. And, as he visited them in the run-down houses to which they had been relegated, houses on some of the city's filthiest alleys, Emerson found that their diseases and mortality were the most devastating.[10] Dr. Charles Lee came to comparable conclusions about

New York's free blacks. "The fact that only 79 persons of colour are taxed out of 15,102 taxpayers in 1835, shows conclusively the generally impoverished condition of that race. Indeed, a striking feature in the population of New York, as well as all our principal cities, is the degraded and wretched state of the blacks; not one-tenth, according to the best calculations, have any regular employment, but depend on transient jobs, stealing, begging, and public charity for support."[11]

Mortality differentials between the races in urban prisons could not be blamed on poverty. Reports of the Eastern State Penitentiary in Philadelphia indicated that, in an 1837 inmate population that included 232 whites and 154 blacks, three-fourths of the deaths were among the blacks. This was not attributed to any differences in treatment given the two races, but rather to the presumed innate character of the blacks, "whose health and habits are known to be degraded and vicious to the last degree." By 1849, however, some analysts were attributing these continuing differentials to the longer sentences given to black prisoners, as well as to the poorer physical adaptability of blacks to prison conditions, especially to odors, sedentary occupations, and lack of sunlight.[12]

The northern free-black population expanded despite the calamitous mortality rates. James Fenimore Cooper noted, however, that there could have been no such increases in the large cities had not large numbers of blacks moved in from other places. They were drawn to New York, he thought, by its extensive opportunities for employment, chiefly at that time as house servants and laborers on ships, and to Philadelphia by the attractive philanthropies of the city's Quakers and German groups. In the absence of such augmentation from outside, Cooper concluded, "their moral condition, their vagrant habits, their exposure, their dirt, and all the accumulated misfortunes of their race," along with their infrequency of entering into marriages, all militated against the perpetuation of the free blacks as long as "society exists under the influence of its present prejudices."[13]

As the century went on, southern spokesmen considered the deplorable social and demographic plight of the northern free blacks to be one of the most telling arguments for slavery. Recognizing this, abolitionists and other reform groups in the large northern cities multiplied their inquiries into the number and condition of the blacks. These resulted, among other things, in numerous statistical tracts aimed at trying to bring about improvements. Meanwhile, substantial numbers of concerned whites were exploring alternatives to emancipation.

The most promising of these alternatives for many political leaders and intellectuals was the colonization movement. This colossally ambitious project aimed at shipping the entire slave population back to Africa. Early enthusiasts regarded this as a solution which could reconcile feelings of humanity toward the black with the desire to protect southern whites from being overrun by any mass emancipation. However, by the 1830s, realists among them had to confess that colonization could no longer be regarded as a practical solution to the "black problem." Its achievements had proved to be paltry in comparison to the needs. Whatever real benevolence lay behind the gesture, statistically it was not an effective social or demographic solution. As Tocqueville tersely reported in 1835, "In twelve years the Colonization Society has transported two thousand five hundred Negroes to Africa; in the same space of time about seven hundred thousand blacks were born in the United States."[14]

It was evident to all, from the successive census enumerations, that, in the South far more than in the North, the black population was far from stationary and was steadily increasing. While there was no clear information, at least before 1810, as to how much of this was due to natural increase, observers frequently commented upon "the astonishing number of births, to the south, among the negroes." As part of this there were abundant, and sometimes authoritative, allegations that the whites themselves contributed to the number of these births and thereby to the complexity of racial relationships. The physician Thomas Ewell, for one, reported that southern "superintendents or overseers generally cohabit with the negro women . . . , and with such success, that but few women of the farms fail having white children by them."[15]

In the 1820s Matthew Carey took note of the "great disparity of the increase of the two races" in Maryland, Virginia, the Carolinas, and Georgia. Between 1790 and 1820, he found, while the white population "increased by 57 percent, the slaves increased 81." For Carey, it seemed clear that any increase of the free population of a slave state by immigration "is checked by the curse of slavery." Southern whites were well aware of the continuance of this differential through much of the antebellum period. Meanwhile, they also had to live with the knowledge that northern whites consistently increased in number even more rapidly than did the southern Negro slaves.[16]

To some southerners, it made good business sense in the nineteenth century, at least in the short term, to stimulate the natural increase of the slaves. To accomplish this seemed to require a certain benevolence on the part of the masters. Rural South Carolina correspondents of David Ramsay indicated in 1809 that in their districts, at least, such a policy was already in effect and working. "The black population increases every year. More slaves are born than die . . . and kindness with proper attention to their food, clothing, and habitations, will increase their number." The register kept by Joseph J. Murray of Edisto Island parish in that state recorded the birth of 74 black children on his plantation between 1792 and 1808, of whom 53 still lived at the latter date, 33 of them females. This was a far better survival record than that of the white children of the nearby community, where only 122 out of 212 babies still lived. Comparable increases were reported at other plantations in the district and in certain other rural areas of the South.

The same magnitude of black increase could not be claimed for southern port cities. There, high mortality rates prevailed among the free-black populations as well as among recently arrived slaves. At least some Charleston physicians in 1808 genuinely looked forward to the end of the slave trade as a medical and statistical blessing that would substantially cut down on that mortality. However, a Savannah doctor found the death rate was high among settled blacks as well, mainly because of "the precarious attention they generally receive in sickness."[17]

Those who tried to obtain more information of this sort found that very few southern communities bothered to keep official vital statistics of the blacks, particularly of the slaves. Adam Seybert noted in 1818 that even the census enumerators paid little attention to obtaining significant statistics about the slave population. "The slaves are returned, in the aggregate, without any discrimination of sex or age; they have been only regarded as property." At the same time, Seybert believed that a general tendency had set in, following the federal prohibition of the slave trade, to clothe and feed slaves better, and generally to treat them better than previously. The trend would, he thought, have a number of demographic consequences.

It will be interesting to notice the effects of these changes on their increase; it is certain that the powers of generation must be promoted by them. The masters will also add to the proportion of the females; hitherto, the slaves consisted principally of males who were capable to labour; few females were employed, because refined calculation had taught the masters, that it cost less to buy grown up slaves than it did to raise them; it is probable in future, the rate of the increase of the slaves will be nearly the same as that of the free [white] population.[18]

Indeed, well before midcentury—in fact, by the time the migration of thousands of slaves, with their masters, had been completed to new plantation sites in the Deep South and Southwest—this expectation had been more than realized.

## Southern Expansion and Medical Institution-Building

The nineteenth-century expansion into the new areas of the South went through the same stages as the push westward—through successive periods of Indian wars, land surveying and distribution, settlement and seasoning, and community development. As elsewhere, the opening of new territories was accompanied by large hopes, but in most places real life was crude, boisterous, often filthy, and usually filled with anxieties and back-breaking labor. From 10 to 20 years were needed before the hectic early activity settled into fairly regular patterns of living and the makeshift original facilities were replaced by something more adequate. However, by the 1840s, even in the newest parts of the South, many of the large plantations had shaken down into fairly smooth routines of existence and production, while members of the scattered communities which had taken root after the War of 1812 had achieved relatively settled lives. Dr. S. C. Farrar in 1849 described the sort of transformation that had occurred since his own arrival at Jackson, Mississippi. Within some 18 years, wild speculation in lands, banks, and business had flowered and then largely ended; disorderly saloons, or "doggerys," had long enlivened almost every crossroad, but now had mostly disappeared under temperance pressures; schools, churches, and other appurtenances of civilized life had taken root; "now we enjoy more composure, we are better lodged and fed. . . ."

Medicine, too, changed drastically in a relatively short time. The processes of medical buildup in the new areas of the Deep South and Southwest followed much the same patterns as they had in the region around the Great Lakes and the upper Mississippi Valley. This involved an influx of restless or unsuccessful regular physicians from the Northeast and the Old South, together with sectarians and quacks of every hue. The early regular practitioners gave the South the reputation of being the most extreme center of "heroic" therapy. However, Farrar thought that by 1848 the day of these indiscriminate measures was fading throughout the region. In Jackson, at least, he reported that the physicians "resort less to the lancet and heavy doses of calomel. We rely more on aperients, diaphoretics, opiates, salt water enemata, cold drinks, sponging with cold water, effusions of cold water, sinapised foot baths, occasionally dry and wet cups and blisters, but above all, on the use of quinine in sedative doses.'' Under combined social and therapeutic changes, he felt that people had become less liable to disease, and, when fevers did come, they were more manageable than in earlier years. The important thing in the physician's new confidence, Farrar thought, is that "we have become better acquainted with the pathology and treatment of Southern diseases.''[19]

Like their peers in other new sections of the country, southern practitioners were community leaders and builders as well as medical men. As such they often played key roles in the early business, educational, governmental, and scientific life of the South's growing towns and cities. At the same time, they joined together professionally to form medical societies, found medical journals and schools, launch hospitals, and help organize the mechanisms of local social welfare and public health.

From the mid-1840s, such medical institutions began to multiply rapidly. Early in that decade, it was reported that not a single regular medical journal was being published south of Charleston in the East or Louisville in the West, but by 1860 every sizeable southern city had acquired one or more such periodicals and often a sectarian journal or two as well. Similarly, regular medical schools in the region multiplied from four to around a dozen in the 20 years before the Civil War, while medical societies proliferated even more. Urban medical-care institutions, which were few and far between early in the century, gradually included increasing numbers of clinics, asylums, inoculation and quarantine facilities, and marine hospitals, together with private hospitals for blacks in eight or more cities and similar facilities on large plantations. Overall, where the scientific and professional institutions of medicine were sparse prior to the 1830s, by 1860 many a southern town could point with pride to having some of these basic facilities. Several, including Savannah, Augusta, Richmond, Mobile, Nashville, and Memphis, with nuclei of active and capable physicians serving such institutions, joined Lexington and Charlottesville in achieving at least local medical repute. However, only Charleston, Louisville, and New Orleans seemed to have been comparable to the large northern or midwestern cities in the diversity and extent of their medical facilities and institutions.

This antebellum medical institution-building in the southern towns, like community-building generally, was accompanied by much the same competitive enthusiasm and rhetoric as in other new areas. The launching of a new hospital was almost as much a community event as the coming of a new railroad. Promoters of new proprietary medical schools at Nashville, Mobile, and other locations filled their prospectuses with extravagant visions of the anticipated medical and scientific glories which the institutions were expected to bring their communities. Editors of associated medical journals publicized one new faculty or another, and extolled their expected advantages to prospective medical students. Some of the spokesmen saw the rising institutions filling genuine needs in the medical life of the South. Others seemed to visualize them primarily as bastions of a distinct "southern" medicine.[20]

## Medical-Demographic Data-Gathering in the South

Partly as a reflection of the early paucity of medical institutions, the number of nineteenth-century southern physicians who did any kind of medical investigation or writing before 1840 was far smaller even than in the North. Richard Arnold of Savannah was envious of the seemingly large number of northern doctors who not only had time for such inquiry but also had easy access to good medical libraries. By contrast, he complained, in the South "practice engrosses almost all the attention, and cut off from books, comparatively, there is not that incentive to write here as at the North."[21] Less sympathetically, some felt that southern physicians simply had a constitutional dislike of serious investigation. John Bell of Philadelphia, intimating that this was a real problem, suggested in 1846 that southerners should "declaim less . . . and study more." He thought that individuals could help their profession by launching much-needed local and regional medical investigations, keeping a "regular and faithful record of cases, divested of verbose speculation." More broadly, they should blanket the South with the same kinds of systematic inquiries that were proving so fruitful in other regions.[22]

Whatever their disadvantages, certain southern physicians did find some opportunity to contribute to medical and demographic knowledge. For them as for their northern colleagues, the results turned out, during these antebellum decades, to be increasingly quantitative. Southern physicians who kept abreast of the literature were becoming aware of the rise of numerical medicine as well as of political arithmetic or statistics generally; Josiah Nott thought that England's *Medico-Chirurgical Review* was particularly responsible for bringing these subjects to the attention of his southern colleagues.[23] Whatever the stimuli, in the South as elsewhere, at least a few curious medical men were already gathering facts about populations, diseases, and the phenomena of natural history. If the region had more than its quota of calomel doctors and mindless bleeders, it also had a share of avid Baconians, Humboldtians, and other data collectors, breeds whose contributions became increasingly conspicuous and important during the 1840s.

In 1826, the Charleston architect-engineer Robert Mills compiled an exhaustive summary of the *Statistics of South Carolina*—political, economic, civil, military, and natural, as well as medical.[24] Moreover, Charleston's remarkable early tradition of quantitative medical studies, which had owed so much to John Lining, Lionel Chambers, and David Ramsay, remained alive in the mid-nineteenth century through the activities of a small new coterie of statistically minded medical scientists. Several of these, such as F. Peyre Porcher and St. Julien Ravenel, were known partly for their contributions to the natural sciences. John L. Dawson, on the other hand, as city registrar made important innovations in the keeping and use of local vital records, while he also collaborated with H. W. Desaussure in 1849 in conducting a comprehensive city census. These men, with the cooperation of the local medical society and civic officials, helped give Charleston a special reputation among cities of the South, as "the only one whose [vital] statistics have been kept for any length of time with accuracy."[25] Meanwhile, Robert W. Gibbes led a valiant, if not entirely successful, state effort in the 1850s for a workable vital-statistics registration system.

Porcher, Gibbes, and Peter C. Gaillard had been among the several South Carolina students of Pierre Louis. Other southerners who had trained under or were influenced by the Paris clinicians included James L. Cabell in Virginia, Josiah Nott in Mobile, John Y. Bassett in Huntsville, Alabama, and a few others. These physicians helped spread an appreciation of the numerical approach in medicine even as they worked to elevate southern medical institutions.

The young Savannah physician John LeConte particularly tried to stir up southern interest in statistical investigation. In 1846 LeConte made a substantial analysis of French and English cancer data which showed, among other things, the significance of age in the disease, its much greater incidence among women, and its progressive rate of increase in the population. He also lectured among the local medical profession to urge them to adopt simple statistical methods. Not too much should be attempted or expected along this line at first, he cautioned, since statistical science was still "in its infancy. This is the period for collecting facts, for multiplying observations, for establishing the basis for wider and higher generalizations."[26]

Few physicians who had any ambitions for the medicine of their region disagreed with LeConte.[27] Still, prior to the mid-1840s, relatively little systematic medical fact-finding was undertaken outside of Charleston. The collective hygienic condition of the rural South, of the plantation population, was conspicuously uninvestigated. This was partly due to the inadequacy of plantation records, and partly due to the failure of southern medical writers to interest themselves in whatever other records were in existence. A number of attempts were made to improve both situations.

Careful record-keeping was generally acknowledged to be one of the desiderata of a well-managed plantation, along with decent housing, food, clothing, and medical care for the slaves. Some meticulous owners did, indeed, keep elaborate "plantation books" in which, along with their business accounts, they maintained detailed records of such basic things as crop acreages, weather, and health of the slaves. Alexander Telfair of Savannah instructed his overseer to set down "the names of the sick; the beginning, progress, and finishing of work; the state of the weather; Births, Deaths, and everything of importance that takes place on the plantation."[28]

While large plantations seem to have been better than small ones about keeping such records, in general this function was badly neglected during the antebellum period, especially while unsettled conditions prevailed in new areas of the Deep South and Southwest. In the mid-1840s Thomas Affleck, the Mississippi planter and almanac compiler, put on the market a standard record and account book designed for use on cotton and rice plantations; these sold at $2.50 to cover a plantation of 40 field hands, $3.00 for one of 80 hands. However, in 1851 Affleck had to admit that it was still "extremely difficult to arrive at correct sanitary and statistical results, anywhere in the South, from the want of correctly-kept plantation records."[29]

Meanwhile, the southern medical profession as a whole showed relatively little interest in digging out and studying whatever information had been kept. Recognizing this, some editors of the new southern medical journals went to great efforts after the mid-1840s to reverse the situation, partly as a matter of sectional loyalty, partly in order to collect interesting material for their journals. However, authors whose articles included extensive statistical material often still encountered serious obstacles to getting them published. On the one hand, many southern editors proved reluctant to include tables or rows of figures because they thought that their readers would find them unappealing, and on the other hand, southern printers were found to be so prone to error as to make the statistical data useless.[30]

During the early 1840s southern physicians became aware of the data-gathering examples offered by recent European and northern medical-topographical and urban sanitary inquiries.[31] Though relatively few such inquiries were as yet under way in the South, at least some of the region's doctors were spurred to this type of investigation by a call from the American Medical Association for city sanitary surveys. The association's publication of 11 such surveys late in that decade included reports on Charleston, Louisville, and New Orleans. In turn, this compilation provided the stimulus for a still more systematic southern effort to gather such data.

In 1848 and 1849, Erasmus D. Fenner of New Orleans decided to branch off from ordinary medical journalism to publish an annual work which would deal with the collective medical and demographic experience of the entire region. To launch this venture, he asked physicians to furnish reports of the medical topography, meteorology, and diseases of their respective communities. Fenner then gathered the contributions together in the *Southern Medical Reports.*

These volumes provided valuable, heavily quantitative insights into the midcentury South. The project also proved to be a pioneering exercise in data-gathering for many if not most of the participants. For some, perhaps their only previous contact with scientific fact-finding had been their experience with census marshals. Several of the southern states had not yet conducted geological, botanical, or zoological surveys, and some had not even begun to consider the creation of vital-statistics registration systems. E. M. Pendleton of Sparta, Georgia, noted the complete "absence of everything like sexton's reports, records of births, deaths, etc." to help the would-be canvassers of country regions.

While Fenner's volumes brought together much new sanitary information about Charleston, New Orleans, and other cities, they were especially noteworthy for the light they shed on the health conditions in rural sections of the South. Some physicians documented both the medical cases and the rude social and political life of their backwoods patients. Others tabulated the numbers of churches, newspapers, Masons, and Sons of Temperance, along with the various species of medical practitioners. Some ferreted out figures of fertility, disease, and death on the plantations, while others searched the recent records of small-town sextons. A few listed local plants, provided weather observations, and characterized the geological characteristics of their communities.

Even though the *Southern Medical Reports* had to be discontinued after 1850, the enterprise was remarkably successful during its brief existence in promoting an essentially objective type of medical fact-finding in the South.[32] Many of its contributors seemed to relish their new Baconian roles, and several knowledgeably invoked the names of Quetelet, Louis, and Shattuck in the course of their statistical searches. Some of them, including Fenner, helped materially to make New Orleans one of the most robust and productive centers of demography activity in mid-nineteenth-century America.

### Demographic Problems and Enthusiasms in New Orleans

New Orleans emerged in the 1840s, not only as the largest and most vigorous commercial hub of the antebellum South, but as a city with a highly active, creative, and contentious medical life. Both the business and the medical communities proved to have lively interests in demography and statistics. Conspicuous in the former group was the publicist, J. D. B. DeBow. A newcomer to New Orleans in the mid-1840s, DeBow sought to further both his own and the city's economic prospects through the gathering and dissemination of data—economic, political, and demographic. In the process he became interested in helping elevate the quality of southern statistics. As one step toward this, he promoted and headed the new Louisiana State Bureau of Statistics in the late 1840s, though that body proved short-lived. DeBow accomplished far more over the years by writing and soliciting quantitative contributions for the pages of his *Commercial Review of the South and Southwest* (popularly known as *DeBow's Review.*)[33] By the mid-1850s, when he was appointed superintendent of the Seventh Census of the United States, he was widely known around the country as a statistical enthusiast. His contributions to the census were not particularly innovative, but he did recognize the desirability of such long-range improvements as a permanent census bureau. However, that institution remained several decades into the future.

Almost equally conspicuous as enthusiasts of quantitative knowledge and methods in New Orleans were certain physicians, private and public.[34] To be sure, few if any physicians of the city found time for clinical studies using Louis's numerical method, despite the wealth of opportunity for such investigations in the wards of Charity Hospital. However, the admission and discharge records of that institution were extensively mined, by Fenner, William P. Hort, and others, for what they revealed of the distribution and extent of diseases in the city, particularly its recurrent devastating epidemics.[35] The New Orleans doctors were also greatly concerned at this time with vital statistics because of the light which such data might shed upon the hygienic status of the city.

The medical journalist Bennet Dowler had a far more comprehensive concept than most of the scope and uses of vital statistics. For one thing, Dowler shared with DeBow a large sense of the special mystique of New Orleans, and particularly of its key destined role as the gateway to the American interior. As captivated as Mark Twain was by the great river which flowed past the city, Dowler challenged Samuel Forry's interpretation of the army statistics—that the Mississippi was generally less salubrious in its lower than its upper reaches. "The Hindus worship the sacred Ganges," he complained, "and the Egyptians adore the beneficent Nile, while certain sanitarians and epidemic expounders, less devout, inaugurate a myth on the banks of the lower Mississippi, namely, 'the Angel of Death,' whose power increases 'in proportion as southern latitudes are reached.' "[36]

At the same time, Dowler was concerned that the tides of strangers, most of them immigrants who came up and down the river to the city, were giving New Orleans a bad name. City fathers had worried about this for several decades, but the problem appeared to be getting worse with ever more numerous sick poor transients dying in the beds of Charity Hospital and swelling the city's mortality rates.[37] However, the absence of official vital data made it difficult to document the situation with any precision. As a stopgap, Dowler in 1840 offered a comparison of Charity Hospital's record of transients' deaths with death records of the city's permanent, well-to-do, population which he obtained from cemetery inscriptions. His predictable finding, that far more of the permanent residents lived to ripe old ages, led him to conclude that New Orleans in reality was an entirely salubrious community and did not deserve its reputation as the "Necropolis of the South."[38]

Dowler's demographic activities extended beyond these dubious graveyard calculations to a professed interest in all of the "perturbations which social physics exercise over vital statistics."[39] His mature concerns, in fact, turned out to be about as wide-ranging as those of the

Belgian demographer Adolphe Quetelet. During the 1840s, as he considered the intended scope of a large study he was planning to carry out on what he called vital statistics, Dowler proposed to deal with "phrenology, ethnology, psychology, social physics, climatic agencies, the perturbations of immigrations, and emigrations, the geographical distribution of races, the density of population, mortality, marriage, births, the mean duration of life, the physical comforts, as food; also pauperism, industry, capital, education, not to name that all-comprehending subject vaguely denominated civilization." This expansive subject matter would in later years, of course, be divided up between such scholarly disciplines as sociology, psychology, anthropology, demography, and public health, but for southerners as well as northerners during the 1840s, it was often conveniently embraced by the term *vital statistics.*[40]

Dowler expounded on some of these broad matters rather loftily in pamphlets and articles in the New Orleans press. He also performed a useful continuing function as an acerbic critic of the naive statistical practices of some of his fellow townsmen. As a busy editor and physiologist, and an increasingly active political polemicist, he never found the time to compete his magnum opus on vital statistics, but he did participate in the campaign to obtain official vital-statistics registration.

By midcentury, after years of local neglect and indifference, Dowler and other leaders were able to convince their colleagues in the New Orleans medical community of the importance of improving vital statistics. In 1852 both the local and the state medical societies petitioned for uniform state registration.[41] Unfortunately, these proposals were so swept up in the political and medical debate over local sanitary reform that no legislation passed. Accordingly, reliable official vital statistics could not be obtained in Louisiana for several decades. Nevertheless, in New Orleans as in other American cities, the imperfect vital data that were available were used, with some additional information, to fuel the efforts to obtain public health improvements.

Unlike some cities, even the great outbreaks of cholera and yellow fever between 1848 and 1854 did not permanently help the cause of registration in New Orleans. They did spur a lively sanitary reform movement, one which included a vigorous search for relevant facts and figures. However, a ruinous division of opinion among the medical profession of the city, particularly over what to do about yellow fever, left the public and the legislature with little confidence in physicians, little interest in registration, and little support for sanitation or boards of health.[42] As the epidemics raged, doctors presented the spectacle of contagionists and anticontagionists arguing with each other publicly over the origins of yellow fever, the extent of the mortality, and proper control measures. Advocates of quarantine were vilified for suggesting a measure which threatened to ruin commerce. Proponents of vigorous internal sanitation were castigated for proposals which would allegedly squander the city's money and set up an unneeded bureaucracy, as well as for being alarmist and disloyal. Nevertheless, in its desperate need to do something, the city had at least to consider the suggestions of both groups.

Apart from Fenner, the best known and most passionate partisans of the "sanitary idea" in New Orleans—of a comprehensive, ongoing, municipal public health organization based on statistics—were the physicians Edward H. Barton and J. C. Simonds. In order to make any progress toward such a goal, Barton and Simonds saw early that their first objective would have to be the extensive education of the public and of city officials. Nothing less than an overwhelming mass of data about the true hygienic condition of the city would enable them either to make an impression on the voters or to overcome the do-nothing mentality of the merchants and their supporters. It was essential to get New Orleans citizens to accept the unpalatable fact that the city did have a serious excess of disease, to approve the establishment of statistical machinery which would determine just how much and in what areas, and then to adopt well-known sanitary methods to eliminate the causes of the excess.

Simonds and Barton had originally been loyal believers in the basic salubrity of New Orleans. However, under the influence of Massachusetts sanitary statistics and reform activities, they changed their minds. Barton, for his part, came to believe that the use of statistics, patiently assembled and studied, could be a "great leveller." He saw such data as a body of truth which would eventually wipe out all of the a priori assumptions, the guesses, the speculations about epidemics. He thought that, if anything could, their use would eliminate the low opinion so many people held of the medical profession. Of more immediate pertinence to New Orleans, however, he argued that sound statistics could put an end to "the indiscreet and ridiculous bragging about our sanitary condition" by the mayor of the city and by certain leading citizens.[43]

Like reformers elsewhere, Barton and Simonds were short on tact and patience and tended to rub many of their Creole neighbors the wrong way with their dogmatic and self-righteous approach. Many resented being told that New Orleans was just as unhealthful a place as northerners alleged it to be, and they did their best to discredit both the reformers and their statistics. Simonds particularly roused local sensibilities by setting New Orleans' record of mortality for 1851 side by side with the far better record of Boston. These figures showed that, while the populations were almost the same, New Orleans suffered nearly twice as many deaths. This was not surprising, Simonds argued, for the two cities demonstrated "in every view connected with Hygiene, Sanitary Police, and Vital Statistics, conditions almost diametrically opposed." Boston was notable, he thought, for its extensive social welfare arrangements, its inhabitants' personal self-discipline, and its thorough system of vital statistics, all part of a highly developed "effort to protect and preserve human life." New Orleans, by contrast, was marked by a deplorable neglect of social order and system, by the extreme personal license of its citizens, and by its lack of effort to obtain vital statistics.[44]

Prominent among the physicians who opposed Simonds's and Barton's sanitary reform proposals were Bennet and Morton Dowler, Samuel Cartwright, and Abner Hester. Morton Dowler, whose vitriolic style was excessive even for that period of history, dragged the discussion to a very low plane with his personal attacks on Barton in the medical press. However, it was Bennet Dowler, with his own acerbity plus a healthy skepticism, who probably caused the sanitarians their greatest trouble. Dowler could have had little reason to oppose Barton and Simonds if the latter individuals had had a plan which seemed promising against yellow fever. Unfortunately for the cause of public health reform in New Orleans, and in the South generally, yellow fever was not a filth disease. Though no one yet knew why, the standard sanitary measures that were so effective against the excesses of mortality from cholera, typhoid, or dysenteries were ineffectual against yellow fever. To be sure, his arguments were heavily loaded with opinionated and selective data drawn from his own New Orleans graveyard statistics, but they were effective. As Barton gloomily confided to a northern correspondent in 1852, Dowler's writings have "done much injury to the true cause of sanitary reform here—his *picked* lives from the cemeteries have misled public opinion, and thrown great obscurity upon the subject."[45]

The New Orleans sanitary reform effort came to a climax following the great yellow fever epidemic of 1853, when a special sanitary commission was formed. The five-member commission was composed of Barton as chairman, Simonds, and three other physicians sympathetic to reform. Through questionnaires, personal investigations, and statistical analyses, the commission proceeded to conduct the most extensive sanitary survey of any American city up to that time.

The commission's report of 1854 included discussions of yellow fever etiological theory, quarantine, and methods of sewerage and trash removal, all prepared by members of the commission. By far the longest section was Barton's quantitative review of mortality, meteorological factors, and local unsanitary conditions. Barton concluded by recommending the completion of major sanitary works in the city and the creation of a health department or board with authority to supervise ongoing sanitary measures. Such a board would be paid, would be protected from political pressures, and would be composed of physicians. The department would be expected to supervise vital statistics, along with records of city dispensaries, sanitary inspections, and meteorological data. However, Barton was vague about the day-to-day responsibility for applying such information; although there was to be a secretary, he was not given the authority that would be necessary in order to be effective.[46]

As it turned out, the New Orleans survey was a premature exercise. To be sure, its report was widely circulated and received high praise from sanitarians outside New Orleans. Within the city, however, it was harshly rejected by its medical opponents, while city and state officials virtually ignored it. In fact, the commission even had to sue the city for reimbursement of its expenses. Barton, crushed by the failure of his efforts, had a physical breakdown and abruptly left New Orleans.[47]

Ironically, one of the commission's least popular proposals was salvaged when, in 1855, the Louisiana legislature passed a quarantine act. As part of the specific quarantine provisions for the port of New Orleans, this act created a state board of health as the administrative body. For a few years, this body also attempted to expand its scope somewhat by undertaking general sanitary activities. Among these, it made a new effort to obtain a registration system. With the medical profession, the Board of Health was persuaded of the important benefits to be obtained from the "startling records of the vital statistician."[48] Nevertheless, the board proved powerless to do anything substantial either about registration or about any other sanitary matter. As a result, by 1861 it quietly reverted to carrying out its modest local quarantine functions.

### Southern Ambivalence toward Medical Statistics—Josiah Nott

New Orleans' inability to face up to sanitary realities and its cruel rejection of its leading medical reformer reflected a basic southern difficulty in accepting the objective idealism of the statistical method. In fact, Barton, Fenner, and the other physicians who were trying through numerical analysis to get at the various kinds of facts about medicine and disease in the South experienced progressively increasing tension between that idealism and the fundamental ideologies of their slave-oriented society. For a good many of these individuals, while statistical precision and objectivity remained abstract desiderata to which lip-service was given, specific application of statistics to medicine was increasingly influenced by the physicians' racial prejudices and practices or those of their neighbors. Even the most scientifically inclined of antebellum southern medical men, while starting out with strong proclivities for statistics as a critical tool in the advancement of medicine, eventually tended to submerge these aims under their essentially propagandistic uses of data to support preconceived ideas. The career of the gifted scientist-physician Josiah Clark Nott is a striking instance of this.

Few southern physicians contributed more than Nott to the medical growth of their respective local communities; few typified southern medical aspirations and racial attitudes more fully; and few used statistics more extensively or more equivocally. Between 1837 and 1861 Nott had a highly successful medical and surgical practice in Mobile, Alabama. As a professional, he helped establish both the local medical society and the Medical College of Alabama, besides operating his own private hospital for blacks. He also found time to conduct research in ethnology, hypnosis, and various aspects of medicine.

Nott's early investigations included a certain amount of clinical research, an extremely rare occurrence in the antebellum South. Although originally an admirer of the localized pathology of Broussais, he ultimately was influenced as well by Pierre Louis's skeptical pathology and even more by the latter's numerical methodology. In Mobile, Nott, like many other southern physicians, put his knowledge to use studying yellow fever, a natural choice considering the ubiquity of that disease along the Gulf Coast; five epidemics struck that city between 1837 and 1844 alone. With his professional colleagues, he performed autopsies on many of the victims of each outbreak. In 1844 Nott compared his pathological findings in 16 recent cases with those obtained by European authorities. He took a certain satisfaction from the fact that his observations closely coincided with those made by Louis during the Gibralter epidemic of 1828, except that a peculiar lesion of the liver which Louis associated with yellow fever had been subsequently proved to be present in other fevers as well. In addition, Nott's findings allowed him to go beyond Louis in differentiating yellow fever from periodic or malarial fevers.

Nott's evaluation of yellow fever therapy involved a combination of current pathological knowledge with accumulated statistical experience. Recent French research, along with his own practice, suggested to Nott that it was generally inappropriate to treat yellow fever by bloodletting. Since the malady was never accompanied either by inflammation, plethora, or active congestions, he felt that it was "not a disease which demands active depletion, either by blood-letting or purging." At the same time, the huge mortality that was being registered in every yellow fever epidemic in the South made it apparent that none of the common drug treatments of the day were of any value. Quinine had reportedly been used with *"immense success"* in the New Orleans epidemic of 1847 and elsewhere, but, Nott noted, "somehow or other about 3,000 persons have died there" in spite of using the drug. In turn, he cautioned, even though mercury remained the most popular medicine, no more faith could be placed in it than in quinine. True, as its advocates argued, both "experience and statistics" were in favor of mercury, but just as many opponents of the drug were using these same measuring sticks against it.[49]

Nott's scientific observations received mixed receptions. His conclusion that yellow fever was transmitted by minute insects or animalcules was a hypothesis that few of his southern contemporaries (or northerners, either) would accept. On the other hand, his statistical conclusion that "the susceptibility of Races to yellow fever is in direct ratio to the fairness of the complexion," seemed to accord with most antebellum experience with the disease.[50]

Anthropologically, Nott embraced a scientific view of race which tended to reinforce racial prejudices but which at the same time proved repugnant to many southerners on religious grounds. Well before the death of Samuel G. Morton in 1851, Nott had become the principal southern spokesman of Morton's "American School" of anthropology, one in which the measurement, comparison, and classification of skulls was a prominent activity.[51] While this group was genuinely interested in the comparative features of all races, its finding that the negroid race had the smallest cranial capacity quickly became an element in the attempt to justify slavery scientifically. Their perception of these cranial differences also led Morton, Nott, and others of the group essentially to reject the Biblical account of the creation of man and to substitute for it a concept of separate creations of each of the distinct racial groups or species.

Within this scientific position, Nott devoted much effort to examining the black as a member of a separate and inferior race. Accordingly, a major part of his research was the compilation of "negro statistics" which could serve to confirm well-established preexisting impressions about the race and its medical peculiarities. He thus exhaustively studied the bills of mortality for evidence that the black under slavery lived longer and suffered less from disease than when he was in a state of freedom. He dug out data to confirm "the baneful influence of cold upon the race, [showing] that, in America, the Negro steadily deteriorates, and becomes exterminated north of about 40° north latitude." And he searched for other figures "to prove that races are influenced differently, not only by the temperature of various latitudes, but by morbific agents."[52]

With other ethnologist-physicians, Nott was also intrigued with the racial nature and diseases of the mulatto, though unlike many he considered such individuals as hybrids. He concluded that, as offspring of two distinct races, the Caucasian and the Negroid, the mulatto was constitutionally frail, unable to resist disease, and doomed to extinction. Statistics already at hand pertaining to the calamitous mortality of free blacks in northern cities tended to bear him out, Nott thought, though he conceded that he lacked specific data on the mulattoes themselves. Unfortunately, he found that "the habits and condition of the Mulattoes in the South render it extremely difficult to obtain satisfactory statistics" about them.[53]

Whatever the statistical evidence that was brought forward, it is certain that the bulk of the antebellum medical profession did not favor the doctrine of separate creations. The enthusiasts actually were only a tiny band who had come under the influence of Morton or had been swayed by the endorsement of Louis Agassiz. In the South, Robert W. Gibbes, Samuel Dickson, Richard Arnold, William Usher, and perhaps a few other practitioners were willing to support the idea publicly.[54] However, most of the doctors had no desire to question established religious doctrine. Samuel Cartwright, for one, countered Nott's argument with his own scriptural interpretation of the origin of black separateness and low status. Blacks, he asserted, were simply descendents of Canaan, who had been destined by God to occupy an inferior place as slaves and "knee-benders," and could never be happy in any other condition.[55]

In the North, similarly, some in the scientific and medical communities agreed with Morton, Agassiz, and Nott, but Asa Gray and many others tended to be more comfortable with orthodox religion. Reflecting the latter, Samuel Forry firmly rejected Nott's position on mulatto hybridity in favor of James Cowles Prichard's well-known scientific rationale of the basic unity of the human race. Forry also pointed out that measurements taken by Friedrich Tiedemann tended to refute the idea that black crania differed from those of Caucasians. Almost as damaging to Nott's arguments, however, in Forry's eyes, was the inadequacy of Nott's "so-called statistics," particularly his reliance on selected data from other authorities and his failure to obtain large numbers of authenticated personal observations.[56]

Lunsford Yandell of Louisville thought that Forry had thoroughly and "triumphantly" demolished Nott's statistical claims for separate creations, though a somewhat greater mass of data might have been desirable. In any case, he was sure that ultimately "statistics must decide the question."[57] Clearly, this was an overly optimistic expectation. Perhaps the only thing that could be accurately stated about this particular issue was that Nott's statistics on race were not of the same caliber as his earlier clinical data on yellow fever. At the same time, taken in the aggregate, even his polemical uses of racial numbers were a substantial cut above those of most other southern medical writers, including those who were energetically promoting a self-conscious sectionalism.

### The Nature and Number of "Southern" Diseases—Samuel Cartwright

Even if slavery had not existed, the South would have gone through its period of local self-sufficiency and excess pride, just as the West did; in fact, Daniel Drake had strenuously fostered these attitudes in the lower Mississippi basin as much as in the upper.[58] However, given the context of a society committed to slavery, southern medical regionalism took on a strength and permanence that was far greater than the western variety. As this commitment deepened and the region drew further apart from the North, southern medical men increasingly used their figures in the defense of their region and its ideology, though some saw no need for statistical justification.

Numerous professional spokesmen during these decades insisted on the unique character of "southern" diseases, on the inadequacy of northern or European medical texts for dealing with them, and on the general incompetence of those trained outside to understand them. They tried to interest southern physicians in making serious studies of these peculiarities and in generally elevating their profession.[59] Particularly strident, however, were those whose primary energies went to puffing one or another of the new southern medical schools. Some of these individuals deliberately linked the growth of their schools with the solidifying political sentiments and aspirations of the South. Subsequently they went to great lengths, during the 1840s and 1850s, to undermine the reputations of established northern schools in the eyes of southern students, a tactic which culminated in 1859 with a substantial exodus of southern students from medical schools of Philadelphia and New York.[60] While northern medical educators and editorialists had no means of direct retaliation, virtually all of them vigorously rejected the premises of a distinct medical regionalism, and most deplored the stiffening of what John Bell characterized as "state's-rights medicine."[61] For many northerners, the arch representative of this viewpoint and of its excesses was Samuel Cartwright of Natchez, Mississippi, and later of New Orleans.

Indeed, Cartwright was something of an "original" even for the South. He made an early reputation as a colorful and often extravagant individual whose extreme pronouncements would have done credit to those of his fellow southern contemporary, Davy Crockett. However, he also claimed a certain status as a medical scientist through his uses of statistics. After a number of years of private practice, Cartwright took the grand tour of Europe in the mid-1830s with his family. There he was influenced to some extent by Louis's clinical methodology, but much more by the arithmetic demonstrations of the French sanitarians. He returned to Natchez to become one of the South's most enthusiastic and outspoken advocates of statistical medicine, though far from the most meticulous. Cartwright instructed southern medical students in the potential of statistical inquiry—"in reality, the Baconian philosophy applied to medicine"—but he did little to prepare them for the painstaking discipline it involved.[62] His own practical uses of medical numbers did not really go very far in demonstrating the statistical method, but they were undeniably imaginative.

Cartwright drew upon a variety of local data sources for his numerical medical studies: the Natchez bills of mortality for a comparison of the effectiveness of regular medical practice with the irregular; and his own patient records for a profile of drinking habits and effects in Natchez.[63] In an unusual 1840 inquiry, he combined folklore with census data. In this, he used the principles of that "new and interesting science, called by the French, *Political Arithmetic,*" to try to verify the belief that the *Jussieua grandiflora,* a floating plant of the lower Mississippi Delta, possessed important health-preserving properties. The plant had long been reputed locally to inhibit consumption, typhus, and inflammatory affections to some degree, but especially malaria. For his demonstration, Cartwright simply pointed to 1830 census figures, which showed that the parishes in which this plant flourished did indeed have a larger proportion of children who survived infancy, and more people who reached 100 years of age, than did adjoining areas of the delta. With this presumed evidence, Cartwright proposed the systematic cultivation of *Jussieua grandiflora* in all sickly and low-lying districts of the South which were not easily drained or otherwise planted. Before long, he suggested, this single plant might well contribute almost as much to the well-being of the region as cotton already had. However, few of Cartwright's contemporaries seem to have paid much heed to this idea, and the experiment apparently was not tried in any southern community.[64]

Cartwright nevertheless remained the "idea man" par excellence of antebellum southern medicine. Some of these ideas were patently preposterous, others merely eccentric, but still others gave off a ring of plausibility or even genius to his contemporaries. In 1853, he proposed what he considered to be a cheap and safe way of preventing yellow fever in southern port cities, assuming that the disease was indeed introduced from abroad. The idea was to stop using newly arrived immigrants as laborers or draymen at the docks, since these individuals had proved to be so susceptible to the disease. In their place, Cartwright suggested using blacks, because experience and statistics had shown that they much less often contracted yellow fever. In short, he urged that officials "insulate the shipping with well-acclimated negroes, and let no other class of people act as stevedores, or to come within a specified distance of the wharf."[65]

This matter-of-fact proposal paralleled DeBow's suggestion that the rapidly increasing excess in the slave population be utilized to build southern railways and provide the labor in anticipated factories in the region.[66] Both of these proposals made sense, particularly in southern port cities. However, neither was systematically implemented, since the South remained predominantly agricultural.

Meanwhile, the subject of differential immunity of the races to various diseases was increasingly interesting to southern physicians. E. D. Fenner considered it "universally admitted" that white newcomers from the North needed a two to three year period of acclimation before they could gain immunity comparable to that of native southerners to virtually any endemic fever.[67] Barton was essentially in agreement, though he conceded that this time period could not yet be determined "to a mathematical certainty." Nott saw that the phenomenon of acclimation was a complex one, but he was persuaded that statistical analysis would soon reveal differences in immunity attributable to disease, geographical location, and race. However, as late as 1860, northern reviewers found that no substantial studies of acclimation had yet been done. So far, wrote Edward Jarvis, those who support the concept of acclimation "found their faith rather upon general observation than upon actual measurement or enumeration."[68]

Cartwright, for his part, made it his special business, during the 1840s and 1850s, to investigate the question of black susceptibility to disease within the context of "state's-rights medicine," but he provided little statistical support for his findings. From the mid-1840s on, in fact, Cartwright's interests in statistical medicine as a presumedly objective process were clearly subordinated to ideological and political considerations. In 1846, at the height of sectional bitterness over the Mexican War and over proposed national expansion into the Southwest, he made a preliminary outline of the main facets of southern regional medicine as they were understood in the lower Mississippi Valley. At that time he expressed himself in a relatively moderate tone.[69] However, within a short time, following northern criticism of the address, Cartwright began expressing "state's-rights medicine" in an increasingly belligerent manner and in explicit terms of white superiority.

It was evident that the largest part of the practice of a great many antebellum southern physicians, particularly outside the cities, was "among the colored people."[70] Yet the medical profession was slow to study the diseases of the blacks or the effects of the various therapies on them. To be sure, empirical evidence had been collected early, suggesting that blacks were far less subject than whites to certain maladies, notably yellow fever. However, blacks appeared to be stricken more often than whites with other diseases and also to have higher fatality rates. The federal census of 1830, for instance, found 1 case of blindness in every 2,650 whites in the United States, while the ratio among blacks was 1 in 1,584.[71] However, relatively few specifics about other black diseases were readily available before the 1850s.

Cartwright's 1851 paper on the principal diseases and physical characteristics of blacks, therefore, was an original contribution which filled a certain need. At the same time, it was one of the most notorious and extreme examples of medical racism. Ostensibly a scientific treatise, it proved rather to be a crude polemic on the inferiority of the black. Starting with an examination of legitimate disease conditions, it went on to devote much more space to the nature and handling of certain "social" diseases of blacks, particularly to "drapetomania, the disease causing slaves to run away," and to "dysaesthesia Aethiopis," or rascality.[72]

Northern physicians seem to have been alternately amused by these whimsically outrageous additions to medical terminology and incensed by Cartwright's violent sectionalism. The rank and file of southern physicians probably agreed with his formulation of southern racial views. However, some were embarrassed by it and tried to discredit it as medical nonsense.[73] A few criticized Cartwright essentially for not applying basic statistical methods. One critic was disappointed with Cartwright's heavy reliance on hearsay reports, while E. N. Fenner regretted Cartwright's failure to document his views quantitatively or to "verify them by recent observation and comparison." Still another reviewer was highly skeptical of Cartwright's claim that his "cholera powder" (made up of calomel, pepper, and camphor) cured 99 out of 100 cholera sufferers, mostly blacks; moreover, slaves to whom it was given as a preventive could not even swallow the mixture.[74]

No other physician approached Cartwright in the status he enjoyed as an authority on southern medicine, though S. L. Grier, A. P. Merrill, and a few other individuals also published their observations on the diseases of blacks. Like Cartwright, moreover, none of these produced objective scientific works on the subject. They made some note of the extensive incidence of consumption, typhoid, tetanus, pneumonia, and dysentery, but they were especially interested in drawing attention to the prevalence of marasmus, trismus, dirt-eating, worms, and other conditions which they thought to be "peculiar" to blacks, diseases which set the race apart. None produced any very extensive figures on these diseases, though Grier agreed that such data would be desirable.[75]

Despite its obvious shortcomings, the federal census of 1850 was thus a most welcome addition to the information about black diseases. It also provided comparative figures on disease incidence among whites and blacks in a single census year. For the most part, readers probably found few surprises; the figures only confirmed the accepted impression that for most diseases there was a much greater ratio of deaths among blacks than among whites. "This is in accordance with the well established fact that in all countries the laboring classes suffer greater mortality than others." On the other hand, the census indicated that blacks often managed to live to ripe old age; the South was already thought to have a much greater population of elderly blacks than elderly whites. However, these figures turned out to be only apparent. Georgia analysts, among others, quickly pointed out the familiar propensity of slaves to exaggerate their ages in order to gain early retirement from their duties.[76]

In addition to the census, other sources of information comparing the two races became available when a few southern cities and states began to publish bills of mortality or registration reports. Meanwhile, a small number of physicians were interested in the long-range disease experiences of whites and blacks. In Virginia, Alfred Tebault kept his own record of periodic fever cases among a group comprised equally of the two races. Over a four-year period, the blacks suffered only a quarter to a third of the number of attacks from the disease that the whites did. More elaborately, E. M. Pendleton of Sparta, Georgia, throughout most of the 1840s kept sufficiently accurate personal records to permit him to analyze the comparative incidence of all diseases of the two groups. Pendleton found that exact ratios were impossible to determine, since plantation owners generally called doctors in to treat only the most serious cases in their slaves. Nevertheless, there still appeared to be "more cases and a greater diversity of disease among the whites than the blacks," and conversely, since "the Caucasian seems to yield more readily to remedies than the African," the death rate of the former was considerably less.[77]

Awareness of such statistical differences in the incidence of and mortality from the various diseases may have persuaded some physicians to distinguish in applying their therapies to the two races. Actually, empirical considerations alone led them for most diseases to bleed blacks less than whites and to give the former smaller doses of calomel or other drugs.[78] However, southern physicians generally seem to have paid less attention to therapeutic data than to broader hygienic and demographic figures which had bearing on the interests and ideology of their region.

## Sectional Rivalry and the Calculus of Disease

Of great interest both in the South and the North were various attempts that were made to compare the incidence of disease in the two regions. The question of relative salubrity was very much a part of the debate over larger sectional issues, but accurate information on the matter was in short supply for many years. From the 1830s, however, a number of compilations of medical information, particularly the extensive census and army statistical reports, opened up rich resources for the debate.[79]

The 1830 census's enumeration of the blind did not favor either of the two sections. Its enumeration of the deaf and dumb, however, gave a decided advantage to the South and Southwest, which had reported far fewer cases. The differential between northern and southern blacks with respect to this condition proved particularly interesting. In the free states of the Northeast the census indicated an incidence of 1 case of deafness among every 1,002 blacks, while the southern states reported a proportion of 1 in 3,402, and the Southwest 1 in 4,558. T. Romeyn Beck of Albany, New York, who uncautiously took the figures at face value, could see that they gave decided support to the southern regionalist view. "If physical causes have the slightest effect in producing this malady, does not the above statement prove that the condition of our free blacks is infinitely worse than that of their brethren at the South?"[80]

Another study was equally provocative, since it too came at a time when abolitionists were trying to challenge the validity of the image of a well-treated black population contentedly multiplying in southern captivity. In 1827, two young New York physicians, John D. Russ and Nathaniel Niles, compiled data showing that the average annual mortality among slaves in Baltimore was 1 in 77.78, while that of free blacks was over twice as great, 1 in 32.08. The authors felt that this disproportion was "worthy of particular notice, and probably arises from the care bestowed on the slaves by their masters, their comparative temperance, and the more regular course of their lives, contrasted with the idleness, intemperance, and improvidence of the free blacks." Figures for the same period showed a 1 in 39.99 rate of mortality among the whites of Baltimore, also noticeably greater than that of the slaves. From this the authors concluded that, "so far as regards the personal condition of the slaves, their situation is by no means so deplorable as has been generally imagined."[81]

The case for the salubrity of the North received a decided boost from the issuance of Samuel Forry's army statistics in 1840. This compilation showed that "the annual ratio of intermittents and remittents is five-fold greater in our southern than northern latitudes," while deaths from inebriety at the southern military posts averaged between 5 and 10 times greater than those in the North.[82] Southerners, again, however, found greater satisfaction in 1850 census figures, which showed not only lower overall mortality ratios in their region than in the North, but far greater longevity, judging from reported numbers of centenarians.[83]

Comparative figures for consumption proved to be mixed. Army statistics consistently showed greater mortality from this disease among the troops stationed in warm states than among those serving in cold areas. Yet, the 1850 census showed mortality ratios for the disease increasing progressively as one moved northward from Texas to Massachusetts. Bennet Dowler spoke for many southerners in hailing these latter figures as a vindication of the southern environment. The experience of a mere handful of soldiers, he argued, "cannot invalidate the climatic and vital statistics of more than twenty-three million people." Northerners who studied the data found them hard to dispute. However, some took comfort in the popular belief that, in those places where consumption was worst, the great endemic fevers were less prevalent, and vice versa. Both the 1850 and 1860 censuses seemed to support this notion. However, Charles A. Lee reminded physicians that these antebellum census statistics were so imperfect that they were essentially useless for comparing any regional diseases and mortalities; DeBow himself had to admit that well over a quarter of the country's deaths had not been reported.[84]

From the northern point of view, the most disturbing of the various census deficiencies were those which came to light in connection with the 1840 enumeration of the insane and idiots. In 1842 Edward Jarvis was one of several, North and South, who analyzed the official figures from that count. Jarvis found initially that there was a "very similar" incidence of insanity among the white populations of the two regions. He also noted, however, that in virtually every state the reported total of insane and idiots was far short of the actual known or estimated number, in some places by as much as 58 percent.

At the same time, Jarvis was baffled by an enormous disproportion in the amount of insanity reported among Negroes of the two regions: in the South only 1 out of 1,558 blacks was found to be insane, but in the free states the ratio given was 1 in 144.5. Looking further into this huge apparent difference, he found that much or all of it was due to gross errors in many of the tabulations of cases for the free states. In the case of Worcester, Massachusetts, 133 white inmates of the lunatic hospital had been improperly listed as "colored," while Waterford, Connecticut, was credited with seven insane blacks even though no blacks lived in the town. Similar errors with respect to the insane turned up for dozens of other northern towns, while figures of the deaf, dumb, and blind also proved to be extremely faulty.[85]

Jarvis's first reaction was basically one of chagrin that the United States had failed to produce a model statistical report. He was "disappointed and mortified" that his country's statistical name abroad should be tarnished by such a shoddy and imperfect national document. It appeared, however, that the report could be readily corrected from the original returns in the Department of State. Accordingly, Jarvis urged that this be quickly done in order to salvage some measure of the country's statistical respectability.[86]

However, statistical accuracy turned out to have less priority in this instance than the demands of current regional and racial politics. Southern analysts understandably welcomed an official document which offered such conclusive testimony to the virtues of life under slavery. An unidentified author in the *Southern Literary Messenger* particularly savored these apparent proofs of the injuriousness of free society to the black race.[87] Obviously there was little inclination in the South to question a report which showed their "peculiar institution" to be 10 times as favorable to the mental health of the black. As a result, Secretary of State John C. Calhoun, whose department had made the original errors, found the uncorrected figures far too useful to the southern cause to listen to any suggestion that they be amended.

Northerners, of course, quickly protested what they considered to be a grotesque southern exploitation of erroneous data. The Massachusetts Medical Society conducted its own inquiry to determine the real incidence of insanity among its black populace. Henry Ingersoll Bowditch, undoubtedly the most passionate abolitionist among Boston doctors, longed "to shake the *Southern Literary Messenger* for its inhuman article" by writing something himself, but he found that a new and longer article by Jarvis on the subject served very well. When the American Statistical Association decided in the fall of 1843 to petition Congress for the necessary corrections, Bowditch ensured that the essence of Jarvis's article was incorporated into the petition and that copies of the document were made available to all congressmen.[88]

Elsewhere, James McCune Smith drew up a similar memorial on behalf of the free blacks of New York, while groups in Philadelphia and other communities also petitioned Congress to amend the offending data.[89] The House of Representatives ultimately requested Calhoun to investigate the matter. Predictably, however, the latter succeeded in completely whitewashing the original report. He further angered the northerners, moreover, by using the figures in official 1844 diplomatic correspondence with the British government to justify the extension of slavery into Texas.

Jarvis subsequently criticized the bulk of northern physicians and statisticians for remaining "so passive" throughout this incident. Southern statisticians, meanwhile, continued to refer to the 1840 census report up to the Civil War, and they stoutly defended the accuracy of its data against all critics.[90] Bennet Dowler, for one, suggested that northern statisticians stop wasting their sympathies on the slaves. For him, the data abundantly proved that the vital condition and progress of southern blacks under slavery was far better even than that of the population of France or the British aristocracy. By contrast, he concluded, "the statistical history of the blacks of the North; their unparalleled deterioration, their frequent insanity, dementia, blindness, deafness, pauperism, premature death, their decrease, or minimized ratio of increase, their physical degeneration and tendency to extinction . . . would seem incredible, did not every decennial enumeration of the population give the same result."[91]

Despite the apparently convincing nature of these figures for southerners, most of their spokesmen continued to find it necessary to bolster their position with new accumulations of information; as George Fitzhugh put it, to "prove the failure [of free society] from history and statistics." To be sure, some zealots, such as the South Carolina planter James H. Hammond, felt that no quantity of arguments the North might be able to muster could stand up against the rightness of the South's proslavery position. He argued, "Ninety-nine facts may constitute a falsehood: the hundredth, added or alone, gives the truth." Nevertheless, other southerners preferred to respond to the North's arguments with the rational weight of statistical evidence.[92]

During the mid-1850s, Samuel H. Dickson of Charleston, for one, decided to challenge repeated assertions of northern publicists that southern whites had been degenerating physically and intellectually in their slave-oriented society. To test this, Dickson gathered figures on the height and weight of 223 young men in local educational institutions, men who were mostly natives of South Carolina and who were all of mixed northern European ancestry. His data suggested that the hybrid white Carolina male compared very well physically with representatives of the parent racial stocks: the Carolina students averaged over 5'6" in height, which was well above the minimum for army recruits in England (5'4") and France (5'1"). Extrapolating from these figures, Dickson proclaimed that "neither in morals nor intelligence, neither in active courage or passive endurance have we degenerated from our loftiest ancestry." Limited though his figures were, he was satisfied that the results provided effective answers to the "foul calumnies and atrocious falsehoods" which had been circulating in the North.[93]

Opponents of slavery also appealed to statistics almost as consistently as to rhetoric. In fact, such figures fueled the northern attacks on slavery just as they bolstered other reform movements of the day. One such attack was the polemic of Hinton Rowan Helper, whose collection of "incontrovertible facts and statistics" was intended to prove that slavery had kept the South backward, depopulated, and impoverished.[94]

At the same time, statistics sometimes were used not to inflame but to show possible ways out of the regional confrontation. Horace Bushnell was one who, as late as 1860, really thought that the problem would take care of itself, provided that tempers could be held in check long enough. The Hartford clergyman found the clues to this hopeful opinion in the population statistics of the 1850 census, specifically, the large and rapidly increasing excess of northern whites. For various reasons, Bushnell believed, this large population would soon find it more attractive to move into the slave states than to continue migrating to the western areas as they had been doing. At the same time, signs pointed to the likelihood that the slave would very shortly become an impossible economic burden for the South, rather than an asset. With these two developments reinforcing each other, Bushnell predicted that all slaves would thus be voluntarily emancipated within a few decades. In turn, since he was part of an inferior race and unable to compete with the dominant Anglo-Saxon, the black would ultimately become extinct in the United States.[95]

Few northern physicians can have believed with Bushnell that slavery would really disappear through the operation of some imperceptible demographic movement which was to be as painless and "silent as the movements of the stars."[96] Many, however, did feel that the northern moralists should stop meddling in the South's "peculiar institution." Most basically agreed with their southern medical colleagues about the essential inferiority of the blacks. Most found it easy to concur with S. B. Hunt of Buffalo, who suggested that "the doctrine that 'all men are created free and equal' is an anatomical, physiological and scriptural impossibility." A majority of northern as well as southern white physicians had little doubt that they actually were members of a superior race. As such, they played significant roles in America's vigorous mid-nineteenth-century pursuit of its extraterritorial "manifest destiny" as a nation.[97]

# *6*

# Manifest Destiny and Medicine

The powerful motivations which propelled antebellum Americans westward and southward in large numbers, despite all of the hazards of climate, disorganization, and disease, were by no means spent on reaching California. Indeed, the movement to the Pacific was only one manifestation of a restless national outreaching toward an even more broadly conceived manifest destiny. Some individuals, seeing America's neighbors still living under repressive forms of government, felt that the United States had a duty to actively help liberate at least some of them, by force if necessary. Armed American bands along our northern borders considered that they had a right to try to detach Canada from Great Britain. And, well before the 1840s southern interests argued vigorously that America's manifest destiny included a large role in the lands to the south. Still others considered that national involvement of various kinds even further afield had quite surely been predetermined.

For generations numerous Americans had made their livings and satisfied their wanderlusts through careers as sailors, traders, and shippers, probing even farther in their schooners, barks, or clipper ships in the search for markets for American goods, and bringing back endless exotic objects or tales from distant lands to stir the blood of stay-at-homes. Beginning in the nineteenth century, moreover, following some of the paths of commerce, earnest Protestant missionaries had been setting out for certain of these same countries in hopes of converting "heathen" souls. Along with both groups, and serving at least as symbolic protection for the merchant ships, the businessmen abroad, and the missionaries, American naval vessels were to be found pushing farther and farther through distant seas of the globe. And, as these and other activities expanded—as America's foreign interests grew—the national sense of manifest destiny strengthened progressively.

Medical men became as important to these forms of national outreaching as they were to the settlement of the West. Doctors often believed in and sometimes became spokesmen for the ideology of manifest destiny. Their medical expertise helped make the various extranational undertakings feasible. And, as they went out among alien peoples, the physicians spread their professional knowledge. While Europeans were still asking who ever read American books or who had heard of any other American cultural or intellectual accomplishments, inhabitants of not a few non-European countries were already beginning to benefit practically from certain American exports of these kinds, including medical ideas and practices. At the same time, the physicians took along with them the strong national propensity for observation and the compulsion to report their foreign experiences in quantitative terms. In short, insofar as the aspirations of manifest destiny were translated into actual demographic movements and vital events, members of the medical profession assumed important roles as measurers and analysts of the various phenomena.

## Medical and Statistical Aspects of the Mexican War

American physicians probably were about as divided over American expansionist policy of the 1840s as was the general populace. While many opposed the use of force against neighboring nations to acquire new territory, particularly when the latter might facilitate the extension of slavery, others regarded at least some kind of intervention as both inevitable and desirable. Mexico—presumably sinking rapidly into anarchy, immorality, and backwardness under the very eyes of the well-ordered, progressive, and self-righteous Anglo-Americans—was an obvious focus of attention. Many, accordingly, thought that it was America's moral duty to lead Mexico into paths of civilization, democracy, and Protestant values. Relations between the United States and Mexico were made increasingly uneasy throughout the decades of the 1820s and 1830s by the pressures of the thousands of American emigrants who poured into various parts of Texas.[1] Conflict became inevitable when the independent Texas that these settlers created was incorporated in 1845 into the United States.

American physicians resident in Texas were frequently active in the rebellion of that province from Mexico, and other medical men also adopted expansionist views toward Mexico. Southern doctors were particularly sympathetic, as were some military medical officers stationed in the Southwest. In 1842, Samuel Forry concluded, among other things, that the adverse Mexican climate made inevitable the day when the United States would have to involve itself substantially in Mexico.

> It requires not the gift of divination to foresee the destiny of Mexico and the States south of it, whose inhabitants, enervated by climate, conjointly with other causes, will yield, by that necessity which controls all moral laws, to the energetic arm of the Anglo-Saxon race. The future history of these States would seem to be typified in that of Texas.[2]

After war was declared and American armies began pushing into northern Mexico in 1846, medical officers detected considerable sentiment among the locals for separation from the central Mexican government and attachment to the United States. William B. Herrick, surgeon with the First Regiment, Illinois Volunteers, reported that this was largely because the Mexican armies habitually plundered the towns through which they passed while the Americans paid fairly for subsistence. However, he thought it was both premature and dangerous to admit such people to American citizenship. "I do not believe the Mexicans, as a mass, are, as yet, sufficiently far advanced in civilization and intelligence to admit of their establishing and sustaining a truly republican form of government."

Herrick and his fellow medical officers also discovered, on the other hand, that the Mexican environment was not all as unhealthful as some of its detractors had supposed. Army physicians frequently made medical-topographical inquiries into the weather, disease, natural resources, and other features of the country as they passed through. At least a few of them held up their findings for comparison with Humboldt's data on Mexico. Robert Newton even made original observations of the body size and structure of the Mexican people.[3]

Of more immediate concern in 1846 and 1847 was the health of the American troops going into Mexico. Well-established military procedures by then provided for the routine generation of a variety of quantitative medical data bearing upon this: daily morning reports of the sick, hospital registers, monthly and quarterly reports on patients. To be sure, the information-gathering processes suffered from all of the usual uncertainties of combat conditions, including the occasional capture by the enemy of returns from given units. Despite such difficulties, regular medical officers were noted for submitting their statistical reports with "remarkable regularity and accuracy." Among the volunteer forces, however, record-keeping was spotty, and surgeons could not be counted on for full or regular medical reports. Accordingly, the condition of the volunteers at any particular time could only be estimated in quite general terms.[4]

As a matter of fact, the volunteer units included many unfit individuals, since few if any had undergone physical examinations. Had the usual recruiting standards of the regular army been followed, more than a third would have been rejected. The approximate comparisons the surgeon-general could make between the medical experience of the volunteers and the regulars were startling. Once in service, the regulars naturally lost greater proportions in dead and wounded than the volunteers, since the former generally took the brunt of the hardest fighting. When it came to disease, however, the ratio of incidence proved to be roughly twice as high among the volunteers.[5]

For the volunteers it was an "exceedingly sickly" war from the start. The 2d Mississippi Rifles, for instance, cruelly exposed to winter weather before ever leaving Vicksburg, saw its original complement of 885 shrink by 167 without even facing the enemy; there were 80 deaths from disease in a staging area near New Orleans, another 28 during a four-week voyage to Texas, and 59 more in Texas, all before the regiment had been in service six months. A volunteer regiment of Tennessee cavalry had much less mortality; it suffered only five deaths on its three-and-a-half month march overland from Memphis across Arkansas and Texas to Matamoros, a distance of some 1,500 miles. But the regiment suffered greatly from disease: 350 cases of measles and considerable venereal disease while still in Memphis; diarrheas and colics most of the time; and "immense" amounts of intermittent and remittent fevers while going through Texas, though the fevers were kept under control by quinine.[6]

As they arrived in Texas, generally at Brazos Island, the various regiments were moved to encampments along the Rio Grande below Matamoros to prepare for the forthcoming campaign. The training of the volunteer units, however, was drastically set back by the debilitating diseases which ran through the camps; field commanders reported that as much as half of the total force was sick at any one time. Many began to blame the local environment for this sickness, and American newspapers began to feature stories about the unhealthfulness of the lower Rio

Grande. Army surgeons who looked into the matter confirmed that there were problems for some of the troops in acclimating themselves to the hot weather and to the local intermittents or remittents. But by far most of the disability and mortality resulted from diarrhea and dysentery. These could not be blamed on an unhealthful climate, but rather on "imprudence of the men"—on poor diet, bad water, lack of personal cleanliness, and inadequate sanitary police. Some doctors pointed also to the weak constitutions which many of the men had brought from civilian life, compounded by their frequent intemperance and dissipated habits.[7]

During the year and a half of war, the army found that there were considerable variations in mortality between troops from the respective sections of the country. On the one hand, the approximately 22,600 volunteer troops from seven northern states suffered a total loss in deaths from disease of 2,931, about an eighth. However, 22,900 volunteers from nine slave states had 4,315 deaths from disease, or over a fifth.[8]

In any case, the commanders recognized how urgent it was to get the troops out of the Rio Grande encampments and into some sort of field activity. Once this was done, a marked decline in the sick list became apparent. William B. Herrick, noting the wide fluctuations in the sick report of his First Regiment, Illinois Volunteers as the regiment finally moved down through northern Mexico, began to generalize about "the importance of keeping an army constantly moving in order to secure the health of soldiers." Correcting his reports for the number of hospital cases, he concluded that in his regiment the average sickness while on the march late in 1846 was only half what it was during the periods in camp.[9]

Whatever the case may have been, the poor overall health of many of General Taylor's troops certainly slowed down his campaign in northern Mexico. In turn, Scott's army in the south also encountered its share of maladies, principally ordinary camp diseases, dysentery, diarrhea, intermittent and typhoid fevers. As it pushed inland toward Mexico City, the army found the high tablelands of central Mexico refreshingly salubrious. The most worrisome medical problems of the final phases of the war focussed on Veracruz, disembarkation point and main supply terminal for Scott's army, for Veracruz had traditionally been one of the continent's chief sites of endemic yellow fever.

Following capture of the city, a large general hospital was established in Veracruz to serve Scott's army. Patient statistics quickly showed that here again diarrhea and dysentery were the most prevalent and damaging of the diseases. But some cases of yellow fever were also admitted almost from the beginning; over the first year 421 cases were treated, with 122 deaths. The head of the hospital, Surgeon John B. Porter, kept a close watch on these cases. And, at the end of the war, he was understandably gratified that his staff had been able to keep the yellow fever mortality rate consistently below that of New Orleans' Charity Hospital—28.9 percent versus 36.1 percent.[10]

Back in the United States, American medical men and public officials were kept on edge throughout the war by any talk about yellow fever. New Orleans physicians had very special reasons for their interest in Veracruz. Even before the war, New Orleans doctors had come to think vaguely of the medical affairs of Mexico and the West Indies as falling within their own special "professional domain." War made this a reality. New Orleans became, in fact, the focal point of most of the country's troop movements to and from Mexico. The thousands who moved to and from the Rio Grande area in 1846 included enough sick individuals to keep the city's hospitals full and its physicians busy. And, when military operations were undertaken in the south of Mexico in 1847 and 1848, the troops moving to and from Veracruz likewise needed considerable medical attention in New Orleans. The movements also reopened the city's perennial heated discussions over the etiology of the dreaded yellow fever.

Contagionists warned that New Orleans now had to be on the alert against a possible large-scale importation of yellow fever, direct from Veracruz. Special precautions were indeed taken by the Board of Health during this period, though anticontagionists did not share the sense of danger. One of the latter, E. D. Fenner, saw here a golden opportunity to test and refute the contagionist view. Through 1847 and mid-1848, Fenner kept a careful watch and medical count of the troops going through New Orleans, particularly the returning shiploads of sick, wounded, and discharged. Those individuals who came back suffering from yellow fever were put under close watch at Charity Hospital or elsewhere in the city. The climax came in mid-1848, following the signing of the Treaty of Guadalupe Hidalgo, when the entire American army of around 30,000 left Mexico, largely through Veracruz. Most of these troops entered the United States at New Orleans. Among this number, Fenner and the Board of Health located only 50 men with yellow fever, 20 of whom ultimately died. Most important for New Orleans and for the case of the anticontagionists, the disease did not spread. The large movement from Veracruz had been concluded *"without affording a single instance in which yellow fever was communicated from one person to another."*[11]

The military withdrawal from Mexico was by no means the end of antebellum American medical concerns in Latin America. In fact, American physicians continued to maintain strong interests in various corners of this "professional domain." Some set themselves up in practice abroad, often about as soon as American businessmen appeared. Others, travelling through the area for their health, prepared reports on medical-topographical details of one or another country. Several such reports appeared on Cuba, whose annexation was increasingly being urged. As early as 1844, John G. F. Wurdemann found that Americans, with their "restless spirit," had been settling on that island in fairly large numbers and were gradually introducing American ways. And he intimated that the typical American traveller there often tended to flaunt "his republican self-importance."

Neither Wurdemann nor most other physicians were prepared to go so far as to interfere militarily in other countries, unlike the young eclectic J. C. Bates, who joined a tiny 1850 expedition of southern adventurers in an abortive invasion of Cuba.[12] However, a number of American physicians did obtain positions with foreign governments during this period. Among them, J. Lawrence Smith went in the late 1840s as scientific consultant to the sultan of Turkey, and Israel Moses a few years later became surgeon-general of the army of Nicaragua. During the Crimean War, moreover, several dozen young American physicians signed with the Russian army's medical service, a step that medical editors endorsed as a concrete means of reducing America's surplus of doctors.[13]

## Death and Disease on the Panama Crossing

America's antebellum medical interests in Panama proved to be of a greater magnitude than those in most of the other Latin American countries. This was particularly true during the 1850s, when Panama became a transfer point for large numbers of individuals on their way to California. The Panama route did indeed sometimes save precious days for those eager to get to the gold fields. It also proved to be fully as dangerous to health as going across the Rockies or around Cape Horn. There are no good data for comparing the medical experiences of the various routes. However, the special nature of the Panama crossing served to concentrate an unusual amount of suffering and mortality within a small area.[14]

During the early 1850s, as many as 5,000 passengers for California were reported crossing the Isthmus from Chagres to the city of Panama monthly, at first laboriously on foot but eventually by railroad. In the latter city, 2,000–3,000 could often be found congregated for varying periods while waiting for their onward passage to California. Early observers, agreeing that the Isthmus was "the worst of unhealthy places," estimated that well over half of the transient Americans who passed through that "gauntlet" fell ill. Several small private hospitals were opened in the city of Panama to care for those who could pay, along with a public hospital for the many destitute. But these provisions admittedly did little to reduce the considerable mortality from disease.

A number of American physicians came to Panama at this time in the service of steamship companies and of the United States Navy. Certain of these physicians kept rough tabs on the emigrants' sickness and deaths, and some made personal surveys of the topographical circumstances which presumably contributed to the toll. However, good medical figures were not obtainable for the transients.

Some data were kept for the American and English employees of the Panama Rail-Road Company. John A. Lidell of New York, who ran a hospital for these employees, analyzed its early experience. During a typical four-month period in 1851, Lidell's hospital admitted 382 of the sickest employees. Many were suffering from acute dysentery and congestive fever, but the largest number, 250, had a malady that Lidell called climate or remittent fever, but which was popularly referred to as Panama Fever.

Lidell discovered that the overall health record of the railroad company's American and European laborers followed a pattern that was readily predictable. Realistically, the company could count on them for only about one good month of work. In their second month in Panama, half of them could be found on the sick list or otherwise much enfeebled by illness. And, "before three months have passed away a large proportion will either have died or been sent out of the country as unfit for further labor." Accordingly, almost every two weeks some 200 of the hospital's patients were loaded on ships bound for New York.[15]

The American presence in Panama was clearly a growing but also a precarious one. Even if one could not measure it very accurately, the nation had a human stake in Panamanian hospitals and cemeteries just as it had an economic investment in the railroad and steamship lines. In any case, those who had responsibilities in the area realized that if America's interest was to be a permanent one, the huge mortality among foreigners would have to be reduced. To accomplish this, Panama would have to be drained and sanitized as well as commercialized and otherwise Americanized. Any large-scale economic development virtually demanded this.

Following completion of the Panama railway, American engineers looked anew into the feasibility of a ship canal which would follow the same general route. A shortage of local labor clearly would be a major problem for such an immense project. But equally serious, it was now apparent, were "the diseases incidental to foreigners, especially of the white race." The great toll which these diseases took on Americans in Panama during the 1850s helped delay a decision on the canal for several more decades. It also provided a substantial argument for those who were beginning to push the case for building a transcontinental railroad from St. Louis to San Francisco.[16]

## Medical Aspects of Naval Expansion

The American navy had a considerable interest in Panama during this period, for its ships as well as American merchant vessels stopped there frequently. The navy had greatly expanded the number of its ships and the range of its activities in the several decades following the War of 1812. By the 1840s it was looking after American interests in the Mediterranean, in the East Indies, along the West African coast, and in South American waters, as well as in or near the Caribbean. To command its enlarged fleet, the navy more than doubled the number of its line officers during the 30 years after 1815.

The need for qualified medical officers grew proportionately. Within the United States alone, physicians had to be provided for each of the new naval hospitals. Other medical officers had to be detached for occasional special duty, such as the Wilkes expedition in South Pacific waters between 1838 and 1842 and Perry's 1852 expedition to open Japan. But most of all, physicians were required for the more routine patrols of the navy, for cruises that sometimes took them around the entire world. Nevertheless, the number of naval medical officers remained almost stationary, with only a nominal increase from 120 to 136 between 1815 and 1848. As a consequence, it was usually only the largest ships that had the luxury of surgeons or enlisted medical personnel.[17]

Following the creation of the navy's Bureau of Medicine and Surgery in 1842, there was marked improvement both in medical record-keeping and in the scientific value of reports submitted by such personnel. On ships which had medical officers, surgeons and their enlisted assistants established daily routines of recording the illnesses and accidents, the treatments given, the drugs dispensed, and the meteorological phenomena encountered. Periodically, they prepared statistical summaries of their ships' medical experiences. These accounts were often accompanied by narrative commentaries on such matters as shipboard ventilation, environmental factors encountered which affected disease, and the physical and moral effects of excessive drinking among naval personnel. Often the reports to naval headquarters were subsequently eagerly sought after for publication in the country's medical press.[18]

Some of the ships' surgeons also had keen eyes for the popular market in travel literature. These included surgeons William S. W. Ruschenberger and G. R. B. Horner, as well as the better-known arctic physician-explorers Elisha Kent Kane and Isaac Hayes. Such men published long, partly medical, and sometimes exciting accounts of their far-flung voyages, narratives which stirred the imaginations of midcentury Americans.[19]

Certain medical officers also took advantage of opportunities to pursue somewhat broader scientific activities. Most frequently these took the form of making observations on the medical topography of Minorca, Rio de Janeiro, Singapore, Monrovia, or other ports visited by the ships. Some individuals inquired into the flora and fauna, climate, and geological or agricultural resources—information that would be helpful to subsequent naval or commercial visitors. Others collected specimens of interest to ornithologists, anthropologists, or other scientists. Particularly significant were the skulls obtained from ancient cemeteries near Lima by surgeons William S. W. Ruschenberger, Henry S. Rennolds, and Waters Smith.[20]

Often, however, the navy's antebellum physicians were frustrated in their efforts to gather any very significant medical or scientific information abroad, particularly in Asian and African countries. Since their visits to any given port were usually short, they rarely had the time to dig very deeply into anything. At the same time, scientific institutions or other sources of reliable data were virtually nonexistent. Surgeon George Clymer noted in the 1850s that the scientifically minded surgeon was almost completely stymied in trying to gather medical-topographical information along the West African coast. There were no meteorological registers to be found, no previous investigations of climate, no local studies of hygiene, sanitation, or disease. In sum, he concluded:

> The coast offers few statistics, and little information that is full, accurate, and reliable. . . . Failing, as does the coast of Africa, in all these essentials to knowledge, the subject of hygiene, as resulting from climate, locality, soil, and its productions, is here . . . a matter, not of science, but of vague, conflicting, individual opinion and conjecture, from which, at best, but approximate inferences can be drawn.[21]

### Rise of the Foreign Medical Missionary Enterprise

Comparable conditions naturally confronted many of the antebellum American physicians who went abroad as missionaries. To be sure, missionaries did not always include scientific investigation as part of their expected activities. Still, they could usually learn more about the countries they went to than did the naval surgeons, simply because they normally stayed considerably longer. If the medical missionary was usually as hard put as his nonmedical associates to point to actual conversions to Christianity that he had effected, at least the numerical extent of his medical practice among the local population provided a specific measure of the Western scientific and cultural influence that he exerted. Meanwhile, though his direct medical interventions can have done but little to modify the overall mortality patterns among his parishioners, his teachings of hygiene may well have been beneficial.

From its beginnings in India and Burma in 1812, the American Protestant foreign mission enterprise expanded steadily until, by the late 1830s, it had created scattered stations not only in those countries, but in the Near East, China, the Sandwich Islands, Africa, and Southeast Asia. While all missionaries were called on from the very first to administer help to the sick, John Scudder, who sailed to India in 1819, became this country's first regular medical missionary abroad. A scattering of other physicians followed in subsequent years. Around 1840, 14 regular physicians were reported serving missions in 10 different non-Christian countries. But the editor of the *Missionary Herald* was "pained" that few candidates were presenting themselves for medical openings at several additional stations. As late as 1849 there were still only 26 such physicians overseas at American missions. Nevertheless, the United States was already the leader in this particular form of benevolence, since there were at that time only about 40 medical missionaries from all countries put together.[22]

It seemed obvious at an early date that physicians were needed at mission posts if only to look after the other missionaries and their families. Nobody seemed to keep exact figures, but experience quickly showed that, living as they frequently did under primitive conditions, these individuals were shockingly vulnerable to the local diseases. In the Middle East, nine missionaries had died by 1843, and others became so ill that they had had to be returned to the United States. Among the first generation of American missionaries in India during the 1820s and 1830s, the average individual was estimated to have died of disease or to have been forced to leave the country after only five years of service. Deaths there were usually greater among females than males, but many of both sexes who survived managed to continue work only in a state of precarious health. Reports from Liberia in 1845 indicated that 42 of the first 62 American missionaries to that country had died, mostly within a few months of arrival. The largest part of the remainder had returned home in shattered health.

In response to these catastrophic results of service abroad, missionary societies at home were urged to pay greater attention to the physical condition of candidates for missionary work. Members of the societies also began to prepare medical advice for individuals going out to the field. Those who already had experience in the field were asked to send back suggestions, such as those prepared by Dr. O. R. Bacheler at his post in South India. Bacheler thought that there was relatively little that could be done about the crushing depression frequently brought on the missionaries by their social and cultural isolation in strange countries or by their lack of success in obtaining converts. But physical ailments could be reduced by obtaining decent housing, by avoiding excessive exposure to sun and rain, by bathing and exercising regularly and otherwise observing good personal hygiene, including following a hearty but rational diet.[23]

Not unexpectedly, members of the various medical sects urged the adoption of their particular therapies as answers to the heavy missionary morbidity and mortality. As a group, medical missionaries were reasonably well trained and predominantly orthodox in their therapeutic philosophy. But some of their nonmedical associates were happier with irregular therapies. Missionaries from India to Africa testified to the value of the water cure in the tropics, while missionaries in various other countries often turned to homeopathy. Similarly, advocates of botanical treatment maintained that the proper course was to bar regular physicians, with their calomel and lancets, from the mission stations, and to provide instead copies of Samuel Thomson's book and supplies of botanical remedies. The *Thomsonian Recorder* editor, Alva Curtis, argued, in fact, that this would be the greatest service that one could perform for the missionary enterprise.

> Send Thomsonian practitioners to the tropics, and there will be far less cause to complain of the sickness and death of missionaries and emigrants. This assertion can be proved erroneous only by a fair experiment.[24]

Apart from differences over treatment, of course, there were differences in some antebellum circles over whether to send out the missionaries in the first place. Herman Melville was one of those who was distressed by the frequent hostility between the latters' rigid ways and the easy-going cultures of the primitive peoples of the Pacific islands. Even an orthodox physician like Ruschenberger, who believed that the spread of the missionary efforts in China would eventually result in enormous benefits for American trade, felt that in other places it was easy to overdo such benevolence. The Sandwich Islands, with 28 missionaries by 1827, had in fact become grossly overburdened in this respect, he thought. This amounted to one missionary for every 3,871 persons in the population, or almost four times the number of clergymen then serving Americans themselves. The Hawaiians would be better served, Ruschenberger observed, by sending them skilled mechanics, agricultural specialists, or more physicians.[25]

Little if any controversy arose over the employ of medical missionaries. Even critics of normal missionary proselytizing had to concede that there could be a place for American healers abroad. American religious authorities realized early that a missionary who was a physician was in a position to accomplish "much more than if he had been simply a preacher." However, for this very reason, they continually had to caution such men not to forget their primary mission of saving souls. Captain Charles Wilkes felt that such doctors could do much to treat diseases introduced among primitive peoples by Western sailors. And he was surprised that the British missions in Polynesia did not include any physicians.[26]

Medical spokesmen in the United States also generally looked with favor on the medical missionary. More than one pointed out that this field could offer abundant work for almost any number of unemployed physicians. But, more broadly, as participants themselves in the philanthropic impulses of the day, medical leaders applauded departing medical missionaries for undertaking the purest kind of benevolence—taking both Christianity and science out to backward nations. These individuals were felt to be particularly promising for dispelling moral darkness, since their religious role tended to be unobtrusive. But, at the same time, they were ideally situated to diffuse the broader benefits of American civilization, and notably its medicine.[27]

Many a medical missionary gave his new parishioners their first glimpses of a variety of Western tools and scientific instruments. Not a few hung thermometers on the porches of their clinics. Some managed to bring microscopes, camera obscuras, or other instruments with them. American benefactors occasionally enabled a missionary to get equipment useful in teaching, such as the set of chemical apparatus sent to O. R. Bacheler in 1849. From Madura, India, John Scudder reported in 1848 the recent arrival from the United States of a melodeon, a lathe, and a small orrery, an event that understandably "excited a vast deal of curiosity." And at other stations, missionaries may well have emulated W. S. W. Ruschenberger, who took the initiative of introducing phrenology into upper-class Siamese and Cantonese circles, including making skull measurements with callipers. His success in interpreting character from these readings became a source of great astonishment and entertainment.[28]

But medicine itself was the greatest scientific attraction in most cases. The poor of Canton, Beirut, and certain other centers had already encountered European missionary or government physicians. But in many places Americans were the first to dispense Western drugs and medical advice. Typically, the medical missionary began practicing in a room of his own house, but later he often obtained separate quarters for a dispensary. Dan Bradley set up a two-room floating dispensary on a Bangkok klong, with one room set aside for treating female patients. Meanwhile, in Canton, Peter Parker's dispensary quickly evolved into an ophthalmic hospital.

Even before the dispensaries opened, the medical missionaries were frequently overwhelmed by large numbers of patients. Occasionally, the physicians enlisted other missionaries to help them. As early as the mid-1830s, moreover, wives were being employed to overcome cultural barriers by doing much of the treatment of female patients. Some physicians at an early date set about the task of training local young men to assist them. These efforts included the conducting of courses in medicine and the preparation of medical text material in indigenous languages. By 1839 Gerrit P. Judd was writing an anatomy text in Hawaiian, and in 1848 O. R. Bacheler published a short treatise on anatomy, medicine, and surgery in the Oriya language of India.[29] While the ordinary missionary doctor usually had to make do with only a small collection of medical books, more volumes were needed if he was to do much medical instruction. Medical or missionary societies back home sometimes mounted drives for such texts and sent them out as donations, perhaps along with a skeleton or anatomical drawings, as occurred in the cases of the Liberia and China missions.

As with physicians at home, medical missionaries' practices varied from place to place depending somewhat on local demands and on their own training or interests. Some who remained generalists treated fevers, dysenteries and diarrheas, rheumatism, and other common conditions. Others decided to specialize primarily in eye or skin diseases, or later goiter. When they could obtain vaccine, many performed vaccinations. And most, even with a minimum of instruments or equipment, were eventually called on to set fractures and perform a variety of other operations: prominently excisions of tumors, lithotomies, amputations, and removal of cataracts. More elaborate operations could be undertaken when benefactors from America sent out additional instruments. Several medical missionaries stirred up great local enthusiasm when they introduced the painless surgery of anesthesia at their stations. O. R. Bacheler in Balasore and Peter Parker in Canton began using crude homemade ether inhalers in 1847 with considerable success, though both switched to chloroform by 1849.[30]

Missionary doctors were characteristically courageous, hard working, and resourceful. They kept up as well as possible with medical developments at home. And they had much incentive to apply their knowledge in an orderly, systematic manner. Once the local language was learned and the dispensary put into operation, no part of their everyday work was more important than the careful recording of events. The entire future of any given dispensary, in fact, could depend on keeping the congregations back home informed about the numbers of the "heathen" who came in as patients as well as those who attended the religious services.

Newly arrived physicians sometimes apologized because there was "so little of order and method" in the hectic early months of their mission life. But they could not afford for long to neglect their record-keeping, official reporting, or private correspondence home. Some individuals apparently did not keep medical records apart from the general mission books in the early stages. But the expansion of dispensaries demanded full separate registers of cases, treatments, drugs, and other matters. In Canton, particularly full records were required by the local British and American members of the society founded to support the missionary hospital. To satisfy this need, Parker assigned a number to each new patient and recorded all treatment on the individually numbered cards. From them he subsequently prepared detailed quarterly statistical reports on patients, diseases, finances, and library acquisitions.[31]

While the missionaries' primary lines of communication back to the United States were with the religious bodies that supported them, physicians maintained some connections as well with the medical community. Medical journals often kept track of physicians in overseas missions, and when the latter began publishing medical reports, as in the case of the Canton mission, the editors frequently inserted statistical abstracts from the reports.[32] Communications from individual missionaries, which included accounts of personal medical experiences or remarks on the various countries, were considered newsworthy.[33] Some of these took the form of general medical topographical reports. Many included figures on the incidence of local diseases. Through such communications, the American medical community became particularly familiar with three of the antebellum foreign missions.

### Missions and Morbidity in Liberia, Hawaii, and Canton

Liberia and its statistics had become known to many Americans from the 1820s on through the exertions of the American Colonization Society and the various state colonization societies. As the colony's population slowly grew, reformers back in the United States realized that physicians were much needed. "If Africa is to be civilized and Christianized," wrote one editor, "science and art must be introduced there." Occasional white doctors provided medical care in the colony up to midcentury, but much of the time the colonization societies had great difficulty in recruiting physicians. During the early 1850s, therefore, reform circles were fascinated by the Massachusetts Colonization Society's decision to educate and send out several black physicians. "A purer act of benevolence was never undertaken," thought one white physician. While dissension in American medical schools forced such students to get some of their training in London, at least two of the blacks were finally readied to sail in the spring of 1854.[34]

In Liberia, missionaries, physicians, and officials directed many of their reports to the nature, virulence, and extent of the so-called acclimating fever, a severe form of intermittent or remittent fever. There was general agreement that Liberia was medically a very unfortunate location for the colonization effort. Early experience revealed that most of the American blacks who immigrated to the country were attacked by the fever soon after arrival and were disabled for long periods. One physician reported that a sufficiently strong religious faith apparently mitigated the effects of this fever and often made the hardships of the immigrants more bearable. But others saw quinine as affording the most effective remedy, one that could make life in Africa feasible. However, since quinine was not always available in sufficient quantities, the Colonization Society in 1859 sent a number of "receptacle houses" to Liberia. Each one of these was designed to accommodate 100 immigrants, providing them with lodging and food for six months. This would permit individuals to bridge the sickly acclimation period until they felt well enough to be turned loose to cultivate their own plots of land and make their own livings.[35]

Reports of missionaries in Hawaii provided a wealth of detail about the diet, climate, materia medica, and diseases of those islands. Above all, however, reflecting the interest of America's learned men in the demographic fortunes of non-European races, many of the accounts focussed upon the catastrophic decline of the native population.[36] Captain Cook's officers had guessed that there were several hundred thousand inhabitants of the Sandwich Islands in 1779; their median figure of 400,000 was taken as a reasonable estimate by the early nineteenth-century missionaries. By the 1820s and 1830s, after Americans had begun to settle permanently, it was evident that the number had greatly declined. To find out just how many there were, the missionaries conducted a census in 1831 and 1832, and another one four years later—enumerations which furnished precedents for the earliest official census in 1850. The 1836 count showed roughly 130,000 remaining in the native population.

Arrangements were also made to maintain birth and death registers at each mission station on the islands. A compilation of data from these registers by one of the missionaries, W. P. Alexander, thus became possible about the same time as the first censuses. This revealed that there were annually over twice as many deaths as births among the islanders, a differential that was becoming progressively greater. By 1856, in fact, Hawaiian population had dropped to around 72,000. There seemed little doubt that the Polynesians as a race were as doomed as the American Indian.[37]

Medical missionaries who treated the ailments of the native Hawaiians were not of a single mind as to the causes of this decline. Some thought that widespread inbreeding was a factor, though C. F. Winslow believed the opposite when he considered the many exceptionally intelligent and able hereditary chiefs. A quite different view, enunciated by Alonzo Chapin in 1837, achieved much wider currency. Chapin concluded that the devastating decrease in population and physical vitality stemmed directly from all the "changes and innovations introduced from abroad." These included the customs and vices carried by visitors from so-called enlightened and civilized countries, chiefly England and the United States, but particularly the introduction of tobacco, hard liquors, and venereal diseases. The worse of these, syphilis, was thought to have spread through much of the population. There it rendered men impotent, women barren, and led to many still-births or deaths of prematurely born infants.[38]

A variety of other diseases—"dropsies, palsies, and diseases of the lungs"—also contributed to the great mortality and demographic decline of the Hawaiians. Some physicians, noting the "miserable modes of living," laid the high infant mortality to insufficient clothing, improper food, and poor hygienic practices. Luther Gulick, for one, was particularly critical of "nonsensical gibberish" about the inevitable extinction of the Hawaiians and believed they could once more multiply in number if they would only "live physiologically." Horace Bushnell, however, reflecting a common view, saw little hope of any such demographic outcome, for the Hawaiians or for any other "pagan" race or stock, until such time as they had accepted Christianity with its temperate and healthful precepts.[39]

Medical reports from the China mission reflected rather different matters from the Hawaii reports, except, perhaps, the large incidence of eye diseases in each place. Indeed, the Canton reports at first gave particular emphasis to ophthalmic conditions and operations, since Peter Parker and some of the other physicians deliberately gave them most of their attention. But other medical conditions were admitted increasingly over the years. Of these, none had wider ramifications for China, or greater paradox for the mission, than that of opium addiction.

Every newly arrived missionary quickly became aware of the thousands of opium shops in every large Chinese city. They invariably regarded the opium habit as a part of the "barbaric" Chinese ways that they hoped to eradicate with their Christian doctrines. Medical missionaries, who treated at least occasional extreme cases, became especially aware of the physical effects of the habit and frequently alluded to those evils in their reports. Although the Canton ophthalmic hospital did not at first admit many such patients, Parker was aware in 1838 that there were "tens of thousands" of addicts in the city. However, by 1862, along with syphilis, opium addiction accounted for a large proportion of the conditions treated at the hospital.[40]

In 1839 and 1840 the missionary hospital and its personnel were caught up in some of the controversies which touched off the opium wars. During those years the English physicians and merchants of the city were forced to leave when the Chinese government launched its attempt to end the massive opium trade. Americans and some other foreigners were allowed to remain somewhat longer. However, Howqua, the Hong merchant and opium importer who had provided the hospital with free space in one of his buildings, cancelled the arrangement at this time, forcing the hospital to move and eventually to close until the opium wars were over.

Actually, the hospital occupied a highly ambiguous position, both then and later, with respect to opium. While its physicians were busy treating Canton's addicts, several of the British merchants who supported the Medical Missionary Society and the hospital belonged to firms that were heavily involved in the opium trade. And, in the late 1850s, so was the custodian of the society's and hospital's funds. This was Russell and Company, which, with seven vessels plying the Asian coasts, was the only American firm then identified as being engaged in the trade.[41]

In the United States, relatively few Americans were aware before the 1850s, either of the vast opium traffic or its devastating human effects. But some information was gradually becoming available. An occasional writer brought the matter to the attention of the medical profession, sometimes through reviews of the work of the Canton hospital. One physician wondered whether opium smoking was in any way responsible for the large numbers of eye diseases the hospital had to treat. Naval medical officers who went ashore at Canton, Macao, Hong Kong, or other Chinese ports also became aware of the opium problem; and those like Ruschenberger who published books on their travels sometimes included data on opium smoking. But no substantial examination of the subject was attempted in the United States until 1850. In that year the Lowell physician-reformer Nathan Allen put together a historical and statistical tract which used information from a variety of sources—

commercial, missionary, and governmental. Allen presented the opium trade as a medical and social evil which was far greater in magnitude even than slavery. He fixed the responsibility for it squarely upon Great Britain. He also concluded that American missionaries had a direct interest in having the trade eliminated, since it formed such a direct obstacle to the success of their efforts in China.[42]

Despite Allen's exposé, American physicians did not pay much attention to opium addiction, whether Chinese or American. Neither the medical literature nor the official bills of mortality suggested that there was any great cause for concern. However, some individuals recognized that the United States did indeed have a problem. In 1860, informants of Oliver Wendell Holmes reported to him that, in certain western towns, the habit of opium smoking had become "more common" than alcohol consumption, presumably among Chinese immigrant laborers. But some addiction had certainly preceded the arrival of the Chinese, and the amount of it was spreading among all groups of the population. In fact, medical men themselves were beginning to get much of the blame for this situation. This was due to their ever heavier and more indiscriminate therapeutic dosing with opium on a scale they had formerly reserved for calomel. In any case, by midcentury in New York and almost every other sizable city, opium addiction had come into view as "a rapidly increasing vice," though only one of various staggering medical problems which beset the growing urban population.[43]

# 7

## The Medical Demography
## of Immigration and Industrialism

The coming of Chinese laborers to the western United States during the pre–Civil War period was, of course, watched for reasons in addition to their opium-smoking habits. There were, in fact, already some individuals talking about a gathering "yellow peril," one which could ultimately engulf Anglo-American civilization if such immigration continued to be permitted. However, since the incoming Chinese stayed mostly in the Far West, and since their numbers remained relatively small during this period, they caused comparatively little alarm so far, at least in the populous East.[1] Moreover, easterners were already intensely pre-occupied with an infinitely larger and more immediate demographic concern. This was the rapidly accelerating phenomenon of immigration from Europe, a well-nigh irresistible movement which, among other things, was threatening the older American ways of living and leaving gigantic social and health problems in its wake.[2]

European immigration was among the most significant demographic components of America's nineteenth-century shifting from an over-whelmingly rural society to one that was increasingly urban.[3] It was clearly a prime source of the new urban energies. And, from a great many viewpoints, including that of health and medicine, it was also a prime source of the period's new urban headaches.

The flow of population into given centers in the nineteenth century—a movement which included both internal migration and immigration from outside—was immensely facilitated and accelerated by the creation of new routes and modes of transportation and by the parallel mushroom-ing of factories, public work projects, and other sources of jobs. And the

Fig. 3. Emigrants Coming Ashore in New York City in the 1850s. From J. C. Furnas, *The Americans: A Social History of the United States, 1587–1914* (New York: G. P. Putnam's Sons, 1969), p. 383.

reverse was equally true. Acting together in a dynamic symbiotic relationship, the combination of population growth and economic growth went a long way toward revolutionizing America's traditional patterns of community life, toward turning many a small town into a sizable city.

Urban growth in its various facets brought prosperity to a good many individuals. But it also put monumental strains on streets, police, transport, public facilities, services, and institutions of all kinds, including those related to disease prevention and medical care. In fact, the diseases of the inpouring swarms of people, along with the accelerating demands of the new populations on housing, hospitals, cemeteries, charities, water supplies, and waste-disposal systems, generated public health problems on a scale that would have been totally inconceivable in an earlier America. Efforts to find solutions and provide new facilities abounded, though they could only rarely keep up with the constantly enlarging problems in most cities. The statistical propensities of the age, in any case, were eagerly enlisted in the effort to determine the nature and magnitude of the problems. By the 1830s and 1840s, therefore, members of the medical profession, along with reformers and officials who were trying to manage the cities, were already putting a good deal of energy into conducting the medical and demographic measurements that would assist in understanding and coping with developing urbanism.

A major phase of this effort was the far-flung attempt of such individ-

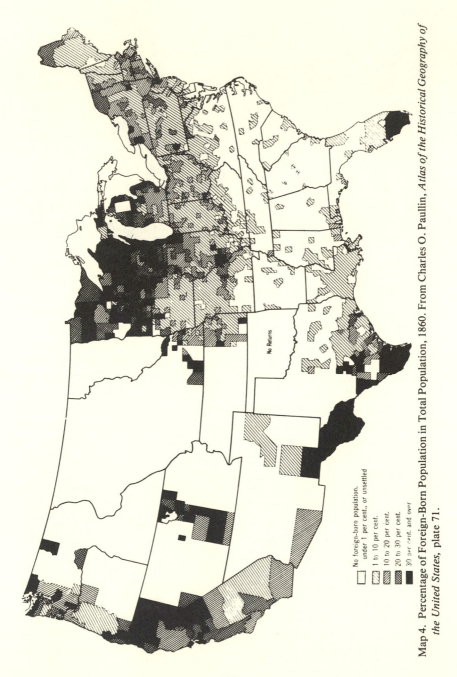

No foreign-born population,
under 1 per cent., or unsettled
1 to 10 per cent.
10 to 20 per cent.
20 to 30 per cent.
30 per cent. and over

No Returns

Map 4. Percentage of Foreign-Born Population in Total Population, 1860. From Charles O. Paullin, *Atlas of the Historical Geography of the United States*, plate 71.

uals to ferret out facts about urban poverty, data which provided them with rational bases for considering the extension of charity, public and private. And, equally important was their collective, but still halting, effort to develop effective means of recording vital events and surveying the sanitary environment in the hope of measuring the excesses of urban disease and death and instituting appropriate measures for coping with them. These extensive medical-demographic activities have been examined in detail elsewhere.[4] There remains to be considered here the perceptions of mid-nineteenth-century demographic observers, especially the physicians, with respect to the immigrants, their diseases, and their relationships to America's changing urban scene, including the expanding world of factories and of technology in general.

### Quantification of the Immigrants and Their Diseases

Americans were consistently of several minds about the swarms of people of foreign origin who became so conspicuous during the century. Political expansionists and captains of industry tended to see them as a positive benefit to the nation and frequently encouraged their movements here from other countries. For these leaders, extensive immigration not only speeded the filling up of the land, but provided needed labor for new factories, fields, and public works. In fact, the statistics which they gleaned from census and customs reports and mercantile journals made clear that these masses of newcomers already constituted an important element in ensuring the future political, economic, and industrial greatness of the country.

By contrast, urban civic leaders, reformers, and physicians tended to have painful reactions to the continuance and expansion of immigration, for these were the men who had to cope with the many-sided and overwhelming onslaught of the people from abroad as they arrived in the United States. To them, immigration often meant immediate and unwanted problems. The adverse effects wrought by this influx on the fabric of American society and ways of life, particularly in the older states, seemed to outweigh any economic advantages. Statistics became essential not only for measuring the problems and drawing attention to them but also for trying to map out effective responses in the community.

Franklin Tuthill, like many medical men who worked for registration and sanitary legislation, had an expansive notion of the sort of questions that the study of vital statistics could settle for the democracy. Along with solving such weighty issues as free love, Malthusianism, and business depressions, he thought that it could also help determine how to "best dispose of the crowds of immigrants that like the waters of a rising tide, roll into every harbor, up every creek . . . a living tide eager to work in its place, but ignorant where that place may be."[5] Other quantitatively oriented social analysts (often referred to as statists) who studied the relevant data were not so confident of finding clear-cut answers. In fact, taken together, the medical and social statistics of immigration were profoundly unsettling.

A certain proportion of the immigrants, of course, particularly during this period, found niches in America with relatively little difficulty or friction. These were the arrivals who came from middle-class backgrounds, had some financial resources on arrival, or had some readily marketable profession or skill. Such immigrants usually paid their own way in society, medically and in other respects, and not a few quickly began contributing directly—as physicians, pharmacists, or chemists—to the functioning of the country's medical establishment.

Much more ambiguous was America's reception of those immigrants who came from Europe's lower classes, who had spent all of their resources just to reach these shores, who had few if any means of bettering themselves, or were burdened by sickness or helpless dependents. On the plus side, of course, not a few of the poor immigrants also were able to find work soon after arrival. And some contributed in their own ways to medical and sanitary growth. For instance, while many Irish laborers furnished much of the sweat and sinew to help build the expanding network of roads, canals, and railroads, others were put to work on almshouses, hospitals, aqueducts, and sewage systems. Nevertheless, at the same time, the bulk of the public health problems which made such construction necessary in the cities was traceable to certain of the new arrivals. As the century progressed, the native-born residents of numerous cities watched with dismay and growing resentment as ever more foreigners who were indigent packed into the available housing and overwhelmed the available public charities and medical facilities. By the 1850s the patient population of most large public city hospitals, for instance, was well over half composed of recent immigrants, and in some, such as New Orleans' Charity Hospital, habitually over 90 percent of the patients were of foreign birth.[6]

Specifics about such matters began to be available on a piecemeal basis through newspaper accounts and the individual annual reports of the various institutions. However, it was well into the century before comprehensive compilations of any kind revealed much about the overall impact, either of immigration or of other demographic forces, in most communities. Conspicuous among the compilations that did begin to provide this type of information were the special censuses conducted in some cities. But, of these, none provided such a systematic and wideranging demographic profile of the community as the Boston census of 1845.

The Boston census was one of several creative contributions to orderly city and state management made by the bookseller, legislator, and statistical innovator Lemuel Shattuck. Shattuck's extensive proposals in the 1840s and 1850s for ongoing sanitary-data collection and comprehensive health activities by permanent public health administrators proved to be premature. However, he did succeed admirably in obtaining a reliable vital-statistics system for Massachusetts.[7] And his census proved to be the outstanding American model of the kinds of demographic inquiries that were needed by urban communities.[8]

Shattuck's 1845 census of Boston was designed to be "a general survey of the people, embracing such facts and illustrations as would truly exhibit their condition, and their means of progress and prosperity, and as would suggest measures for their modification and improvement." Its inquiries thus included such customary matters as occupations, commerce, and industry, as well as such new subjects as educational and cultural bodies, government, housing, pauperism and crime, charities, and religious institutions. Shattuck also made a special inquiry into vital statistics and from it a lengthy numerical analysis of public health because of his conviction that no other kind of information was as crucial to "that great mass of human beings that congregate in this growing prosperous city." Using a formula introduced by William Farr, he estimated that, if 2,585 was an accurate figure of the deaths in Boston's population of 114,000 in 1845, then there must have been some 72,380 cases of sickness, or one death for every 28 illnesses. These figures suggested that, with an average duration of three weeks per illness, the equivalent of over 4,000 years of productive life had been lost. Translated into monetary terms, at $1.00 per day, Boston's annual loss from sickness calculated out at over $1.5 million.[9]

With the census, Shattuck was also able to quantify such things as the decline in Boston's preeminence as a port: in only five years, between 1840 and 1845, while the population as a whole climbed from 85,000 to 114,000, the number of seamen based in the city dropped from about

3,212 to 2,600. At the same time he found that the high proportion of widows in the population was as noticeable as it had been to Cotton Mather nearly 150 years earlier. He ascertained that, in that age of uplift and reform, some 25 percent of the city's children were not attending school. His data revealed that Catholics had already become the largest religious segment of the population (26 percent), with Unitarians (16 percent) and Congregationalists (13 percent) trailing noticeably. And a question about the temperance movement elicited the information that since 1841 "39,083 persons have signed the pledge of total abstinence."

During the next few years, the demographic complexion of Boston changed even more. Shattuck, for one, was both "appalled and astounded" by the magnitude of the changes that occurred in only five years, from 1845 when foreigners made up 32.6 percent of the whole population, to 1850 when the percentage had jumped to 45.6. The tenement housing occupied by the immigrants continued to be by far the most densely packed and by far the most rife with disease of any in the city. In addition, the foreigners had come to constitute 58 percent of the paupers, 90 percent of the vagabond children, 70 percent of the dramshop keepers, and 63 percent of the persons sent to jail. In the city's medical institutions, the almshouse population, most of it sick on admission, had become 97 percent foreign by 1850, that of the lunatic hospital over 50 percent, and that of the dispensary nearly 90 percent. For Shattuck, immigration had become the direct cause of many of the city's worst sanitary evils. But beyond that, it was a social problem of such colossal proportions and profound implications as to be "sickening [to] every man in whose veins courses any puritan blood."[10]

Shattuck was only one of many Americans of the old stock who, viewing such statistics of this period, called for some degree of limitation on the flow of foreign immigration, particularly the entry of paupers, invalids, and criminals. Since sanitarians and physicians were among the closest observers of this influx, it was not at all strange that many of them reacted with deep-seated nativist emotions. For instance, as mental hospitals increased their proportions of foreign born—poor Irish in the Worcester asylum increased from 10 percent of the total in 1844 to 31 percent nine years later—superintendents increasingly scrutinized their statistical data to determine the relative effects of therapy on foreign and native patients. And in 1855 Edward Jarvis's statistics of lunacy in Massachusetts disclosed so many indigent foreigners flooding the state institutions that Jarvis recommended erecting separate hospitals to accommodate them.

Americans increasingly balked at the situation which was forcing their governments to make such provisions. Most medical men, like the rest, bristled at allegations that the poorhouses of Europe were being emptied of undesirables at America's expense. They were frustrated that the local head taxes levied on disembarking immigrants covered only small percentages of the cost of hospital services. By the 1850s there was broad agreement that it was "asking too much that we should be required to erect and endow asylums at an annual expense of hundreds of thousands of dollars for the protection and support of foreign paupers." With this in mind, many physicians joined their neighbors in advocating legislative action to control immigration. Others became directly involved in political aspects of nativism. John Griscom, for one, hoped in vain that the nativist American Republican party would carry him back into the office of City Inspector of New York in 1844. And the editor of the *Boston Medical and Surgical Journal,* Jerome V. C. Smith, was actually elected mayor of Boston in 1854 on the Know-Nothing ticket.[11]

While the nativist movement did indeed have some success in bringing about restrictions, it could by no means turn back the entire flow of immigrant poor into the cities. The financial cost of taking care of the sick and indigent newcomers thus remained an immense continuing burden for many communities. At the same time, apart from this economic imposition, many members of the old stock were deeply concerned with the impact of the newcomers' diseases in their human and medical aspects. Humanitarians were early made aware of the great suffering which disease and death caused among the immigrants. Meanwhile, physicians and public officials became aware that the immigrants' diseases could and did spread among the native populations, sometimes very widely.

As a group, the immigrants who landed at New World ports suffered extensively from such common conditions as pneumonia, diarrheas, smallpox, amenorrhea, and depression. Some of the illnesses resulted from the crowding, exposure, or poor nourishment of the long voyages. In the case of the indigent, preexisting conditions were terribly compounded, first by the foul conditions of steerage travel, and subsequently by the equally poor conditions of cellars or garrets into which they often had to crowd.[12] Even if they endured the ocean trip in reasonably good health, the poorer immigrants all too often saw their dreams turn into nightmares in the wretchedness and disease of their life in slums of the port cities. And there were further large measures of sickness, misery, and death for many of those who made their painful way to more distant destinations in the interior of the country. But much of this went unnoticed in official records and reports. In many cases, for instance, apparently nobody bothered even to count the large numbers of immigrants who succumbed from fevers and accidents while helping build the nation's canals and railroads.

From early in the century, wherever they were calculated, the immigrant morbidity and mortality rates loomed so conspicuously large that American observers and publicists felt it desirable to differentiate them from those of the native-born populations. This was not really a scientific matter in many cases, but a step considered necessary in order to preserve the sanitary reputations of the respective communities and ensure their attractiveness for commercial development. Whatever his motivation, at the end of the summer of 1805, a Savannah physician noted that out of 175 deaths reported during the hot season, only 40 percent were among the native born; the lion's share was among European immigrants and northern-born newcomers. And the differential continued to grow. By 1820 the bills of mortality showed that over 80 percent of the deaths among that city's white population were among nonnatives. It was entirely understandable that, not only in Savannah but in New Orleans and in other southern port cities, the constancy of these high mortality rates helped materially to instill "great caution and just apprehension" among potential white immigrants throughout the antebellum decades.[13]

Officials of northeastern ports found it similarly desirable to make clear the normal good health of their native-born populations as opposed to the obviously sickly state of many of the nonnatives. New Yorkers, for instance, by 1804 were specifically attributing the excessive numbers of deaths appearing on their bills of mortality to destitute immigrants and transients.[14] And, in the mid-1830s, Charles Lee pulled together numerous statistics which showed the same thing, though by then on a much larger scale.

Lee's 1836 summary for New York epitomized the tendency of his medical contemporaries everywhere to view the demographic situation of the immigrant population in a selective manner. They were, after all, little interested in the relatively well-off segments of that population who could afford to live in much the same manner as the bulk of the native American middle class or even the respectable artisan classes. Rather, as alarmed crusaders, they focussed their concern upon those poor immigrants who could not live up to those standards. Accordingly, Lee highlighted the desperate plight of the many thousands of "poor foreigners

who annually land in this city, destitute of the comforts and even necessaries of life. . . . A large proportion seek the cheapest lodgings, where,
huddled together in filth, and destitute of proper nourishment, they
perish in large numbers.''[15] It may have seemed like good economics in
1830 for someone like Matthew Carey to urge that Europe send its
paupers to the United States to expedite the ''completion of those grand
instruments of national prosperity, canals and railroads.''[16] But such a
proposal overlooked the fact that so many of the paupers who actually
were coming never went farther than these festering slums of the ports
where they landed. It also overlooked the prices that these urban centers
were having to pay merely in medical care and sanitary arrangements.
And it ignored the sense of alarm which some of the immigrants' diseases
aroused among the native-born population.

Native-born Americans were particularly upset over the apparent
introduction of certain epidemic diseases into their communities by the
poorer immigrants. Of these, cholera, in its successive waves between
1832 and the mid-1850s, was by far the most frightening and devastating
for the country as a whole. Despite the medical profession's prevailing
belief in the miasmatic origins of cholera, by 1850 increasing numbers of
contagionist physicians as well as laymen were remarking upon the
unmistakable sanitary significance of the vast streams of immigrants
who had travelled inland just ahead of the cholera. Daniel Drake and
Austin Flint, watching the immigrants moving down the St. Lawrence
and along the Great Lakes, knew that the cholera which followed them
was not just a coincidence. The immigrants who were spreading inland
from New Orleans were almost equally numerous; and some medical
reporters noted that ''the steamboats ascending the Mississippi and its
tributaries are infested with cholera.'' While cases of the disease were
reported to be scarce among the occupants of cabins, sickness and death
were very heavy among the crowded deck passengers, though many of
the deaths never found their way into the bills of mortality.[17]

In 1854 Stephen Smith reviewed this demographic aspect of the epidemic for the members of the Society of Statistical Medicine in New
York. It was perfectly clear, he felt, that the cholera had been introduced
into America on the vessels used by the immigrants. Then, from the
ports—chiefly New York, New Orleans, and Quebec—it had followed
''the great routes of emigration'' taken by the immigrants, along the
turnpikes, canals, rivers, and railroads. It was obvious that summer was
the time for cholera. But so far, Smith concluded, statistics had not
revealed ''any very definite law of progression'' of the epidemic. All that

the American experience could tell was that it was "governed apparently by the temperature of the weather, the course of the emigrants, and the condition of the towns where they took up residence."[18]

The spread of diseases other than cholera, even including yellow fever, was also sometimes blamed upon the immigrants.[19] But none of the midcentury maladies were so closely associated with the foreign newcomers as typhus. Typhus, one of the century's classic "filth diseases," and widely known as ship fever or jail fever, was an almost constant threat wherever large numbers of people were thrown closely together, and conspicuously in such places as the immigrant ships, the urban slums, and the camps for canal or railroad workers. Though still poorly distinguished from typhoid fever, the disease was more or less endemic in moderate amounts in East Coast cities through the early decades of the century, but there were years when it sometimes ran wild through tenements, almshouses, or hospital wards. And periodically, the arriving ships reported horrendous losses of passengers during passage. Ninety-four out of 132 passengers perished from typhus on a trip of the *Sybilla* in 1833, at the end of which crew members not only had to remove the dead but also to cleanse the filth of the living.[20]

The sizable increase of immigration starting in the mid-1840s brought a great increase in typhus as arrivals of other such vessels, grossly overcrowded and "laden with disease, pestilential human misery and filth," accelerated in number. Newspaper accounts playing up the horror of these voyages caused considerable public apprehension, as did subsequent cases which broke out among natives. New York City was especially shaken by the spread of typhus through Bellevue Hospital in 1848, during which outbreak, in addition to patient casualties, two-thirds of the assistant physicians fell ill from disease and one-third died.[21]

The medical profession did not yet know about the role of lice in causing this disease. But they learned enough other information in 1847 alone—through observation, experience, and statistics—to be able to handle it increasingly effectively. In New Orleans, where 8 out of 10 of the patients at Charity Hospital late in 1847 were immigrants suffering from ship fever, doctors found that removal to clean surroundings and the provision of good foods would restore most patients to health with little medication. Daniel Drake journeyed to Quebec in the summer of 1847 to observe the Canadian procedures; while the gross mortality among the immigrants there was great, he found that there was little spreading of the disease wherever adequate space, ventilation, and cleanliness could be provided. Elizabeth Blackwell reported that, with the assurance of these same conditions at Blockley Hospital in Philadelphia, and with the use of a "modified antiphlogistic plan, sometimes stimulating, and frequently simply expectant," the mortality from typhus was held to 10 percent or under. And a committee of the New York Academy of Medicine gathered statistics partly to assure the general populace that there was little danger from typhus so long as proper cleanliness and ventilation were maintained.[22]

These facts, widely accepted by physicians, were directly responsible for much of the midcentury interest in measuring and improving ventilation as a public health measure. In the context of the typhus danger, for instance, the AMA's 1850 committee on public hygiene stressed anew William Farr's recommendation that every living or sleeping chamber provide at least 512 square feet of space per person in order to ensure minimum adequate ventilation. The accumulation of physiological and chemical wisdom from Sanctorius to Liebig had demonstrated the quantities of human excretions which were constantly being given off into the air—some 100 pounds of "pulmonary and cutaneous [secretion]" alone from each individual per month, apart from feces and urine. Obviously, neither the packed immigrant ships nor the slum tenements offered the kind of space which was considered necessary to protect the occupants from concentrated doses of their neighbors' exhalations and, hence, from disease.[23]

Authorities estimated that 1 out of every 20, or 5 percent, of the immigrants from Great Britain in 1847, and conspicuously the Irish, perished on shipboard before ever reaching America. This was patently an extreme year. After 1847 the official figures on immigrant mortality were usually closer to 1 percent of the number of passengers, with .7 of 1 percent, or 2,774 out of some 370,000, recorded for 1853. At the same time, the shipmasters' returns, which were the bases for these figures, were known to be contradictory and unreliable at best—one number being given to the customs boarding officers, and another to quarantine officers—while passengers frequently reported yet another. Moreover even in nonepidemic years, conditions on certain of the transatlantic ships, the converted freighters, were well-known to cause much higher mortality than the norm. John Griscom in 1853 summarized the horrible prospects on such infamous craft.

> Of those who embark for an Atlantic voyage, on any one of a certain class of ships, *one in every twelve* of them but steps into a coffin; nearly nine percent will either never reach the promised land, or will die soon after.[24]

Of those who did survive, very large proportions had suffered some form of sickness or the other. In New York City, between 1848 and 1851, the State Board of Commissioners of Emigration hospitalized annually an average of 13,500—about 1 of every 15—of the most seriously ill immigrants. But uncounted others struggled ashore with ailments that were only slightly less serious, and of those many were in the hospitals within a few weeks after landing. Contagionist physicians, of course, found that arrival of the sick immigrants greatly enhanced their arguments for quarantine and other local port restrictions. And at the same time, in every port city, humanitarian sentiment grew for improved federal law or international standards for shipboard facilities and conditions. American legislative enactments of 1847 and 1848 reflected congressional awareness of the situation. But both medical and lay writers pointed out serious continuing problems: gross overcrowding, inadequate sanitation, poor cooking facilities. The American Medical Association suggested, in a memorial to Congress, that requiring a physician on every passenger ship would be beneficial. (It would also help reduce the presumed surplus of physicians.) But many felt that considerably more than this was required.[25]

As a result of the various pressures, the Senate in 1854 established a special committee to look into the matter of sickness, mortality, and sanitary provisions on immigrant ships. Under its chairman, Hamilton Fish of New York, this committee conscientiously gathered a considerable mass of testimony, much of it in reply to a 14-point questionnaire. Ultimately included in its report were statistical data from customs officials and quarantine officers, along with information supplied by consular officials, sea captains, merchants, officers of immigrant benevolent associations, mayors, and representatives of the medical profession. Medical communications came from the Philadelphia Board of Health and three individual physicians—Griscom and Isaac Wood of New York, and Samuel Cartwright of New Orleans. The long communications of Griscom and Cartwright, taken together, constituted a detailed treatise on maritime hygiene. Cartwright dealt particularly with such desiderata as basic sanitation, good diet, and the prohibition of alcohol, though he also lobbied for the increased use of New Orleans as a port of entry; Griscom stressed the dominant role of adequate ventilation to eliminate ship fever and reduce other diseases. Both strongly endorsed the committee's proposal to obtain standard statistical information about passengers and their health.[26]

The committee's inquiry resulted in passage of a new federal law in

1855. This legislation attempted both to limit the numbers of passengers carried by the various sizes of vessels and to establish minimums of space and ventilation for each passenger. It provided for increased numbers of privies on shipboard, for central cooking arrangements, and for other sanitary improvements. And it specified that ship captains should be required to submit regular reports on the number of passengers on each voyage, together with information as to age, sex, occupation, homeland, and berth occupied, plus any deaths with their causes. It did not require individual vessels to have physicians. In fact, there were no effective means for enforcement of most of the law's provisions. As a result, even the requirement for the bare statistical reporting of the passengers, their diseases, and their mortality was impossible to ensure until the twentieth century.

### Hygienic Aspects of Technology and Industrial Expansion

Having uncovered some of the data of immigrants' miseries, diseases, and death, antebellum sanitarians and humanitarians began looking to technology as well as to legislation for means of prevention or cure. Griscom himself was foremost in the introduction of instruments to measure the adequacy of ventilation in immigrant ships and tenements. And as the popular awareness of conditions grew, inventors came forward with improved ventilating devices. The steamboat, already available, could do the most to improve immigrant health by cutting the one-to-three-month trip down to a few days; but during the pre–Civil War period most individuals were still being transported across the Atlantic in sailing ships. Once in this country, however, their distribution to various sections was increasingly facilitated by the new mechanical means of transportation—steamships and railroads. In fact, like the native-born, the immigrants found their lives and their health increasingly affected by many aspects of the new technology. Despite the lingering protestations of Jeffersonian agrarians, America was rapidly absorbing the factory system and the Industrial Revolution in all their manifestations.

Certain economists and enthusiasts argued that the United States, with its far lesser density of urban populations, would not be subjected to the horrors that the Industrial Revolution had already spawned in Great Britain.[27] However, the philanthropists, health reformers, dispensary physicians, and others who worked among the city poor were not always convinced by the argument. In any case, Americans of all kinds found

Fig. 4. Vaccinating on an Immigrant Train Going West. From *Harper's Weekly* vol. 27, February 10, 1883, p. 85.

themselves so deeply affected by gathering industrialism as to ensure a demand for statistical information on the subject. Of these, not a few were concerned with the diseases and medical problems that were related to it.

In the mid-1830s Benjamin M'Cready of New York City touched on some of these concerns in the course of a medical inquiry into the jobs performed by Jacksonian-period Americans. M'Cready found few previous American statistics to help him, though Charles Thackrah had recently (in 1830) investigated the subject in England. For the United States, some data on the professions were to be found, mainly in biographical dictionaries. But information on common laborers and farmers was sparse and mostly general in nature.

For the fast-growing class of artisans, M'Cready was hopeful of finding mortality and perhaps even morbidity figures in the records of the different mechanics' unions. Apart from the Cordwainers Benevolent Society, however, he found that few of these groups had any data. In the hope of making future studies more complete, he urged upon other union secretaries the importance of preserving full records of their members, but for his present purpose he had to be satisfied with sparse replies to written inquiries.

Lacking in concrete statistics, M'Cready's 1837 report thus gave only a generalized impression of disease in the occupations of America's early industrial period. It was considered common knowledge that the professions, with obvious advantages, suffered less disease and lived longer than mechanics or laborers; but clergymen were healthier and more durable than either physicians or lawyers. As could have been anticipated, agriculture received the palm as "the healthiest, and the most natural of all employments." While the farmer suffered a variety of ailments, he got more exercise, better air, and better food than city laborers. Seamen, though having some of the same advantages, suffered much from exposure and accidents, and were notoriously short-lived. Carpenters, who usually worked in the open air, were often long-lived, but city cabinetmakers, exposed to dust, rarely lived beyond 50 years. Moreover, the health and longevity of almost all urban artisans—goldbeaters, watchmen, shoemakers, and others—was felt to be seriously impaired by intemperance.

Common laborers, most of whom by the 1830s were immigrants, were assumed to be even more intemperate than artisans. And, since not a few of them lived in filth and poverty, they were the unhealthiest and among the shortest-lived. City laborers had the health hazards of squalid tenements to contend with. But canal, drainage, and railway workers often suffered equally or more heavily, from fevers, exposure to the elements, and inadequate food and clothing.[28]

M'Cready thought that public works contractors and city landlords alike had a responsibility for the health of the common laborer, a group upon whom the progress of all the great internal improvements had become very dependent. It was no secret that there was much neglect of this responsibility in the materialistic self-serving of the age. The essentially conservative message of the social reformers—that a society which placed such a high premium on bodies to get the nation's urgent

work done should heed the figures on preventable deaths and sickness—
was all too often unheard by those toward whom it was directed, the
doers and shakers of the age.

It was a noisy age, filled with the prodigiously hectic excitement of
building and launching new enterprises, speculating and searching for
markets, inventing and using machines to harness nature. Jacksonian
physicians and statisticians were as aware as anyone of the impatience of
the times, the widespread mania for money-making, the propensity for
work, the habit of fast walking, driving, and eating—traits which had
become nationwide and were presumed to be making the United States
great.[29] But there was a need, many thought, for such impulsive traits to
be controlled.

The physicians Luther Bell and Josiah Curtis marvelled at the audacity
of Boston's new breed of entrepreneurs—"men of giant energies, of
boundless faith, of far-seeing calculation [who] sit down in the counting-
rooms with a surveyor's sketch and a few engineer's levels [and] decide
that a town shall be built." But all too often men like this let it go at that.
Once the streets had been laid out and the assorted buildings erected, it
was left to someone else to take care of the human needs in such towns.
Some observers, like Bell and Curtis, felt it was properly the role of the
medical profession to step in at this point and make the appropriate
hygienic arrangements. Others, however, pointed out that the sanitary
planning really should be done ahead of time.[30]

Franklin Tuthill of New York considered that prior public-health
planning was precisely the sort of job for the statistical expert, and he
formulated a grand vision of this role. In his view, this expertise would
be needed at each step of every great enterprise if these latter were to
succeed. In the excitement of competition and progress, practical men of
affairs would not have "the leisure or the patience, to fumble over folios
of figures." They should turn these matters over to the statists, those
"calm cool heads [who can] take the observations, make the calculations, issue the orders, and guide our destinies." Essential to progress
was the Baconian ordering of facts by the "ciphering closet-men."

> The busier the multitude, the quieter must be the solitude of the thinker,
> who directs them. The greater the building on which the laborers engage, the
> more nice and accurate must be the "laying down" and "taking off" and
> "figuring up" of the draughtsman.[31]

Antebellum planners and dreamers did get some of their schemes, say,
for hygeian cities or for vegetarian communities laid out in octagonal

patterns, onto the drawing boards. But few if any of those communities approached closely enough to reality to require the advance services of the statists. The kind of towns that Curtis and Bell had in mind—the newly laid out mill towns of Chicopee, Paterson, Manchester, and others, but conspicuously Lowell, the model for the others—all brought in the statists or sanitary planners *after* they were built.

From the beginning, of course, there was great interest in the question of just how healthy any of the new factory towns were, planned or unplanned. M'Cready's principal point about these towns was that, in the 1830s, they did not as yet display the sanitary evils that had long since plagued the British industrial scene. American manufacturing towns, he found, were still small in size; relatively few young children were being employed in the mills; female workers, while extensively used in the factories, apparently still had their morals intact; and the mortality of such towns was thought to be no greater than that of the rural districts. To be sure, mill towns were growing so rapidly that most of them had serious shortages of housing, particularly for the immigrant workers. But so far, as of 1837, M'Cready concluded, "the experience of our country is not unfavorable to the healthfulness of factory labor."[32]

M'Cready knew that this situation could change. In fact, some observers were persuaded that the well-advertised favorable circumstances of female mill workers in early mill towns had already changed. Some worried that life in the female boarding houses of factory towns was leading to seductions and licentiousness. Others began to draw attention to the long working hours, lack of exercise and ventilation, and wan appearance of the female workers. It was bad enough to have conditions that affronted the Jacksonian ideals of both individual morality and hygiene. But, according to the Boston editor Orestes Brownson, the millwork so impaired the women's health that many were leaving their factory jobs within a short time and returning to their original farmhouses to die prematurely.

Since Lowell was singled out by Brownson and other critics, a number of clergymen, officials, and other residents of that city felt the need to defend the community's reputation. Medical men became closely involved. Some of these tried to answer the critics through statistical information. Bills of mortality had been compiled and printed by the city physician by the mid-1830s, but they remained admittedly scanty for many years. When the physician Elisha Bartlett became mayor, he thus had to look beyond the official reports for information about health in the mills. In the course of a 1834–1835 investigation of typhoid fever cases in Lowell, Bartlett distributed simple questionnaires about health to girls in several factories. Then, in 1839, following some of the critical Boston articles, he sent out a new questionnaire, from which he received over 2,600 replies. Bartlett concluded from these that health conditions in the mills were generally good. But some individuals, looking at the results of Bartlett's own questionnaire, were by no means so sure, for fully a third of the replies indicated that the respondents' health had declined since beginning work at the factories.[33]

Other physicians also offered some modest statistical insights into Lowell's health. Among these were John O. Green, who in 1846 pulled together in tabular form, data on the previous 16 years of the city's mortality. In his remarks Green contented himself with only a generalized appeal for shorter working hours based on a simple hunch that factory labor leads to shortened life. However, Nathan Allen, who looked briefly at similar data a few years later, concluded that, if adequate bases for comparing were available, the manufacturing environment of Lowell would not prove any more injurious to health than places with other kinds of occupations.[34]

A far different order of inquiry from any of these was Josiah Curtis's 1849 survey of the city for the American Medical Association. Unlike Bartlett, Green, or Allen, Curtis approached the subject of Lowell's health with more of the thoroughness and method of the dedicated statist. Going beyond the bare bills of mortality, Curtis looked for answers in the experience of dispensary physicians, as well as in records of the local hospital since the latter's opening in 1840. Going beyond the booster statements of the politicians, he looked for the informed testimony of home missionaries as well as of mill owners. In 1849 he found the latter generally to be "high minded and humane gentlemen [who wanted] to have the matter fairly treated and the exact truth made known." The oldest and largest of the Lowell firms, the Merrimack Corporation, gave Curtis access to its mills and opened its books on matters such as hours, wages, and factory housing, along with records of employee sickness and death. From these, Curtis found that the rapid turnover of employees—the average duration of employment was nine months—made it impossible to draw very accurate public health deductions. But ventilation, an obsession he shared with Griscom and other sanitarians, was another matter. Inspection of the actual space in the corporation's workrooms made it clear that there was totally insufficient air space per worker and very poor provisions for air circulation.

Outside the mills, Curtis cataloged the sanitary ills of the city as a whole, particularly the overcrowded housing, which, because of the rapid influx of foreigners, had become as serious as in many older communities. A full-time health officer and registrar was needed to bring the full extent of these conditions to public notice. Merely the crude data that were available made it clear that already in the model city of Lowell, the shrine to industrial enterprise, there was much that needed sanitary attention. The crucial figures were the more than 800 deaths and 16,000 attacks of illness which occurred in Lowell over a three-year period and which were estimated to have been preventable. Without even calculating the pecuniary significance of such a loss, it seemed obvious that the industrial princes of the United States could use sanitary and statistical guidance.[35]

The spreading of textile mills, and indeed of shops or factories of all kinds, had the directly observable and predictable result of a proliferation of serious accidents caused by the machinery. Jacksonian bills of mortality reflected the considerable variety of these mishaps. And physicians' waiting rooms were increasingly filled with patients who had been injured either in the mills or in connection with some other of the "bold mechanical enterprises which characterize the times."[36]

Accidents involving the new modes of transportation were particularly conspicuous. Not a few Americans, like Harriet Beecher Stowe, who described the canal boat as "the most absolutely prosaic and inglorious" way to travel, had been swept up by the splendor of the steamboat and the excitement of the railroad. But early travel by either also involved a certain amount of danger. Boiler explosions on steamships plying the inland waterways sometimes resulted in frightful suffering from the flying debris and scalding water.[37] And on land, quite apart from the occasional major train wreck, so many people were losing life or limb under the wheels of the trains by the 1850s that such accidents were no longer considered newsworthy. The casualty statistics which were collected in a few states by the Civil War began to stir up some demand for better safety provisions, emergency care, and compensation for the injured. But there were no American figures as yet on the medical effects of simply riding on railroad trains—no measurements of discomfort, fatigue, spinal and muscular derangement, eye or nervous strains—few yet worried about such matters.

Conversely, of course, certain social and scientific benefits were made possible by the spread of railroads. Proposals were already in the air, for instance, that the railroads be utilized to expand opportunities of suburban living for the middle class and to facilitate philanthropically supported therapeutic excursions out of the slums for the lower classes.[38] Meanwhile, well before the Civil War, there was already considerable appreciation that the coming of the railroads, together with other advances in transportation and communication, signalled remarkable benefits to the conduct of medicine itself.

On the one hand, the new networks of turnpikes and canals, the fast-moving steamboats, and the even swifter railroads helped physicians to spread their practices far more widely than before, while a corps of peripatetic physicians used the new means of travel to move rapidly from one medical school to another hundreds of miles away in successive school terms. On the other hand, rapid transportation and, from the mid-1840s, rapid communication in the form of the telegraph made the literature of the physician—his journals and books—far more attainable than ever before. And, as this occurred, other nineteenth-century changes greatly expanded the opportunities to obtain all sorts of knowledge. The development of efficient mail and express systems, for instance, was a great stimulant, not only to the growth of colleges and medical schools but to the flourishing of native publishing houses, the spread of public schools, and the growth of literacy.

Rapid transportation, of course, also revolutionized the distribution of drugs and medicines from factories through wholesale warehouses and retail outlets—druggists, physicians, or peddlers—to the ultimate consumer. In fact, by 1850, a conjunction of the new facilities made it easy for anyone to obtain drugs and medical equipment rapidly. One enthusiastic Hoosier could hardly say enough good things about the medical benefits of "these happy days of railroads and electric telegraphs. Now, if a man wishes an ounce of morphine or quinine, or a lot of surgical instruments, he [simply] walks to the Telegraph Office . . . and the express will deliver [his order] into his hand, at his own room, in a short time."[39]

The technological explosion of which the multiplication of rails, steamships, telegraph lines, and looms was a part did not yet pay many direct dividends to American statisticians or demographic calculators. To be sure, table-sized European-made calculating machines were becoming available by 1860, and George Scheutz's first great "difference engine" was obtained by Albany's Dudley Observatory in 1855, while Scheutz's second was put to work in London by William Farr to help prepare the English life table of 1864. Americans, however, continued for some time to make most of their statistical calculations manually with pencils and paper.[40] In any case, by midcentury, a significant proportion of these calculations had to do with the changing medical and demographic aspects of antebellum women, their diseases, and their children.

# 8

# Women in Antebellum
# Medical-Demographic Change

For all the importance of immigration, far-reaching urban growth, and fast-moving industrial development, no mid-nineteenth-century demographic issues were of more interest and concern than those pertaining to women: women's place in men's society, women's diseases, their roles in marriage, and their fertility. A large majority of American women probably felt that they had no choice but to acquiesce in the ambiguous conventions of the day which, on the one hand, increasingly placed them with their feminine traits and child-bearing capacities on an idealized pedestal and, on the other hand, firmly perpetuated women's historical subordination to men. However, some women were beginning to challenge the status quo of gender relationships on broad ideological grounds, while others were doing so within narrower contexts of medicine, hygiene, and demography. These latter individuals, along with the males who supported or opposed such aspirations, argued their cases to an increasing extent on the basis of numerical fact-finding and analysis. Certainly, statistical methodologies, however crude, were recognized as being fully as essential to the elucidation of these sociosexual matters as of any other demographic phenomenon.

## Women's Rights and the Growth of Female Medical Practice

One of the most tangible as well as symbolically important foci of the women's movement was the realm of health and medicine. To be sure, women had to start virtually from scratch in the effort to make for

169

themselves places in the formal and institutional part of this realm. Accordingly, prior to 1860 they did not become more than a very small fraction of the whole number of trained antebellum medical practitioners. Nevertheless, those numbers have a special bearing upon the period's medical demography.

From a purely economic view, there was no ostensible justification for female practitioners in a profession that was already plentifully supplied with male personnel from regular medical schools, and in which seemingly endless numbers of irregulars and quacks were also buzzing like insects around the available patients. However, other factors were coming into play by the 1830s and 1840s. For one thing, a large segment of early Victorian society had drawn a clear line beyond which it was immodest and improper for male physicians to go in treating female patients, even in delivering their children. Many a woman of the period thus chose to put up with the most excruciating pain rather than permit such doctors to examine or treat her chest, abdomen, or pelvic regions. In turn, many a physician was so embarrassed by this part of his practice that he did everything possible to encourage stoicism in his female patients. The training of female physicians seemed to many to be the long-term solution to the problem of adequately coping with these delicate sensibilities.[1]

However, more than sensibilities appeared to have been affected by the shifting of much of America's obstetrical practice, earlier in the century, from the hands of the midwife to those of the male physician. Certain statistics, in fact, seemed to show that the shift had been an unfortunate one in terms of infant survival. For instance, Boston at midcentury, with mainly male-delivered children, was reported to average one stillbirth in every 14 births, while La Maternité Hospital in Paris, with only female attendants, had but half that rate. For those who were impressed by such figures, the readmission to and adequate training of American women in midwifery thus seemed to be a matter of some urgency. This, together with training in general hygiene, was indeed all that most antebellum female medical activists called for.[2]

The first medical degree earned by a woman was awarded to Elizabeth Blackwell in January 1849 by the Geneva Medical School. Geneva was located near the heart of upstate New York's religious revival belt, the famous "burned-over district," and only a few miles from the site of America's first women's rights convention, which had been held in 1848. For a decade or more before those events, however, women had been eager participants in the health reform movement, and some had been applying Ralph Waldo Emerson's doctrine of self-reliance as earnestly in the furtherance of personal health as Margaret Fuller expounded it in transcendentalist tracts. Steadily expanding numbers of women, particularly disciples of Sylvester Graham and William A. Alcott, began spreading around the countryside, giving public lectures to other women on physiology, anatomy, diet, and the like. These lectures often attracted audiences of several hundred, among them female school teachers who passed the information on to their girl students.[3]

Many of the lay lecturers, as well as many of the generation of females who followed Blackwell in obtaining medical degrees, were heavily involved in the women's rights movement.[4] This clearly had an effect upon their reception by male orthodox physicians. Understandably few antebellum regulars supported the "metaphysics of woman's rights" at all enthusiastically. Still, some did perceive that well-educated female physicans might have their uses. They might, for instance, play a positive role in reducing the impact of quackery upon women in general. One male practitioner also thought that, if medicine were opened to able women, fewer females would become public charges. And some males actually thought that women were perfectly competent, so long as they confined themselves to female conditions.[5]

Most regular physicians, however, adamantly opposed allowing women to leave their "proper" sphere of home and hearth. They regarded the often revolting details of everyday medical practice as being totally incompatible with true femininity. Moreover, as a pursuit that required "exercise of the highest intellectual power," it was assumed to be clearly beyond woman's capacity. As a result, those females who nevertheless ventured to enter medical practice in the early decades typically found themselves ostracized and jeered at by the male regulars, treated on virtually the same terms as irregular practitioners and quacks.[6]

This hostile viewpoint by itself effectively kept all but a very few females out of regular medical schools before the Civil War. In turn, it led directly to the establishment of a number of women's medical institutions. Meanwhile, sectarian medical schools, notably eclectic institutions, gave a conspicuous welcome to female candidates. As a result, by far the largest proportion of first-generation female practitioners got their training at one or another irregular college.[7]

Male physicians were understandably chagrined when money and other support seemed to be readily available, both for the female institutions and for aspiring female students. Within a few years, sympathizers were claiming that the demand for female physicians was "widespread and increasing," a claim that gained added authority with the realization that such doctors might also play important roles in the foreign missionary effort.[8] In 1852, according to one estimate, over 100 women were already practicing medicine in the United States, 35 of them with M.D. degrees, while a substantial additional number had started their medical studies. By 1858 Dan King could identify at least 300 female physicians. However, Sarah J. Hale, the able editor of *Godey's Lady's Book,* was certain that almost any number, "even 800," could be easily absorbed into the profession.[9]

Whatever the actual number of women who became medical lecturers or trained physicians, it represented no more than a tiny proportion of those women who were involved in one aspect or another of antebellum health-related activity. In the South and West, and in immigrant ghettoes everywhere, women continued their age-old role as midwives. As hospitals and asylums were constructed, women were increasingly employed as nurses, and some efforts were made to train such individuals along with the female physicians. Here and there women sold patent medicines or homeopathic preparations in the family store.

Far more extensive was the important medical role that women still played in the home itself, despite the new reliance on physicians, pharmacists, and the like. In many or most homes it was the mother, grandmother, older sister, or maiden aunt who bore the traditional burden of caring for the bedridden, administering medication to the ill, supervising the diet of the well, instructing the children in good hygienic practices, and generally directing the programs of family medical self-help which were such central features of health reform. Simultaneously, in many a church, the women's benevolent societies were the groups which pushed hardest for temperance, public care of orphans or sick poor, reforms to benefit the blind, deaf and dumb, insane, and mentally retarded.

In whatever phases of reform they were involved, antebellum women were avid consumers of reform statistics, and sometimes they were generators of such data. They pored over and were swayed by William Alcott's figures on food, drink, and child health. They were shocked by Griscom's data on city housing and mortality, and by Gouverneur Emerson's analyses of the diseases of Philadelphia's poor. While few became as actively involved in the actual collection of data as Dorothea Dix, many, both in and out of the women's rights movement, were vitally concerned with the so-called statistics of licentiousness, the numbers of abandoned women, prostitutes, and houses of ill-fame that were becoming so conspicuous in the cities.[10] It is not clear whether any male statisticians before the Civil War other than Edward Jarvis employed women to tabulate statistics, in his case, census figures. However, it is certain that women as well as men kept personal journals of the mortality and sometimes of the births in their communities. Moreover, in the privacy of their homes, unknown numbers of women kept accounts of their menstruation, and sometimes of sexual intercourse as well.[11]

### The Health and Fertility of the Early Victorian Woman

While their public statistical achievements were manifestly insignificant beside those of men, the record of Victorian women as patients was something else. Their lives and family relationships deeply affected by a complex of economic and social changes, these women proved liable to a wide range of physical and emotional ailments. Whether or not antebellum women actually developed more ailments than did previous generations, the fact that they thought they did helped make them an increasingly large proportion of doctors' patients.[12]

Middle-class hygienists and moralists were understandably more concerned with women's health than with men's. The high mortality of women and infants during or soon after parturition was by itself a particularly direct threat to the maintenance of the country's rapid population growth and its prosperity, and as such it received increasing attention. However, there were many other sources of concern. The old campaign against corsets, for one, picked up new momentum with the argument that tight lacings could cause all sorts of uterine derangements, troubles that could impair the reproductive capacity and be transmitted to female offspring.[13] At another level, people worried increasingly about the effects produced on "delicate" female nervous systems by their increased exposure to the physical phases of modern living—the cacaphony of city noise, the bustle of travel, the excitements produced by newspaper reading, the tensions produced by their husbands' ventures and risks in business. Some were concerned about the unusual fatigue that women had to undergo in the course of long migrations to new parts of the country. Others fretted over the effects of women's expanding employment in factories.[14]

To be sure, some few physicians professed to be not much worried by these conditions. Elisha Bartlett, of course, had had a personal stake in proving with numbers that factory life at Lowell was not inherently harmful to working women.[15] However, Augustus K. Gardner produced data which seemed to show that employment at the sewing machine was actually a benefit to women's health. Gardner argued, moreover, that regular labor on these devices acted as a "healthy stimulant to the muscles of the lower extremities," and in so doing produced "a tone in the generative apparatus before unknown."[16]

The bulk of commentators, both medical and lay, seemed to think the contrary, that women's health was being undermined by the various new conditions. America's middle-class women, in particular, seemed to be turning into a race of chronic invalids. Some observers perceived that the regular medical profession itself actually played a role in fostering this invalid state. Samuel Cartwright put the problem on a roughly numerical basis. "Statistical medicine proves," he wrote, "that American women grow old, lose their youthful beauty and perish at an earlier period of life than the women of other civilized countries." The reason for this, he concluded, was the general indifference on the part of regular physicians to the minor complaints and chronic ailments of females. As a consequence, women had turned in large numbers to quacks and empirics or undertook to treat themselves by harmful nostrums. Statistics of disease and mortality, he concluded, pointed clearly to the dangers of both of those alternatives.[17]

Health reformers and educators pursued the problem of the sickly female much further and with a rather different view of irregular medicine than did Cartwright. Prominent among their midcentury tracts was Catherine Beecher's *Letters to the People on Health and Happiness.* Beecher, on the basis of her personal experience as patient or boarder at 13 different health establishments, formed the impression that there was "a terrible decay of female health all over the land." Subsequently, she attempted to confirm this impression by polling the married women whom she had encountered at these establishments. Each woman was asked to evaluate her own state of health and well-being along with those of 10 of her closest married female friends, assigning one of three possible descriptions: "perfectly healthy," "delicate or diseased," or "habitual invalid."

Beecher subsequently obtained what she termed statistics from some 200 communities in the free states of the North and Midwest. Under the circumstances, the results were predictable. When the findings were tabulated, only 2 communities out of the 200 showed a majority of women who were in good health. Admittedly, in order to obtain those results, Beecher had made a good many adjustments. Chiefly these amounted to reevaluating the accounts furnished by women who were themselves in good health, on the ground that such persons were "seldom well informed" and could not be trusted to recognize ill health in others. Such adjustments did not make for reliable statistics, though they did reinforce the painful image of a generation of sickly women.[18]

This negative image had distressing implications for the future of what had come to be thought of as the "American" race, for the white Anglo-Saxon Protestant upper and middle classes that dominated affairs. By the 1840s it appeared to many that America's traditionally bountiful human fertility, and with it the country's rapid growth, might well be nearly at an end if matters were not improved. Clearly, the continued production of healthy children, or any children, would be endangered if a substantial proportion of the mothers were pale, lethargic, nervous, consumptive, or otherwise constantly ill. The invalid female unable to bear children, moreover, violated the ideal of true womanhood just as surely as did any deficiency of female piety, domesticity, or submissiveness.

To be sure, as Henry Carey found, the United States in the 1840s still ranked far ahead of any European country in the proportion of married people, in fecundity, and in rate of population growth.[19] Yet, Carey and other observers were disturbed that the maintenance of this high rate of growth apparently owed more and more to the influx of foreign immigrants. Just how much it did and how much was owing to natural increase unfortunately could not be determined from antebellum census data. How to deal with the problem was equally uncertain.

The decline in the native birth rate was accompanied by a gathering trend to less frequent and later marriages, as well as by an expanding and, to some, alarming spread in peoples' knowledge and use of contraceptives.[20] Moralists perceived all of these trends as threats to the nation's well-being, and frequently fell back on the old patriotic rhetoric in order to exhort couples to produce larger families. Many of them also worked to obtain better statistical information that would help the community understand and deal with the situation.

### Birth Registration: An Imperfect Record of Fertility

The desire to know more about the trends in native fertility apparently played only a modest part in the movement of the 1840s and 1850s to obtain effective public vital-statistics registration. For many urban dwellers, birth figures had none of the urgency that mortality data did. Moreover, there turned out to be far greater difficulties in obtaining accurate information about births from physicians and midwives than in getting death reports from sextons or undertakers. As a result, despite the interest of reformers and health officials, both marriage and birth statistics were conspicuously underreported and incomplete throughout the nineteenth century in all but a tiny handful of old communities.[21] In fact, as one expert asserted in 1860, "it would probably be impossible for a large part of the middle-aged men and women in the United States, to prove that their own parents were ever married."[22]

Before 1850 the only large American city with any claim to having fairly adequate official birth data was Philadelphia. There, since 1819, the law had required accoucheurs to report births to the city health office. Physicians had gradually taken over most of the obstetrical practice in the city, but in 1831 there were still 21 female midwives practicing and sending in birth returns, out of 155 accoucheurs. Within another decade that number had dwindled to six. The city of Philadelphia did not at that time issue official registration reports in which birth and death data could be tabulated and analyzed. However, something of the same ends were achieved in a series of articles published by Gouverneur Emerson in the medical press between the 1820s and 1850s. Emerson's commentaries included some of the most substantial American analyses of birth statistics made during the first half of the century.

Emerson was interested in, among other things, the fluctuating differential in the births of the sexes. Philadelphia averaged, during his time, about 7 percent more male births than female. As he watched this phenomenon over the years, he concluded that an unwholesome environment, poor economic or living conditions, epidemic disease, and in fact almost any kind of "depressing" circumstance, could affect the differential, even to the extent of producing an excess of females over males. In short, he noted, the fluctuating proportions in births of the sexes "may be considered as a sort of natural thermometer of the physical comfort and advantages enjoyed by a community."[23]

Emerson also studied month-by-month differentials in births, in emulation of investigations that had been carried out slightly earlier in Paris by Louis René Villermé. The Philadelphia figures, Emerson found in 1836, tended to confirm Villermé's conclusion that the differences were caused by environmental, seasonal, and meteorological influences on conception, chief of which was summer heat.[24]

With respect to health, Emerson's comparison of birth and mortality data confirmed him in the view that extended serious epidemics among adults tended "not only to diminish population directly by the amounts of death, but indirectly, by diminishing fecundity." Or, as he put it somewhat more broadly, "the *maximum* of conceptions will almost invariably be found corresponding to the *minimum* of adult mortality, and vice versa, the *maximum* of deaths agreeing with the *minimum* of conceptions."[25]

In subsequent decades, a small coterie of other medical men who undertook the compilation of vital-statistics reports, registrars such as Edwin M. Snow of Providence and William L. Sutton of Kentucky, made similar analyses of the proportions of the sexes at birth, the months of greatest fecundity, the quantities of stillbirths and illegitimacies. Those in northeastern states also devoted increasing attention to immigrant birth rates, to the countries of origin of the parents, and to the rise in mixed native and alien parentage. By 1860, New England registrars had settled upon a rough formula for figuring the components of population increase: three-eighths of the total was assumed to be due to natural fertility, five-eighths to immigration.[26]

The only state in which any substantial proportion of births was being incorporated into the official registration reports before the Civil War was Massachusetts, though even there it was not until late in the century that as many as 90 percent of the births were included. Elsewhere, concerned individuals were only rarely able to get their communities to do anything about the obvious deficiencies indicated by their reports. The one expedient that was adopted in a few instances was the supplemental baby census. Boston inaugurated semiannual enumerations in 1850, and Providence did so in 1857, while the state of Rhode Island began conducting an annual baby census in the mid-1850s. Still, even such efforts admittedly could not ensure full birth records, and, as expedients, they became progressively less useful as populations grew.[27]

## Genealogy: a Calculus of Heredity and Fertility

The search for supplemental information about births and fertility also led to sources which were private rather than official in nature and scope. By the 1830s and 1840s, Americans' interest in their ancestors had become increasingly institutionalized, with the formation of historical societies, genealogical societies, and libraries. Activities of these institutions helped sharpen the concerns in many communities with the continued fertility decline and with the capacity of the old stock to survive. However, if genealogical resources were to become useful in studying these questions, there would have to be improvements in the data compiled at the family level.

While preparing his history of Concord in the early 1830s, Lemuel Shattuck found that there were as great shortcomings in such data as in the local town and church records. In fact, there seemed to him to have been a substantial breakdown in the maintenance of archives in the average private household. In Shattuck's view, the orderly keeping of personal records was as much of a desideratum for the responsible individual and the family as was the maintenance of a properly moral and hygienic home environment. Thus, even while he was working more conspicuously for public vital statistics in Massachusetts, Shattuck was preparing texts aimed at remedying some of the lacunae in genealogical record-keeping. In 1841, he issued his *Complete System of Family Registration,* a work which provided elaborate instructions, forms, and charts for keeping genealogical information, together with details of current births, marriages, and deaths. An allied work, *The Domestic Book Keeper and Practical Economist* of 1843, was a utilitarian work designed, as indicated in its subtitle, for "those who are willing to know how they live, and who desire to live better."

During the early 1850s Shattuck addressed himself to the record of his own family. The resulting *Memorials of the Descendants of William Shattuck* (1855), proved to be both a model of what a family history should be and a guide to the construction of other genealogies. The economist Henry C. Carey considered it "the most remarkable contribution to vital statistics that has yet been made." In a rich opening section, written nearly 15 years before Francis Galton's *Hereditary Genius,* Shattuck pointed out some of the potentialities of what he called philosophical genealogy, or the science of heredity, a subject he found but little pursued at that time. Going on, he made a unique and detailed demographic analysis of the characteristics of the Shattuck family over the generations. More such genealogical analyses of established families would, he thought, do much to lighten the task of future historians. They would also contribute to the scientific objective of "ascertaining the laws of human life existing in this country, and the changes, if any, that have taken place in relation to these laws in the different periods of its history."[28]

A comparable, and probably even more influential, argument for better genealogical records came out of phrenology. The early devotees of this practice, believing that the various phrenological traits were transmissible from parents to children, made the study of heredity a central part of the lively nineteenth-century phrenological movement. In an 1842 work on matrimony, for instance, Orson S. Fowler noted that the study of phrenology, physiology, and family history would help young people in selecting compatible mates. A few years later, in his work on *Hereditary Descent,* he expanded on this in an effort to revive the science of "parentage."

Like the majority of spokesmen for his generation of Americans, Fowler applauded the wisdom of those of God's laws which ensured the rapid multiplication of the human race. "What magnificent results, from an arrangement so simple! Wastes, but yesterday desolate, today it is beginning to people, and anon will have crowded with homes, hamlets, villages, and cities, swarming with millions, and teeming with life and happiness." That happiness would be magnified for future generations, he saw, if the present generation would practice selective marriage and thereby ensure transmission of only superior traits to its children. "If man can derive benefits from improving his *stock,* how much greater by improving his *children.*"

Fowler drew from scattered existing records, private and public, to illustrate the transmission of the various phrenological traits across several generations. However, the implementation of hereditarian research on any extensive scale required far more extensive sources of information. He thus urged individuals everywhere to keep detailed family biographies, vital statistics, and other genealogical records. More ambitiously, he outlined a long-range proposal for a national repository which would store these kinds of data and make them available through appropriate publications.[29]

Well-maintained state registers of vital statistics, of course, would take care of some of these basic needs. They also had the potential for revealing the presence of hereditary disease, not only in the offspring from a given marriage but throughout society broadly. Once they were established, Edward Jarvis thought, people would begin to consult the registers routinely "to ascertain the purity or impurity of the blood of families . . . [just] as they now consult the registry of deeds to ascertain the clearness or defect of the title to estates."[30]

While the fulfillment of the ideal of complete vital statistics by the states was still decades in the future, the efforts to improve family record-keeping bore more immediate fruit, judging from the expansion of genealogical activity in the next generation. By 1858, in fact, at least one observer believed that as a general rule families had become much more methodical in such affairs and that most now kept "a family record as a matter of reference."[31] The concept of scientific propagation, or eugenic marriage, also struck a responsive chord in midcentury America. Orthodox medical spokesmen as well as irregulars frequently endorsed the concept.[32] Eventually, Darwin's *Origin of Species* fortified the idea among the scientifically minded. For the literate, at least in principle, the desirability of improved breeding of the human species became by midcentury almost as widely accepted an article of faith as the scientific breeding of animals.

At the same time, certain members of the antebellum medical profession showed that there was another side of the coin by documenting instances of mental retardation, birth defects, or criminal tendencies which might be blamed on inbreeding. Samuel Gridley Howe's important 1846–1847 survey of idiocy in Massachusetts provided strong statistical evidence that this condition was the most frequently found imperfection in the offspring of consanguinous marriages. Out of 95 children born from 17 such unions, 44 were found to be idiots, 12 scrofulous, 1 deaf, and 1 a dwarf.[33] During the 1850s, other individuals became more specifically concerned with the practice and effects of consanguinous marriage, and some made questionnaire-type inquiries into the extent of the practice among American whites.[34]

The most extensive survey of this type was the one conducted in 1857 by Samuel M. Bemiss for the American Medical Association. Although this study actually uncovered only 873 cases of consanguinous marriage around the country, Bemiss confidently estimated that the real total would undoubtedly be five times as great. At any rate, the history of the progeny which had issued from this sample alone provided a damaging indictment of the practice. From these statistics, Bemiss inferred conservatively that over 10 percent of the country's deaf and dumb, 5 percent of the blind, and nearly 15 percent of the idiots were offspring of closely related parents.[35] Meanwhile, Isaac Ray noted that, even without statistical verification, "one has only to cast his eye over the list of voters suspended in the bar-room of the tavern, or by the church-door [of America's small towns], to see how large a proportion of the people is embraced in a few leading names seldom met with anywhere else. This naturally implies a good deal of intermingling, and an extensive infusion of common blood."[36]

Not everyone agreed with such findings. The Philadelphia hygienist John Bell found Bemiss's statistics unreliable and virtually meaningless, little more than reflections of long-standing middle-class prejudices against consanguinous marriage. Since individuals with the strongest prejudices were the ones most likely to reply to questionnaires, Bell thought that the data accumulated by Bemiss could not be considered a fair sample, but only "a burlesque upon medical statistics." Carefully collected statistics might well prove just the opposite of the AMA findings. At any rate, he thought that Americans speculating about the subject would be well advised to keep in mind man's success over the years in improving animal lineages through this very practice of inbreeding.[37] And C. F. Winslow noted that in Hawaii the practice had already produced a large, healthy, and highly intelligent class of hereditary chiefs, in marked contrast to the "common natives." But most commentators, if they had read Lewis H. Morgan anyway, would undoubtedly have agreed that the Iroquois Indians had provided the more respectable eugenic example by not countenancing inbreeding, even within larger tribal entities.[38]

None could have quarrelled seriously with the efforts to improve the quality of nineteenth-century American children by means of statistical record-keeping and analysis. But some real differences were beginning to be expressed with respect to the quantities of children being produced. In fact, within the large context of social, economic, and demographic change, of health reform and women's rights agitation, several serious challenges emerged during the antebellum period, not only to the traditional ethic of large families as such, but to the orthodox structure and authority of the institution of marriage itself.

### Marital Discontent and the Arithmetic of Birth Control

Various hitherto submerged dissatisfactions with conventional marital relationships and practices were brought to the surface by nineteenth-century egalitarian ferments and social changes. Their depth was reflected, to some extent, by the vigorous educational efforts of moralists and hygienists to improve the institutions of home, family, and marriage. However, articulate women's righters and their supporters made it clear that far more was involved than educating females to be better homemakers. In fact, that was part of the problem. Fundamental among the female grievances, as reformers saw it, were such basic matters as their lack of legal rights, the frequently harsh routine of their daily labor, the maltreatment and sexual tyranny they were often subjected to by selfish or cruel husbands, and above all, the endless cycle of labor and suffering imposed by repeated pregnancies and childbirths, particularly when they were unwanted.

Divorce was an obvious means for escaping unhappy marriages. However, divorces were not easily obtained in antebellum courts. Even if one were willing to bear the social stigma and economic consequences of such a course of action, most states placed considerable legal obstacles in the way. While a few states made some improvement in their divorce statutes during this period, would-be reformers in other states continued to face formidable opposition from entrenched conservatives. The latter included such well-known individuals as Horace Greeley, who, in adamantly rejecting divorce except for adultery, earned a reputation as a "man of statistics and facts, but not of principles." In any event, constrained both by public opinion and by law, only some 7,000 divorces were awarded annually around 1860, a large proportion in which women were the plaintiffs.[39]

Actually, most of the women who had marital grievances did not necessarily want divorce at all. The more urgent need was for physical and economic relief from childbearing. In the 1830s the reformer Robert Dale Owen pointed out to American married couples that adoption of some means of limiting the number of their children would reduce quarreling in the family over financial matters, would permit decent food and clothes to all, and would greatly reduce the strains on the mother's health. Other reformers soon joined in questioning the standard "assumption that woman was created only, or at least chiefly, to bear children, nurse them, cook, wash, and drudge through life." The iconoclastic physician Charles Knowlton seconded this doubt strongly, and added the observation that the adoption of contraceptive measures would enable thousands of young men to marry who would ordinarily put it off for economic reasons. In turn, he hoped marriage would keep many of these young men away from prostitutes and other forms of licentiousness.[40]

The birth control tracts of Owen and Knowlton, both of which appeared in the early 1830s, pointed the way to achieving such ends by publishing specific details about the crude devices then available.[41] These works were widely circulated in a number of editions and exerted considerable influence. In turn, some medical-reform publicists disseminated the new contraceptive information in their own texts, while irregular practitioners increasingly advised their patients on the use of such devices. One of the latter, R. T. Trall, at an early period, had several

*(margin note: Women's Movement Advancement)*

hundred of his patients keeping records of their menstruation in order to provide a statistical basis for predicting "safe" periods, while Mary Gove Nichols and her husband made contraception an essential adjunct to their concepts of free love.[42]

Despite the logic of its early advocates and the alleged existence of a "vast number" of immediately interested couples, contraception did not have smooth going in nineteenth-century America. Religious and other community leaders were by no means the only ones opposing the measure. Even among the health reformers, many traditionalists were shocked by it. Alcott, for one, was dismayed to find Knowlton's book "in nearly every part of our wide-spread country." It was appalling to him to discover that Knowlton, a fellow New Englander, had so far ignored the conventional ethic as "to teach people, both in married life and elsewhere, the art of gratifying the sexual appetite without the necessity of progeny."[43]

In the eyes of orthodox medical practitioners, endorsement of contraception by sectarian practitioners and advocates of free love automatically made it suspect. Moreover, the enthusiastic commercializing of [*opinion*] birth control devices by unsavory and often unhygienic quacks further ensured its utter disrepute in regular medical circles. Desperately seeking respectability themselves in society as a whole, the regulars retreated behind a mixture of moral, medical, and statistical objections and quickly closed ranks in vigorously opposing any and all forms of birth control. As a result, most antebellum couples who wanted contraceptive information had to look for it outside the orthodox medical profession.[44]

The increasing numbers of families that wished to avoid having children was an understandably unsettling matter for the white Anglo-Saxon Protestant establishment. Here if anywhere, in the eyes of traditionalists, was the ultimate heresy in a new and growing country. It was, to be sure, a subversion of religion. But, even more alarmingly, it represented a threat to progress and manifest destiny, an anti-American development that further jeopardized the traditionally boundless native fertility and contributed dangerously to the already declining native birth rate. It also threatened the traditionally dominant male role in society.

That is not to say that anybody knew exactly how many people at midcentury were deliberately practicing some form of birth control. However, physicians were well aware that it was spreading. In the South, antebellum physicians and planters were widely persuaded that black women had access to some secret nostrum which would either "produce an incapacity to bear children or destroy the foetus in embryo."

E. M. Pendleton, who had his doubts about this, decided to test the assumption by the census findings of 1850. Restricting his test to Hancock County, Georgia, he confirmed that the belief had no factual foundation whatsoever. On the contrary, the data showed conclusively that the blacks had produced substantially more children per capita than the whites. Here was just another proof, Pendleton concluded, that "one well authenticated table is worth more as an argument, than all the plausible theories of the profoundist philosophers of the age."[45]

In New England, William Alcott lamented that there still were no precise statistics of "these crimes without names." He thought that publishing the facts to an indignant nation might bring the practices to a halt. Meanwhile, Alcott could only make a wild guess as to the numbers of births that were being circumvented each year in the United States, and as to the specific measures that were being used to do so.

| Destroyed, yearly, by means of a certain book, clandestinely circulated | ten thousands |
| Destroyed by careless intercourse | thousands |
| Destroyed by violent intentional efforts | thousands |
| Destroyed by accidental means | hundreds |
| Destroyed by poisoning—foreign and domestic | ten thousands |
| Destroyed by instrumental violence | hundreds |
| Destroyed by overworking | hundreds.[46] |

While the amount of contraception itself thus remained a hypothetical matter, there were, as Alcott knew, rather better figures on the extent of deliberate efforts to destroy conceptions already made, that is, to induce stillbirths or abortions. Early in the century some thought that stillbirths occurred predominantly as the legitimate result of physiological problems or illnesses of the mothers, accidents, or other involuntary circumstances. Even if this had been the case, their number was startling. In fact, according to the bills of mortality, nineteenth-century American cities had far more stillbirths than did London; in the case of Boston, twice as many. Stephen W. Avery, who examined the phenomenon in the 1830s, thought that this excess was mainly due to differences in diet, dress, and habits of living in the two countries.[47]

Many other nineteenth-century observers consistently believed that stillbirths were mainly the result of premeditated action. As early as 1807 Thomas Ewell estimated that "thousands of children in the womb" were annually sacrificed through abortions, and others concurred. What-

Fig. 5. The Female Abortionist. From the *National Police Gazette,* March 13, 1847.

ever the actual figure, John B. Beck was of the opinion that most of the women who resorted to the practice were single.[48] Apart from the occasional infanticide, according to Beck, the most frequent means of abortion up to the 1830s were such drugs as calomel and ergot, though none were very effective. Within another decade or so, both the drugs and the instruments that were employed multiplied prodigiously. Judged merely by the large quantities of "flaming advertisements" that struck the eye in the daily and weekly press, by the 1850s abortion had become literally epidemic. In New York City, stillbirths and abortions reportedly increased 140 percent between 1843 and 1853, while in many cities as much as 20 percent of the overall mortality of children under five was being ascribed to these two causes. "So very common," in fact, were the abortion operations performed by itinerant quacks that juries rapidly became reluctant to convict except in unusual cases.[49]

As D. M. Reese confessed in 1857, not a few midcentury medical regulars found it "humiliating to record the widespread prevalence of an evil scarcely known to the generation of our fathers." Facing an intolerable situation, they thus proceeded, in conjunction with clergymen, educators, and other leaders of society, to make the abortion issue a national moral and medical cause. Fortified with statistical ammunition, they prosecuted this cause with much the same fervor that their fellow countrymen took up abolition, temperance, the insane, or foreign missions.[50]

By far the most zealous and statistically informed spokesman of the medical crusade against abortion was Horatio R. Storer of Boston. In 1857 Storer had himself appointed by the American Medical Association to look into the subject, and he spent much of the next two years collecting relevant information. Acknowledging that exact figures on the frequency of abortion could still not be obtained, he nevertheless compiled some impressive findings from census enumerations, vital registers, and reports of abortion trials. Comparative data from Europe demonstrated that the problem was not restricted to the United States. However, nowhere was it worse than in New York City and in Massachusetts, the principal localities which Storer used to illustrate the American situation. Assuming that most *premature* stillbirths were the result of abortions, Storer concluded from the New York bills of mortality that 1 of every 4 stillbirths in that city in 1856 reflected an abortion, a marked increase over the proportion of 1 in 10 only 15 years earlier. Massachusetts showed an average of 1 in 3 in the later year, a figure which was really little if any larger than that for the rest of the country; Massachusetts just had better vital statistics.

In his 1859 report Storer noted that 12 of the states in the Union had no statutes at all dealing with abortion, while in most others the laws were vague and ineffective. In Massachusetts there had been 32 abortion trials between 1849 and 1858 but not a single conviction. Storer hoped that his "startling" statistics would help alter this situation. As such, they did have considerable influence, during the next few decades, in obtaining strong antiabortion legislation throughout the country. They also helped solidify a climate of social and medical opinion that linked the abortion issue firmly to birth control and eventually contributed to the passage and implementation of the Comstock Laws of the 1870s.[51]

The antiabortion crusade did not, of course, reverse the declining antebellum birth rate among the native born, though it did provide some comfort to those who worried about the decline. Antiabortion data-gathering, however, did become a conspicuous aspect of the steadily enlarging effort to obtain quantitative data about human life in the United States from birth through death. These empirical findings were neither better nor worse statistically than those that were used to illuminate almost any other social issue or medical problem of the day. However, they did not measure up in quality to the calculations of life expectancy which were emerging in business and scientific circles.

# 9

## The Length of Lives
## in Antebellum America

Like the examination of birth and abortion statistics, the study of longevity was undertaken within a framework of preconceptions and social
biases. However, investigations into the average length of life seemed to
offer a somewhat greater prospect than some of the other areas of demographic inquiry of attaining the objectivity that statisticians proclaimed
as their ideal. This is not to say that American physicians, statists, or
other scholars were as yet able or detached enough during this period to
pursue that ideal very far. Nevertheless, some began to approach a
certain methodological competence, occasionally perhaps in their individual inquiries into American longevity, but more particularly in a
variety of involvements with life insurance enterprises. Under the exact-
ing demands of business and science, they made at least some progress
both in raising the level of their studies and in building up better bases of
data for future studies.

### The Numerical Study of Longevity

Eighteenth-century European inquiries into longevity raised many
questions but came up with relatively little in the way of conclusive
answers. In fact, so few concrete data were actually forthcoming that
Scotland's Sir John Sinclair in 1802 decided to reformulate much the
same questions for nineteenth-century consideration. What was the role
of occupation, heredity, and marital status in determining longevity?
What was the influence of weather and other physical surroundings in a

given locality? What was the effect of good diet and hygienic practices? And what about medical science itself?[1]

Nineteenth-century Americans responded to such questions with energy and enthusiasm. They ransacked local libraries for historical information on the long-lived. They gathered information about the old people in their respective communities. Some tapped the census or vital reports for any light they could shed on actual length of life achieved. For the well-to-do, at least, the biblical age of three score and ten remained the usual goal. But society was increasingly interested in measuring just how far toward that goal the average American managed to go and in identifying the medical and environmental barriers to achieving it. Moreover, some physiologists were beginning to suggest that society should aim to make 70 a minimum-life-expectancy ideal for all rather than a standard for the favored few.[2]

The subject of longevity received particular attention from those involved in hygiene and health reform. Among medical practitioners, regulars and irregulars alike agreed that shortness of life was to be attributed chiefly to "the disregard of hygienic measures."[3] They sometimes focussed upon abuse of or inattention to some one element—diet, alcoholic drink, climate, clothing, exercise, or sex behavior—as the predominant cause of short life. But most saw that one's best chance for a respectable longevity lay in adherence to an overall package of healthful habits. The hygienists also agreed that it was extremely advantageous not to be poor or live in unhealthful physical surroundings.

Sectarians made a great issue out of the substantial abbreviation of life allegedly brought about by indiscriminate drugging and other practices of the regulars. The former naturally maintained that a faithful adherence to botanic remedies, hydropathy, homeopathy, or some other regime was certain to ensure both health and long life. Homeopaths believed, for instance, that acceptance of their system would bring about the virtual elimination of surgical operations, which were then recognized as very immediate means of decreasing the life spans of those concerned. One homeopathic practitioner, Benjamin Joslin, claimed to have statistics showing "that the average duration of life among those affected with schirrus [sic] and cancer is shortened by operations—that those on whom excision is practiced, die sooner than those who submit to no operation."[4]

Regulars in turn, compiled their own statistics to prove the efficacy of orthodox medicine in enhancing longevity. Among these, Alonzo Clark pointed in 1853 to American as well as British hospital figures as concrete evidence of the triumphs of regular medicine in the nineteenth century. By far its greatest achievement, he thought, was that of "prolonging the years of the life of man more than one-fourth their former average, throughout Europe and America, in the short period of half a century."[5]

Phrenology did not originally include within its scope any special measure for judging potential longevity. However, in 1855 W. B. Powell offered a means for rectifying this. He suggested that the length of the portion of the skull between the ear and eye could "accurately indicate the comparative duration of life." Proceeding to make measurements of numerous living individuals as well as of the crania of several hundred deceased, Powell concluded that persons with a space of about one-half inch in that area could expect an average length of life, while those who measured a full inch could anticipate living to an age of 80 or 100.[6]

Like their eighteenth-century forebears, nineteenth-century Americans stood in some awe of the centenarians around them and never tired of citing examples of long-lived individuals from the past. In fact, few projects enjoyed such perennial appeal among antiquarians as searching for examples of longevity in the pages of the Bible, the classics, or local newspapers, histories, and genealogies. Such compilers, even those with few pretensions to learning, found an abundance of outlets for their compilations in the general or popular press. Even medical and other learned journals found space for interviews with centenarians or other articles on longevity that had few if any scientific features.

The medical press, however, also went beyond this to publish occasional short compilations of the longevity data of special groups—the Moravian congregation at Bethlehem, the Shaker village at Canterbury, New Hampshire, the physicians listed in Thacher's *American Medical Biography*—figures that had both general interest and scientific value.[7] Some of these works were little more than bare lists of names or tables of data. Still, others provided a certain amount of analysis or commentary, often comparing contemporary longevity with the ancient or generalizing about the salubrity of given communities.

One of the most ambitious of the early nineteenth-century studies was made by Joseph E. Worcester in 1825. Worcester brought together data on 98 persons who had lived to the age of 100 or over in New Hampshire and 132 who had died elsewhere in the United States at age 110 or more. He assumed that the living habits of past generations had been more favorable to longevity than those of his own generation, though his data provided no evidence about this one way or the other. His figures did show, he thought, that the New Hampshire population had a consistently greater proportion of centenarians than such countries as Sweden or Russia. The United States as a whole, moreover, was producing a respectable number, considering its newness as a nation. For reasons that were unclear to him, aged women were considerably more numerous than aged men, but of those persons who lived to 110 or more "a large majority" were men.

Worcester lamented that the United States census reports thus far shed but little light on his topic, since they lumped people by age into four large groups. He hoped that subsequent reports could provide "a more minute, uniform, and philosophical" view of the ages of the population by grouping the figures for each sex and color into smaller groups, preferably 5-year groups for those up to 20- and 10-year groups for the rest.

> The census, thus taken, would furnish the means of presenting interesting comparative views with regard to longevity, or the *chance of life,* in different parts of the Union. It would also afford the means of confuting the unfounded assumptions of European theorists respecting the unhealthiness of our climate and the infrequency of longevity; and would probably furnish evidence, that among the agricultural population of the Eastern and Middle states, the chance of life is as great as in any country on the globe, of which the statistics are well known, of equal extent and population.[8]

The federal census of 1830 did indeed provide the improved age classification that Worcester wanted, except in the case of blacks, while the census of 1850 went even further by publishing detailed age figures for all segments of the living population. The 1850 census also gathered several other new kinds of demographic information, but none of the innovations were more significant than the attempt to obtain national mortality data by race, age, sex, occupation, and cause of death.[9] This was a stopgap effort, prompted largely by the slow progress being made in establishing workable state vital-statistics registration systems. And understandably the results of the federal inquiry had as many serious shortcomings as most of the early state systems.

Most conspicuous among these deficiencies were the very high degree of incompleteness of the census's mortality returns, together with the wide range of disease terminologies used by the reporters.[10] While some specialists felt that the deficiencies rendered the whole inquiry virtually useless, others felt that some parts could be salvaged. The superintendent, James D. B. DeBow, in 1854 thus decided, among other steps, to

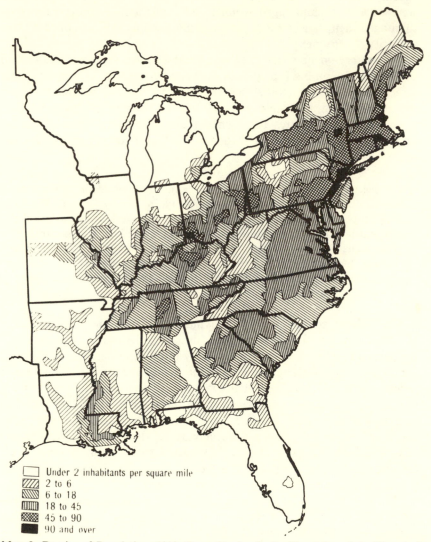

Map 5. Density of Population, 1830. From Charles O. Paullin, *Atlas of the Historical Geography of the United States,* plate 76.

engage Edward Jarvis, the Massachusetts medical statistician, to do what he could to edit and interpret the returns, including their nomenclature. Jarvis devoted many hours of work at home in the effort to reduce the size of the confused mass of disease names and to arrange them under a slightly modified Farr classification. When the mortality report was ultimately issued in 1855, Jarvis found some satisfaction in thinking that he and DeBow together had at least managed to salvage something of the statistical honor of the United States. But he was disappointed that not enough funds had been available to accomplish all of the revisions of this sort that were really needed.[11] And it was equally disappointing to every-one concerned that, with the 1860 census, Jarvis had to be called in once more to try to patch a mortality report that all agreed was flawed and unsatisfactory.

Despite the many enumerators, clerks, and assorted part-time consul-tants who were brought in, the federal census remained an ad hoc operation. Statists, of course, among others, pointed out that both census enumerations and vital-statistics registration activities should ideally be assigned to a permanent independent bureau such as the Office of the Registrar-General in Great Britain. The registrar in charge of such an office would be truly a professional; the medical profession generally agreed that he should preferably be a physician. In any case, in Jarvis's view, he should be "selected for that office on account of his familiarity with the law of population and of mortality, and [because he] has the exact mental discipline and cautious habits of reasoning, which would enable him to discharge the duties of his office in the most perfect manner."[12] A national bureau of statistics was proposed in 1845, and several antebellum superintendents of the census argued the wisdom of having a permanent federal census bureau, but such an agency was not finally created until 1902.

## Taking Chances on Life and Sickness

The nineteenth-century American man's interest in his chances of living to an advanced age focussed usually upon his concern for the odds of contracting and dying from disease. The widespread desire to know just what those odds were gave encouragement to scholars to work them out with ever greater numerical precision. To be sure, there were some observers who maintained that continuing national progress required a citizenry that was "high spirited," daring, and indifferent even to the

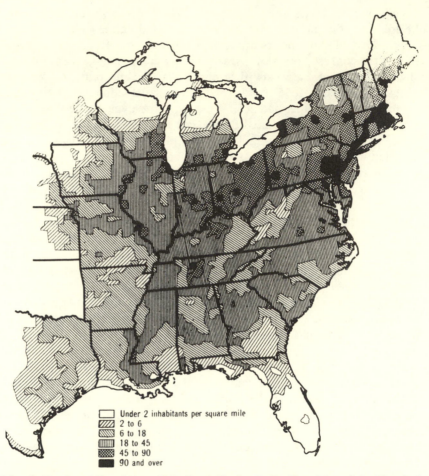

Map 6. Density of Population, 1860. From Charles O. Paullin, *Atlas of the Historical Geography of the United States,* plate 77.

odds of pestilence and death. Charles Caldwell, for one, insisted that "to achieve what is great, man must not tremblingly take counsel of his fears, nor always calculate, with a clerk-like caution, the chances of danger."[13]

Nevertheless, however attractive the potential rewards, Americans did not normally rush blindly into these various risks. Whatever daring they possessed, most individuals were prudent enough to prepare themselves in advance as well as possible. This included the attempt to discover as accurately as possible what the odds of success were. Once these were determined, steps could sometimes be taken to minimize the risks or offset them in some way. Thus, the improved navigational charts produced by Nathaniel Bowditch and his successors greatly reduced the chances of shipwreck which sea captains faced in American waters. Manuals, geographies, and travel accounts provided migrants with comparable information on the hazards to prepare for along their projected routes to the West. And, as part of a trend toward improved business methods, merchants increasingly protected themselves with different kinds of insurance—identifying their risks more carefully to begin with, and adopting mutual insurance when possible as a means of sharing risks.

The businessman's search for ways to protect himself against some of his risks was paralleled by a growing desire of the ordinary citizen to protect himself and his family against the economic consequences of disease. This desire manifested itself in a certain amount of support for early nineteenth-century projects to insure healthy lives against disease. However, a general lack of American sickness statistics throughout this period made all of these projects highly precarious.

The sickness insurance and other benefits of Great Britain's mutual aid and fraternal groups, the so-called Friendly Societies, were, of course, well known in the United States. Similar American bodies, some of which grew out of the British organizations, came into being late in the eighteenth century and to an increasing extent in the nineteenth, and some of them offered insurance or other sickness benefits to their members. Most conspicuous of these groups in the United States was the Odd Fellows, an order which attracted hundreds of thousands of new members during the 1840s, partly because of the appeal of its insurance provisions. By the late 1840s, however, it became apparent that the health insurance benefit of the order in America rested on very shaky statistical and financial ground. The chief problem, it turned out, was its reliance upon British sickness experience. A Boston lodge of the order found itself losing so much money that it voted to start benefit payments only after the first week of any case of sickness. Subsequently, during the 1850s, a national committee under Isaac D. Williamson tried to effect a comprehensive actuarial reform of the Odd Fellows' insurance system, but the effort proved premature.[14]

Attempts made during the late 1840s to launch commercial sickness insurance in the United States were even less successful, and for some of the same reasons. Companies were founded at this time in a number of eastern states, but all failed within a year or two. Four such firms were established in Massachusetts alone in 1847. Since there was then no statistical information available about the state's previous sickness experience to guide them in setting premium rates, the founders fell back on the British experience. However, this quickly proved inappropriate in the Massachusetts setting, and all four firms closed down by 1849. To Edward Jarvis these failures suggested that, contrary to the general preconceptions of Americans, there probably was "more sickness here than in England." The failures also warned American businessmen that they could not afford to take such chances on sickness until statistical information about its incidence and distribution in this country became available.[15]

## Life Insurance as a Medical Concern

America's early life insurance companies did not have to depend upon native statistics to the extent that the health insurance enterprises did. Partly for this reason, when life insurance finally took hold in this country, businessmen found it to be a desirable and lucrative form of enterprise.

While the carrying of insurance on property had been widespread even in colonial times, the insuring of lives against premature death remained an extremely rare practice in this country in 1800 and for several decades thereafter. Despite its considerable popularity in England, the demand for life insurance was slow to develop in the relatively secure setting of a predominantly rural American society. Here food as well as land was abundant, while families traditionally absorbed in their own ways the economic burdens imposed by the deaths of their members.

Whatever the reason, though native general insurance companies proliferated, life insurance firms long failed to take hold. Up to 1800 a few small ministerial associations operated their own private life annuity plans, while English insurance companies sold occasional policies on lives in this country. The latter were mostly for short terms or to cover the risks of specific trips. Scholars estimate that at the beginning of the nineteenth century fewer than 100 commercial policies were in force in all of the United States.[16]

The climate for commercial life insurance remained inhospitable well into the Jacksonian era. A scattering of native companies were organized during these decades, but no more than a handful were at all successful. Only with the emergence of mutual firms in the 1840s did life insurance

come into its own as a business in this country. During the next generation it achieved a rate of growth that had spectacular proportions. By the
close of the Civil War over 70 companies were engaged in this business,
and already they had written an estimated $1 billion worth of life
insurance. Around 400,000 American lives were then covered, while
120,000 new policies were reportedly being issued every year.[17]

The long-range interest of these companies in the medical condition of
the American people was a self-evident matter. If the level of the nation's
health could be elevated, then the average expectancy of life stood to
rise, and with it the profits of life insurance. By the 1840s, in fact, it was
abundantly clear that most of the high-minded objectives of hygiene and
public health—the reduction of sickness and excess mortality, the extension of man's life span, the development of registration systems and
surveys for monitoring trends in vital events—coincided closely with the
fundamental interests of the life insurance firms. For the latter, preventive medicine was not a humanitarian proposition but a business. As such
it represented an extension of the insurance concept into the public
domain.

During the 1840s and 1850s, life insurance companies began to manifest their support of public health measures in a variety of ways. They
became vigorous advocates, both of state vital-statistics registration and
of provisions for collecting mortality data in the federal census. Medical
men in the employ of the companies backed efforts made in the American Medical Association to reform disease nomenclature. In New York
City a number of firms contributed funds for sewer construction and
sanitary surveys. And in some cities they furnished statistics for sanitary
reports.[18] Moreover, in 1861 and 1862, life insurance companies made
substantial financial contributions to the war work of the United States
Sanitary Commission.

In their day-to-day operations, the life insurance firms built up an
increasingly close relationship with the medical profession. The companies early recognized that they were "entirely dependent, in every
fundamental respect, on medical men."[19] For their part, the physicians
were interested in what life insurance had to offer them though somewhat ambivalent about its business methods.

From early in the century medical editors undertook to explain the
nature and function of life insurance. They often urged physicians to
insure their own lives and sometimes put in a good word for some particular company or other. Occasional physicians began to turn up as paid
lecturers or writers of tracts promoting life insurance companies.[20]

However, with the uncontrolled proliferation of life insurance, medical spokesmen eventually found it necessary to warn the profession against unsound companies and fraudulent practices. Some even began to question the wisdom of pouring premiums into any of these corporations "without souls," firms that were growing as rapidly as railroads and were seen to be amassing great wealth at the expense of the ordinary family.[21]

The medical profession's principal connection with life insurance lay in the individual practitioner's employment, either ad hoc or on a regular basis, as medical examiner. Many private physicians seem to have welcomed the added income they received from making these examinations. But some resented being asked to submit potentially damaging information about their patients in order to save the companies from financial loss. Others protested that the fees paid to doctors by companies or their agents were too small. As the companies grew in size there was more than a little suspicion that the physicians were being taken advantage of, that they had become pawns or "instruments in the hands of these colossal corporations."[22]

While there was undoubtedly some truth in this, it was also true that the need of the life insurance companies to screen the physical state of their applicants eventually proved to be a factor, albeit an unmeasurable one, in elevating American health and medical practice. Knowing that a medical examination would be required, potential applicants for policies often became more conscientious in their hygienic practices and more regular in seeing their physicians. Doctors, in turn, gained the incentive to provide a competent level of care if they wanted to be considered for work as insurance examiners. The examinations themselves, however bureaucratic and materialistic their *raison d'etre,* became concrete means of getting physicians to be more thorough in their observation, more systematic in their approach to diagnosis, better organized in keeping their records, and generally more efficient in their business procedures. Meanwhile, records of these individual practitioners, and to an even greater extent the overall quantitative screening experience of the life insurance companies themselves, quickly created a whole new body of data for the analysis of the nation's health and diseases.

From the very early years of issuing policies on life, the physician acting as examiner was asked to determine certain basic information about the applicant for insurance. Basically the inquiry was supposed to find out "whether he labours under any disease, and particularly one which tends to shorten life; whether his habits are temperate or not, and his employment unhealthy or dangerous." Any record of such diseases as consumption, mental disorder, or syphilis was almost automatically disqualifying. Subsequently, individual companies made their medical criteria for examinations increasingly specific and detailed.[23]

Among the various factors, life insurance companies early realized that they "should look at the doctor risk." Most, in fact, from the beginning gave their support to the medical orthodoxy exclusively and made it their practice to reject applicants whose family physicians were known to be quacks or sectarians. No other risk, in fact, seemed "so great as that incurred by insuring a man, who, when he becomes sick, allows a certain class of doctors to trifle with his life."[24]

Naturally, some sectarian practitioners and their patients were interested in obtaining life insurance. These individuals resented the actuarial implication that their systems of medicine were more hazardous to life than any other. Although most sects could do little about the situation, American homeopaths eventually proved strong enough to challenge this policy. By 1865, in fact, they had persuaded at least one firm to charge 10 percent less for premiums from applicants who used homeopathic physicians than from those using allopaths. Another firm founded that same year, the Atlantic Mutual Life Insurance Company, proposed to reduce premiums for homeopaths still further as soon as it had determined by a few years of mortality experience just what were the differences in life expectancy between the patients of homeopaths and allopaths.[25]

### Life Expectancy in the South—Region, Climate, and Race as Insurance Risks

Another medical criterion which companies adopted for evaluating individuals as life insurance risks and for determining the premiums they had to pay was that of geographical setting. This factor also proved to be controversial in its application. The antebellum life insurance industry was overwhelmingly located in the North, and it was northern in its outlook. Most firms focussed their sales efforts almost exclusively upon the propertied and settled classes of that region. The American Mutual Life Insurance Company, for instance, made no apologies for being interested only in the predictable risks of the "old and healthy States." The other regions held so many uncertainties or potential risks to life and health that they were seen as forming a vast actuarial no-man's land.

As one official of a large firm put it in 1848, "We do not allow an insured person to trifle with his life . . . by going into the Southern States during the sickly months, nor by wandering in unsettled portions of the United States." With the gold rush, some companies did consent to insure the lives of emigrants. But such firms covered themselves by charging very high premium rates, and also by the knowledge that many of the emigrants would ultimately be unable to continue their premium payments, a situation which would result in the forfeiture to the company of all money already paid in.[26]

The southern environment proved to be consistently inhospitable to the spread of life insurance. From the mid-1840s to the Civil War a number of southern firms were launched but all remained small and most failed within a short time. Frederick Ludwig Hoffman subsequently characterized southern life insurance of the period as a form of business that was made "decidedly precarious" by the high death rates of the region, a mortality caused by the particular "topography, climate, habits, and the generally backward sanitary condition of the country." Similarly, although northern firms had agents in the larger southern cities, they did not make much effort to write life insurance there, focussing instead mainly upon fire or other forms of property insurance.[27]

Those members of the "better" classes of southern whites who wanted life insurance had to pay higher premium rates than those that prevailed in the North. In 1847 the difference was usually 1 percent, but high mortality during the devastating outbreaks of cholera and yellow fever quickly prompted insurance companies to make added charges. In 1859 the New York Life Insurance Company incurred such heavy losses that it assessed an extra .5 percent for all policy applicants in the southern Atlantic states, and an added 2 percent for those in the Gulf states.[28]

J. D. B. DeBow, C. F. M'Cay, and scattered other spokesmen for southern interests protested that these differential rates were patently unfair. And not a few noted the standing southern claim that the region had produced more individuals, both black and white, who had lived to extreme old age than any other region.[29] Northern analysts, however, had only to emphasize that, because of the low overall level of hygiene in the area, the life expectancy of the southern populace as a whole was decidedly lower than elsewhere.[30] And southerners were in no position to refute this argument scientifically. They had to concede that by and large southern vital statistics were so poor that no solid actuarial case could yet be made for eliminating the rate differences. The one substantial antebellum effort to build up such a case was that made by the Mobile physician Josiah C. Nott.

In 1847 Nott published a number of long articles which sought to prove that the northern life insurance companies used erroneous information about southern white salubrity in setting their rates for the latter region. Particularly damaging, he thought, was their assumption that the hot and humid southern climate acted uniformly upon the entire population in causing disease and death. To counter this assumption, Nott turned to the vital statistics of Charleston, South Carolina. Charleston offered a unique combination of circumstances for his study. For one thing, it was the only southern city in which bills of mortality had been kept "for any length of time with accuracy." In addition, unlike other southern seaports, Charleston's population had been virtually stationary for over a decade, "little disturbed by emigration and immigration."

From his analysis of these statistics, Nott concluded that, despite the bad reputation of its climate, Charleston enjoyed rates of mortality and longevity and a level of health that were no worse than those of Boston.[31] The key factor, he thought, was the high proportion of permanent residents in the city's population. These were individuals who had become acclimated to the adverse climatic conditions.

In the case of New Orleans, Savannah, Mobile, and other southern port cities, the large populations of unacclimated newcomers inevitably suffered formidable mortality under the harsh climatic conditions. However, if one judged those communities by the mortality of their acclimatized native inhabitants, they rather resembled Charleston. Thus, if one only had the figures, Nott thought that even those cities would be found to be basically among the "healthiest in the United States." Moreover, it was mainly this acclimated class of people that applied for insurance.[32]

Nott hoped that the northern life insurance companies would take these factors into consideration. "My belief is, that no good reason exists for charging one per cent more on southern risks, where the applicants live in the seaport towns, and are acclimated, and if these companies will select faithful agents, and competent, honest, medical examiners, the result will prove the correctness of these opinions." At the same time, it was evident to Nott that the South was in no position to do much about this actuarial discrimination. "The Southern cities cannot expect, nor do they deserve justice on the subject of Life Insurance, until their vital statistics are properly kept."[33]

While Nott felt that he could infer enough from the Charleston statistics to justify lower rates for certain other southern whites, he was unable to make a comparable argument for the life insurance rates on Negro slaves. To be sure, his comparison of the mortality statistics of Charleston and Philadelphia persuaded him that the warm Southern climate was highly advantageous to black longevity, and that "the negro attains . . . his greatest longevity in a state of slavery." This suggested that "the black slaves of the South are very safe risks for insurance." However, both of those cities lacked data that were sufficiently detailed to permit definitive calculations of black life expectancy. In fact, neglect of the vital statistics of blacks was widespread throughout both the South and the North, a condition that Nott considered "positively disreputable in this enlightened epoch." However, the lack of this kind of information did not deter the commercial firms from writing a certain amount of life insurance on blacks.

Throughout the period of the slave trade it was a common practice for shippers to insure these valuable cargoes against death during transit. Such insurance was no longer available after 1808, the official termination of the slave trade. However, owners still found it desirable on occasion to insure the lives of particularly valuable slaves. Nott thought that this practice was increasing noticeably in the mid-1840s and that insurance companies were rushing "pell-mell" to try to capture shares of this market. In fact, northern as well as southern companies appeared willing to take risks on some such lives.

Plantation owners sometimes carried a general insurance on their slaves as a part of their overall property insurance, but regular life insurance was seldom purchased on such lives. Nott considered it unsafe from the companies' viewpoint to insure plantation slaves, "because it is impossible . . . to get competent and reliable medical examiners." By and large, it was mostly the slaves that were used on railroads, in factories, or in other risky employments that were covered by life insurance. Companies insisted that, to be considered for coverage, blacks had to be healthy, acclimated, and vaccinated, but even when these conditions were met the premium rates were very high on them. From his own experience in Mobile, Nott summarized some of the slave risks that governed such rates.

> Most of the negroes presented to me for insurance, have been deck-hands of steam-boats, who, besides the danger of being blown up, are exposed to other dangers much greater; at one moment they are employed as firemen,

and at the next, they are rolling cotton bales down the river bank at midnight in a cold rain. Many are consequently attacked by pleurisy, and other acute diseases—they are not infrequently seriously injured by blows from the cotton bales while rolling down the high bluffs, and lastly, they often become intemperate, and contract other bad habits which lead to disturbance of health.[34]

Nott was apprehensive that the indiscriminate insuring of slaves would lead to foul play on the part of masters. Such might well occur when insured slaves became incurably infirm, aged, or otherwise unproductive. Nott suggested that in such cases, to cruel or unfeeling owners, "the insurance money is worth more than the slave, and the latter is regarded rather in the light of a superannuated horse." These owners, he feared, would not hesitate to overwork such slaves and drive them to death, thinking, much "like the Yankee Captain with the insured ship, 'damn the old hulk, let her sink—I am safe.' "[35]

Apparently there is little if any evidence from the final 15 years or so of southern slavery that might confirm Nott's fears for the insured slave. However, the possibility of just this kind of abuse against the insured of any race seems to have remained in the minds of a good many antebellum critics of life insurance. In fact, a New York editor in 1856 considered the practice rather common in some northern areas. According to his sources, the lives of insured persons were "frequently tampered with," albeit subtly, by leading the insured to dissipation, encouraging them to drink to excess, or getting them to participate in potentially dangerous sports such as steeplechases.[36] However, since verification of specific instances of tampering with insured lives was a difficult matter, accurate statistics on the practice remained unobtainable before the Civil War. In any case, such data remained an insignificant part of the broad mortality experience upon which the life insurance companies necessarily sought to base their operations and rates.

### Constructing Life Tables from Nineteenth-Century Experience

For the first several decades of the nineteenth century, the guidance that American life insurance enterprises had as to native life expectancies at the various stages of life was limited to sparse collections of local mortality experiences. This was, of course, almost equally true of European firms. Eighteenth-century British life insurance companies, in fact, long had little besides Edmund Halley's pioneering tables based on the experience of Breslau, Germany, to guide them. Late in that century, English firms could finally base their operations more appropriately upon English life experience as reflected in Richard Price's Northampton tables. Subsequently, as the nineteenth century progressed, more sophisticated life tables were prepared in England, though these, too, were for some time still based upon the longevity and mortality records of single communities, notably Chester and Carlisle.

Only in the early 1840s were the necessary resources of mortality and census data available to permit William Farr to construct a life table representing the experience of the entire English people. Before that time, accurate national tables seem to have existed for Sweden, while Prussia and Austria might also have fashioned them, since they had the required data. The United States, Farr noted, clearly lacked some of the essential statistical resources. "No correct life table can therefore be formed for the population of America, until they adopt in addition to the Census, the system of registration which exists in European States."[37]

Farr came to think of the life table as "a *biometer,* for it gives the exact measure of the duration of life under given circumstances. [It] represents a generation of men passing through time."[38] Nineteenth-century American statisticians, registrars, and health officials found this an attractive concept, and some sought to apply it to the measurement of their public health efforts. However, it was not until well into the twentieth century that vital-statistics registration in this country was sufficiently complete to permit the construction of a reliable biometer reflecting the experience of the entire nation. Meanwhile, nineteenth-century Americans had to make do with imperfect tables, with those based on strictly local experience, and with European mortality experience.

The earliest American tables of life expectancies were prepared from fairly substantial accumulations of mortality data for those times, but they lacked the benefit of information about population movements which would have corrected the figures. Edward Wigglesworth's celebrated table of 1793, compiled from records of 63 communities in Massachusetts in New Hampshire, was actually based on a much broader mortality experience than the English tables of the day. However, Wigglesworth's failure to take census information into consideration prevented his table from supplanting those in the United States. William Barton's calculations of Philadelphia life expectancies, made about the same time from mortality data of Christ Church Parish, had a similar deficiency.[39] Accordingly, while the Pennsylvania Company for Insurance on Lives and Granting Annuities took both Wigglesworth's and Barton's tables into consideration in setting its premium rates around 1809, its officers felt it only prudent also to utilize Price's Northampton tables. Similarly, during the 1820s Nathaniel Bowditch drew upon Wigglesworth's table and the Pennsylvania experience, but he also consulted various European tables when he established premium rates for the Massachusetts Hospital Life Insurance Company.

Wigglesworth's figures of New England life expectancy were confirmed to a certain extent in 1833 by Jonathan Ingersoll Bowditch, not from actual mortality experience but by inference from the ages of whites as reported in the 1830 census. Bowditch's calculation involved a 3 percent correction for population growth.[40] However, Wigglesworth's table continued to be used without these corrections in the process of rate determination by some Massachusetts life insurance firms into the 1840s. By then it was well known that, even for New England, the table's life-expectancy estimates were too low for the younger ages (under 35) and too high for those over 35.[41] At the time the American life insurance industry began its take-off in the 1840s, there was thus no adequate table of American life expectancies that the new companies could use. Lemuel Shattuck concluded simply that "data do not exist, sufficiently accurate, to form a proper table of rates which shall be paid here for such risks."[42]

By way of makeshift arrangements, virtually all of the new American firms based their rates initially upon one or another of the English tables. By 1850 the predominant choice among these was Joshua Milne's Carlisle tables. As it happened, these actuarial expedients proved to be entirely safe for the companies. Hygienists, however, criticized this reliance upon "tables of mortality, prepared in England many years ago, and which never afforded an adequate estimate of the probabilities of life on this continent." It was entirely possible, as Franklin Tuthill observed, that the American mortality experience in 1850 was really not very much different from that of Carlisle in 1785. However, experts believed that there was some difference and that the public as well as the insured were entitled to know how much it was. Eyebrows were being raised in any case at the "enormous" profits that were being made by the antebellum firms, profits more than sufficient to "pay the expenses of a perfect registry system." Profits of such a magnitude appeared manifestly unjust to those who knew that they were based upon out-of-date foreign tables, tables constructed from a life-expectancy experience that many considered too low for the United States.[43]

Whatever impatience or frustration Americans felt about this actuarial situation was relieved to some extent during the decade of the 1850s. By then, improvements in the resources of vital data, public and private, made possible a number of new life tables based upon segments of the American experience, though problems remained. The mathematician Charles F. M'Cay in 1850 constructed a table based upon the vital records of Baltimore, and he subsequently attempted to devise a mathematical law of human mortality that would agree substantially with any existing table.[44] About the same time Levi Meech used mortality returns from the 1850 census to prepare life tables for the white populations of Massachusetts and Maryland, but his calculations were undermined by the large acknowledged deficiencies in the numbers of deaths reported.[45]

A more reliable life table for Massachusetts was constructed by the Boston mathematician and actuary Ezekial B. Elliott. By 1857 Elliott used the Massachusetts state census of 1855 together with the state's vital-statistics reports to produce the first state life table based upon data produced in any of the new registration systems. Elliott compiled his table as part of a series of studies for the New England Mutual Life Insurance Company. However, as an analysis of life expectancies of a general rather than of a selected population, it proved to be fully as welcome to public health analysts as it was to the company.[46]

During this same period Elliott and other scholars also looked into the life expectancies of particular social and occupational groups. Elliott in 1860 prepared a "biometre or life-table for the blind," based upon 1,252 cases furnished by Samuel Gridley Howe from records of the Perkins Institution. Elliott's analysis showed that life expectancy of the blind was noticeably lower than for others. The causes of this appeared to be their "inherent deficiency in vital power," their limited range of occupations and amusements, and their greater exposure to accidents.[47]

In 1857 interest was provoked in academic circles by Benjamin Peirce's actuarial analysis of deceased Harvard alumni. Peirce's life table showed that at most periods after graduation the learned classes represented by the Harvard sample could expect to live from four to five years longer than could the average man. It showed, moreover, that Harvard honor students had higher life expectancies than the run-of-the-mill students. Contemporary medical men wondered whether these differences were due to the effects of dissipation during college, to variations in the amount of exercise given to the brain, or to the patterns of occupations pursued after leaving college.[48]

Far more significant among the private sources of mortality and longevity data were the burgeoning files of the new mutual life insurance companies. By the late 1850s the files of some reflected a dozen years of their policyholders' mortality experience. Actuaries in several firms began to reflect on the meaning of this experience, but it remained for Charles Gill and Shephard Homans to undertake preliminary analyses of the data of any one company, the Mutual Life Insurance Company of New York. It was a matter of considerable moment simply to realize that after only 15 years of operation the files of their firm alone embraced "a larger number of persons than those comprising the entire population from which the Carlisle and Northampton Tables were formed."[49]

Officials of Mutual of New York also realized that they could improve the scientific base of their operation if they could get access to earlier compilations of American mortality statistics, data which until that time were not well known or easily available. To remedy this lack, the company in the mid-1850s commissioned James Wynne to make a comprehensive survey of all available material and bring the significant data together in a single volume. In issuing this work in 1857, Wynne expressed laments similar to those of many another midcentury scholar with respect to the great lacunae in American vital statistics. Nevertheless, the material he did manage to collect was potentially so useful that 17 American life insurance firms in addition to the New York firm were willing to share the expenses of its publication.[50]

However modest, this cooperation proved to be one of the steps which brought the leading commercial companies together in the American life insurance conventions of 1859 and 1860. Along with their other business, these conventions established a committee on vital statistics. This group addressed itself chiefly to preparing a plan for pooling the companies' mortality experience in order to prepare a single authoritative American life table.[51] Implementation of that plan had to be deferred upon the outbreak of the Civil War. However, the project was resurrected after the war and its aims realized in 1868, when Homans constructed the American Experience Table from the pooled data of many firms.

This generation of actuaries—Homans, Elliott, Meech, and their peers —emerged as the most competent of the mid-nineteenth-century American vital statisticians. Their expertise was clearly essential to the growth and health of the new life insurance businesses. At the same time, that expertise and that growth, together, provided an important impetus to the general elevation of the science of vital statistics in this country. And, as methodological refinements found their way into statistics, greater precision became possible in every variety of American demographic inquiry.

# Epilogue:
# Demography and Medicine at Midcentury

The increasingly large-scale data-collection, reporting, and analysis enterprises of the life insurance firms, census officials, army officers, vital-statistics registry offices, and medical societies represent concrete public responses to the nineteenth-century proliferation of vital events and population movements. But the private responses to and intangible perceptions of these phenomena by participants in the various enterprises, as well as by other contemporaries, are no less significant. Not surprisingly, the perceptions of the observers of 1860 were not necessarily the same as those of 1800.[1]

## Toward Demographic Pessimism

As he or she works more or less chronologically up through the nineteenth-century materials, the historian becomes aware of a progressive shifting in contemporary attitudes toward most of the period's demographic events, trends, and energies. For one thing, as the century went on, considerably more people than had been the case at the turn of the century seemed to be asking questions about the implications of demographic phenomena on their lives. At least there were more outlets for airing these questions, and far more published works dealing with them. At the same time, the changing nature of the questions they asked reflected a gradual but steady abandonment of the predominantly optimistic view of those phenomena that many observers in the earlier day had held.

208

Throughout the period, most industrialists and publicists, as well as many policy-makers, thought of population increase as a positive good. And, as this account has shown, expressions of national pride over the progressive growth of population, the filling up of the land, and the expansion of boundaries often found their way into technical reports and professional papers as well as into private correspondence. However, these were increasingly modified or replaced by manifestations of dismay and regret with respect to some of the threatened consequences.

Even if direct testimony were lacking, twentieth-century readers could easily draw inferences about these changing human feelings from the very nature of the events or trends themselves. It cannot have been easy for any nineteenth-century American to accept the fact that, as the century went on, most of the nation's demographic problems, far from remaining static, were growing larger with every generation. It was equally difficult for them to face up to the reality that, for every step taken to bring the material rewards of national growth and expansionism within reach, very heavy costs were being incurred—financial obligations, social disruptions, tolls of disease and death. Many citizens certainly found it hard to accept that the nation's classic family exhortation, "to increase and multiply," was losing some of its traditional authority, and indeed that the procreativeness once thought of as a patriotic duty was threatening to turn into a personal and national liability. It was painful for others to realize that, as populations became more concentrated, society more complex, and people more dependent upon each other, they were threatened with the loss of some long-cherished freedoms and with erosions of their accustomed quality of life. And it was equally painful to have to acknowledge that, while individuals could still move out beyond earshot of their closest neighbors, the United States as a nation no longer had a choice between retaining unchanged a simple Jeffersonian agrarianism or adopting a dynamic urban-industrial way of life.

The complex demographic situation of 1860 gave Americans the opportunity to make various other kinds of choices. And, in most of those cases, at least one of the options presented some segment or other of society with a far from optimistic outlook for the future; sometimes both options were threatening to someone. Because large and continued immigration was clearly still needed to meet the needs of industry for cheap labor, midcentury cities were faced with the prospect of having even more immense and ruinous demands placed upon their institutions, resources,and inhabitants. Since medical and religious leaders seemed intent on the suppression of birth control and abortion in the interest of morality and the renewal of the native white American birth rate, innumerable families found themselves facing the alternatives of going "underground" to obtain contraceptive information or of slipping into ever-greater economic distress. Because the restless land-grabbing of whites in the West showed no signs of abating, humanitarians could see little likelihood of being able to reverse the calamitous decline of the Indians. Similarly, given the growing intransigence of southern and northern extremists with respect to slavery, late antebellum moderates could harbor few realistic hopes of finding a rational solution favorable at once to the demographic future of the two regions and to the black and white populations of each.

The outbreak of the Civil War effectively ended any such remaining hopes. Subsequently, the war's massive and depressing harvest of dead and wounded young men, its vast population dislocations, and its huge economic devastation went on to complicate the country's demographic situation immeasurably for the rest of the nineteenth century. Meanwhile, the wide postwar dissemination of Darwinian concepts among scientists, intellectuals, and the general populace greatly reinforced the pessimistic determinism that had been suggested by the older Malthusian views on population growth.

Nevertheless, despite the intrinsically depressing character of many midcentury demographic projections and ideas, individual observers and analysts were not always necessarily pessimistic about them. This was true of those who were swept up in the enthusiasms of immigrant and emigrant aid, colonization societies, missionary ventures, municipal booster and sanitary movements, or other philanthropic and reform causes. It was equally true of those who became participants in the large demographic data-collection enterprises or who involved themselves with like-minded colleagues in some activity or other which aimed at statistical or demographic professionalism. The antebellum American investigators of medical-demographic phenomena, for instance, tended to be buoyed up by the shared challenges and excitement of their work for censuses, their affiliations with state or life insurance company registries, and their participation in statistical societies and international congresses. And, during the Civil War, the opportunities for such satisfactions were extended further, by projects of the army and the United States Sanitary Commission for bringing together the medical-demographic data of the war.

## Medical Limitations and Demographic Change

By and large, the midcentury medical scene itself was not a very promising one, demographically speaking. In fact, not only the physicians' demographic activities but many of their other positive accomplishments were all too often lost sight of by contemporaries, just as they have been by historians, overshadowed as they were by the enormous problems then confronting medicine. Members of the medical profession could be excused frequent feelings of hopelessness as they contemplated the continuing erosion of their authority, the abysmal quality of medical education, the vituperative conflicts of competing medical ideas and sects, the impotence of most of their therapies, the frustrating failure of their statistics and their scientists to solve the basic questions about disease etiology.

Nevertheless, for all their failures and inadequacies, the physicians of 1860 had more reason for optimism than did their predecessors of 1800. In fact, there had been both concrete and intangible achievements. Certainly medical men in a good many midcentury communities found satisfaction in looking back over the medical-care institutions that they had helped create for the poorer segments of the population. Not a few others felt a sense of professional well-being in the networks of medical schools, journals, and societies that had arisen. More were heartened by the availability of a few truly effective therapies: vaccination, quinine, opium, and digitalis. Surgeons and dentists pointed with pride to certain of their new operations and techniques, especially to anesthesia. Health officers pointed to their encouraging initial successes in pinpointing excesses of infectious diseases among large concentrations of people and in reducing those excesses through environmental and sanitary measures.

The period's new clinicians were also hopeful about the rational approach to disease that they had introduced into therapy, one that was based on greater skill in observation and diagnosis, on moderation, on a recognition of the healing powers of nature, and on the use of numerical methods of analysis. In the short run, this approach admittedly offered the profession precious little specific help in dealing with sickness. For the long run, however, its adherents were confident that the fundamental habits of skepticism, discipline, and systematic research that were implicit in the approach could not fail to lead to greater medical certainty and to decreases in the quantities of disease and death. Indeed, the groundwork that was laid during this period did provide an indispensable base for the medical successes of subsequent generations. As Richard H. Shryock concluded, "We can now see . . . what was hidden to the observers of that era; namely, that science was moving—however slowly in the United States—toward the creation of a type of medicine which would eventually exert a profound influence on the health of the American people."[2]

The midcentury sense of medical helplessness was also somewhat mitigated by the disclosure that Americans' expectancies of life at birth had apparently improved during the previous 60 years. In 1793, Edward Wigglesworth's life table had set the overall life expectancy at about 35 years. Subsequently, E. B. Elliott's table of 1855 showed a figure of 39.8 years. Although both tables were based upon the experience of Massachusetts, they were also regarded to some extent as rough indicators for other parts of the country.[3] The increase of nearly five years was indeed a gratifying one, reflecting at the least, as many observers were aware, improvements in the environment and in the standard of life.

What this increase indicated about the effectiveness of antebellum medical attention was not so clear. Some enthusiasts of the 1850s were ready to claim that medical attention had played a considerable role in improving levels of health. However, many others wondered if it had made any contribution at all. In fact, more than 125 years before Thomas McKeown published his similar findings, an important segment of the medical profession, along with numerous lay health reformers and sectarians, came to the conclusion that, for all its new hospitals, asylums, and clinics and for all its therapies, heroic or rational, orthodox clinical medicine could as yet exert but little direct positive influence upon the course of disease or the occurrence of death.[4] On the basis of this understanding (founded in their subjective gut feelings as well as in their statistics), both groups turned much of their energy toward bringing about an improved popular knowledge of nutrition, exercise, and every aspect of personal hygiene, as well as to ensuring a broad extension of public sanitation and the general elevation of people's physical well-being. In short, they aimed for the time being at preventing disease rather than focussing upon fruitless and sometimes harmful efforts to cure it. Given the imperfect state of antebellum knowledge, both the life expectancy of that period of history and the growth of population were surely influenced more by these educational and preventive measures than by the attempts at clinical intervention.

*Notes*

*Bibliographical Note*

*Index*

# Notes

## Chapter 1. Seeds of a Demographic Science

1 The French physician Achille Guillard introduced the word during the 1850s in a work which he entitled *Eléments de statistique humaine ou démographie comparée* (Paris: Guillaumin, 1855), pp. v-xxxii, 367.

2 For British and American applications of political arithmetic, and other early manifestations of statistical thinking, see James H. Cassedy, *Demography in Early America: Beginnings of the Statistical Mind, 1600–1800* (Cambridge, Mass.: Harvard University Press, 1969).

3 For a short recent summary of the development of the census, see Robert H. Davis, "The Beginnings of American Social Research," in George H. Daniels, Ed., *Nineteenth-Century American Sciences: a Reappraisal* (Evanston: Northwestern University Press, 1972), pp. 154–166.

4 This shift is persuasively argued by Patricia Cline Cohen, "Statistics and the State: Changing Social Thought and the Emergence of a Quantitative Mentality in America, 1790 to 1820," *William and Mary Quarterly,* 3d ser., 38 (1981), pp. 35–55.

5 For example, see Tench Coxe, A View of the United States of America (London: Johnson, 1795); Samuel Blodget, *Economica: a Statistical Manual for the United States of America* (Washington: the author, 1806); Timothy Pitkin, *A Statistical View of the Commerce of the United States of America* (Hartford: Charles Hosmer, 1816); Adam Seybert, *Statistical Annals* (Philadelphia: Dobson, 1818); David B. Warden, *A Statistical, Political, and Historical Account of the United States of North America,* 3 vols. (Edinburgh: Constable, 1819); John Melish, *A Statistical Account of the United States* (Philadelphia: G. Palmer, 1813). The noted journal known as *Niles' Register* had as its full title, *The Weekly Register, Containing Political, Historical, Geographical, Scientifical, Astonomical, Statistical, and Biographical, Documents, Essays, and Facts.*

6 The earliest use of the word *statistics* that I have found in an American medical publication was in the *Medical Repository* for 1807 (Vol. 10), where it occurs both in the index and in the table of contents, though not in the title of the article referred to.

7 "Interesting Particulars of the American Census, Ending May 1, 1801," *Medical Repository,* 5 (1802), pp. 216–218; and W. P., "Health Statistics," *Niles' Register,* 8 (1815), p. 257.

215

8 There is some discussion of birth statistics in Chapter 8.

9 In 1794 Samuel Williams, working from Rutland bills of mortality, figured a doubling period of 19.5 years for Vermont. See his *The Natural and Civil History of Vermont* (Walpole, N.H.: Thomas and Carlisle, 1794), pp. 360–369. Blodget, Seybert, and Warden found the figure for the country as a whole to be somewhat greater.

10 David Ramsay, *The History of South Carolina,* 2 vols. (Charleston: Longworth, 1809), Vol. 2, p. 582; Daniel Drake, *Natural and Statistical View, or Picture of Cincinnati and the Miami Country* (Cincinnati: Looker and Wallace, 1815), p. 27.

At least one early physician predicted serious public health problems as a result of Louisville's growth. "Rapidly as this town augments its population, a few years will find every foot of ground within its precincts covered with houses, forming ramparts that will keep without, that ministering angel of health, a pure and circulating atmosphere, and keep within, the daemon of contagion." Henry McMurtrie, *Sketches of Louisville and Its Environs* (Louisville: Penn, 1819; reprinted Louisville: Clark, 1969), pp. 114, 118.

11 Thomas Hersey, *The Midwife's Practical Directory,* 2d ed. (Baltimore: the author, 1836), pp. 48–49.

12 Benjamin Rush, "An Account of the Progress of Population, Agriculture, Manners, and Government in Pennsylvania," in his *Essays, Literary, Moral and Philosophical* (Philadelphia: Bradford, 1798), pp. 223–224.

13 Jefferson felt that "the greatest part of his [Malthus's] book is inapplicable to us, but as a matter of speculation." Jefferson to Thomas Cooper, Feb. 24, 1804, quoted in E. Millicent Sowerby, *Catalogue of the Library of Thomas Jefferson,* 5 vols., (Washington: Library of Congress, 1952–59), Vol. 3, p. 199; Jefferson to J. B. Say, Feb. 1804, in Albert E. Bergh, Ed., *The Writings of Thomas Jefferson,* 20 vols. (Washington: Thomas Jefferson Memorial Assoc., 1903), Vol. 11, pp. 2–3. Writing in the 1870s, William Farr commented that if Malthus had had advance intimation of America's incredible capacity for agricultural production he might well have modified his equation of population increase vs. subsistence increase. Noel Humphreys, Ed., *Vital Statistics: a Memorial Volume of Selections from the Reports and Writings of William Farr* (London: Stanford, 1885), p. 16.

14 George Tucker [Joseph Atterly, pseud.], *A Voyage to the Moon* (New York: Elam Bliss, 1827), p. 62; Seybert, *Statistical Annals,* p. 54.

15 Timothy Flint, *Recollections of the Last Ten Years* (Boston: Cummings, Hilliard, 1826; reprinted New York: Da Capo, 1968), p. 29.

16 Benjamin Rush, "An Inquiry into the Causes of Premature Deaths," in his *Essays, Literary, Moral and Philosophical,* 2d ed. (Philadelphia: Thomas and William Bradford, 1806), pp. 310–316; Benjamin Rush, "A Charge, Delivered in the University of Pennsylvania, to the Graduates in Medicine, April 19, 1810," *Philadelphia Medical Museum,* n.s., 1 (1810/11), pp. 116.

17 Samuel Latham Mitchill, "Facts and Observations Relative to the Trade from New York to the Fejee Islands; and Especially to the Practice among the People There, of Eating Human Flesh: In a letter from Dr. Mitchill to Mr. Malthus, Dated New York, November 10, 1810," *Medical Repository,* 14 (1811), pp. 209–215; anonymous review in *Medical Repository,* 10 (1807), pp. 206–209. Edmond Cocks errs in his statement that *Niles' Register* was "the first American periodical to review" Malthus's book. Edmond Cocks, "The Malthusian Theory in Pre–Civil War America," *Population Studies,* 20 (1967), p. 346.

18 Thomas Ewell, *Statement of Improvements in the Theory and Practice of the Science of Medicine* (Philadelphia: John Bioren, 1819), pp. 53–65. This section on reproduction is an expansion of a short article which Ewell published in the *Medical Repository* in 1807. The birth control agitation, which gained momentum sometime after Ewell's book, will be discussed in Chapter 8.

19 "Crawford's Animalcular Hypothesis of Epidemics," *Medical Repository,* 11 (1808), pp. 86–87; news announcement of Crawford's course of lectures, *Niles' Register,* 1 (1811/12), pp. 405–406. Crawford's views on population and the survival of the fittest are most fully expressed in the second and third installments of his "Observations on the Seats and Causes of Disease," *Baltimore Medical and Physical Recorder,* 1 (1808/09), pp. 81–92, 206–221.

20 William Currie, *A Synopsis, or General View of the Principal Theories or Doctrines of Diseases* (Philadelphia: Parker, 1815), pp. 48–49.

21 Seybert, *Statistical Annals,* p. 53.

### Chapter 2. Demographic Aspects of Early National Expansionism

1 Henry Hill, "Observations on the Mortality by Yellow Fever, among the Seamen of the United States, Who, with Northern Constitutions and Habits, Sail to Havanna, in Cuba; and on the Health and Longevity of the Native Spanish Inhabitants," *Medical Repository,* 10 (1807), pp. 113–117. An earlier consul, John Morton, compiled a somewhat similar medical post report for Havana. See *Medical Repository,* 6 (1803), pp. 228–234.

2 Apparently at least five of the other ships also had surgeons, though some of those may not have been American ships. Baldwin mentions Drs. John Martin of the *Ganges,* Thomas Bryant of the *Jefferson,* Moore of the *Pekin,* Knight of the *Active,* and Hugh Service.

3 One of the typical works of this period was James Ewell, *The Planter's and Mariner's Medical Companion,* 1st ed. (Philadelphia: Anderson and Meehan, 1807); following the War of 1812 one of the popular publications was Usher Parsons, *Sailor's Physician* (Cambridge, Mass.: Hilliard and Metcalf, 1820). This work passed through several editions under various titles.

4 William Baldwin, *A Short Practical Narrative of the Diseases Which Prevailed*

*Among the American Seamen, at Wampoa in China, in the Year 1805* (Philadelphia: printed by Thomas T. Stites, 1807), p. 22 and passim.

5  Albert Gallatin, "Statement (by the Secretary of the Treasury) of Expenditures for Relief of Sick Seamen, during the Year 1809; Their Amount, and in What Manner Made," *Medical Repository,* 14 (1811), pp. 313–316.

6  The Bureau of Medicine and Surgery of the navy was established in 1842, while the Marine Hospital Service was organized on a centralized basis only in 1870. Establishment of the Office of the Surgeon-General of the Army in 1813, and its continuation after the War of 1812, ensured an earlier central coordination of the medical experience of that branch and the preparation of statistics reflecting that experience on a large scale. From the 1830s, marine hospitals were also built to serve boatmen on the inland waterways, particularly the Mississippi River and the Great Lakes.

7  Mason L. Weems, *Hymen's Recruiting-Sergeant; or the New Matrimonial Tat-too for Old Bachelors* (Hartford: S. Andrus, 1845), preface, p. iii. This work was first published in 1805.

8  The 1802 list of Edinburgh medical graduates did not include a single American, but Benjamin Silliman found 25 Americans studying there in the winter of 1805–1806.

9  British impressment of American ships was done to some extent to prevent migration to America, particularly of seamen and other able-bodied men.

10  Thomas Ewell, "To the Physicians of the United States," *Philadelphia Medical and Physical Journal,* Suppl. 2, July (1807), pp. 200–201. I have been unable to discover what, if any, response Ewell's offer evoked.

11  "Of the Duties of a Surgeon" (extract from United States Naval Regulations, 1802), *Medical Repository,* 6 (1803), pp. 83–85.

12  William P. C. Barton, A Treatise Containing a Plan for the Internal Organization and Government of Marine Hospitals in the United States (Philadelphia: Parker and Nicklin, 1814), p. 215. Barton's detailed proposals for naval medical administration were published late in the war. Ibid.

13  Edward Cutbush, *Observations on the Means of Preserving the Health of Soldiers and Sailors* (Philadelphia: Dobson, 1808). Rush's pamphlet was reprinted in this work.

14  Review, *Medical Repository,* 12 (1809), p. 376. Somewhat similarly, Benjamin Rush in 1810 advocated that individual physicians pay attention to record-keeping because it was good business practice.

> Let me advise you to keep fair and correct entries in books appropriated to that purpose, of all your services to your patients. This will give a just and correct uniformity to your charges, and enable your executors to do justice to your heirs, without those compulsory means which are often the consequence of the careless, or incorrect manner in which some physicians keep their accompts.

Benjamin Rush, "A Charge, Delivered in the University of Pennsylvania, to the Graduates in Medicine, April 19th, 1810," *Philadelphia Medical Museum,* n.s., 1 (1810/11), pp. 119–120.

15 Samuel Akerly, analyzing some wartime New York data, observed that while disease reports of regular troops in his area were apparently fairly complete, "there was much irregularity in the sick returns from the militia." Samuel Akerly, "Medical Topography of the Military Positions in the Third United States Military District," *Medical Repository,* 18 (1817), p. 407.

16 James Tilton, "Real Independence," *Niles' Register,* 6 (May 21, 1814), pp. 191–193.

17 James Tilton, *Economical Observations on Military Hospitals; and the Prevention and Cure of Diseases Incident to an Army* (Wilmington: J. Wilson, 1813).

18 Jabez W. Heustis, *Physical Observations and Medical Tracts and Researches on the Topography and Diseases of Louisiana* (New York: Swords, 1817), pp. 117–118; and Tilton, *Observations on Military Hospitals,* pp. 57–59. Side effects of the overuse of calomel often included inflammation of the mouth and rotting of facial bones.

19 James Mann, *Medical Sketches of the Campaigns of 1812, 13, 14* (Dedham: H. Mann and Co., 1816), esp. pp. vi, 141, 144, 246.

20 Ackerly, "Medical Topography," p. 407. See also Ackerly's earlier report, "Diseases of the Army," *Medical Repository,* 16 (1813), pp. 412–414.

21 Usher Parsons, "Surgical Account of the Naval Battle on Lake Erie, on the 10th of September 1813," *New England Journal of Medicine and Surgery,* 7 (1818), pp. 313–316.

22 William Darlington, Comp., *Reliquiae Baldwinianae: Selections from the Correspondence of the Late William Baldwin, M.D.,* facsimile of 1843 edition, edited and with a new introduction by Joseph Ewan (New York: Hafner, 1969).

23 See the collection of "Papers on the Last Winter Epidemic in Different Parts of the United States," *Medical Repository,* 16 (1813), pp. 246–267, 329–344.

24 Samuel Latham Mitchill, "On the Preservation of the Soldier's Health," in his letter to James Monroe, Jan. 1, 1815, *Medical Repository,* 17 (1815), pp. 340–352.

25 This quotation was attributed to "General Eaton," probably William Eaton (1764–1811), a United States army officer and diplomatic agent to the Barbary States between 1798 and 1805. *Niles' Register,* 6 (1814), p. 191; 7 (1814), p. 54.

26 "Some Account of the Disease That was Epidemic in Some Parts of New-York and New-England, in the Winter of 1812–13," *New England Journal of Medicine and Surgery,* 2 (1813), pp. 241–243 and 1–8; book review, *London Medical Review,* 5 (1812), p. 67.

27 [Nathaniel Niles?], "New England Emigration Society," *Niles' Register,* 8 (1815), p. 39.

28 In fact, the details of the early centuries of this epidemiological confrontation

of European (and African) newcomers with the continent's native populations will almost certainly never be able to be determined with any certainty, since there are few written records for much of that period, either of specific disease outbreaks or of the manifold contacts, direct and indirect, by which the various pathogens might have been transmitted. For challenging discussions of the possible course of this biological confrontation, and of inferences which can be made about it from modern data and scientific information, see Alfred J. Crosby, *The Columbian Exchange: Biological and Cultural Consequences of 1492* (Westport, Conn.: Greenwood, 1972); and William H. McNeill, *Plagues and Peoples* (Garden City, N.Y.: Anchor/Doubleday, 1976).

29 Jedidiah Morse, *The American Geography,* 2d ed. (London: Stockwell, 1792) p. 159.

30 Alexis de Tocqueville, *Democracy in America,* ed. Phillips Bradley, 2 vols. (New York: Vintage Books, 1954), Vol. 1, p. 349.

31 James Fenimore Cooper in 1828 placed these coastal Indians "about on a level with the lowest classes of European peasants." He reported also that some were seamen, though the number by then was probably only 100 or 200. James Fenimore Cooper, *Notions of the Americans,* 2 vols., 2d ed. (New York: Stringer and Townsend, 1850), Vol. 2, p. 279. (The first edition appeared in 1828). Tocqueville, in the 1830s, searched in vain for Narragansetts, Mohicans, or Pequots in New England, and for Lenapes in Pennsylvania, and he felt that he had personally "met with the last of the Iroquois, who were begging alms." Tocqueville, *Democracy,* Vol. 1, p. 349.

32 Cooper, *Notions of the Americans,* pp. 285–286.

33 Jedidiah Morse, *A Report to the Secretary of War of the United States, on Indian Affairs* (New Haven: Converse, 1822), pp. 57, 75. See also Charles Caldwell, *Thoughts on the Original Unity of the Human Race* (New York: E. Bliss, 1830), p. 143. Lewis Henry Morgan expressed a similar view several decades later. Lewis Henry Morgan, *The Indian Journals 1859–62,* ed. Leslie A. White (Ann Arbor: University of Michigan Press, 1959), p. 42.

34 Tocqueville, *Democracy,* Vol. 1, pp. 354–359.

35 See the letters from Heckewelder and Geddes in "Miscellaneous Facts and Observations," *Philadelphia Medical and Physical Journal,* 1, Part 1 (1804), pp. 129–130.

36 Brant's replies to an extensive questionnaire distributed by Holmes are reproduced in Douglas W. Boyce, Ed., "A Glimpse of Iroquois Culture History through the Eyes of Joseph Brant and John Norton," *Proceedings,* American Philosophical Society, 117 (1973), pp. 286–294.

37 W. A. Trimble to J. C. Calhoun, Aug. 7, 1818, in Jedidiah Morse, *A Report to the Secretary of War of the United States, on Indian Affairs* (New Haven: S. Converse, 1822), pp. 256–260.

38 John Barnes, "Case of Variolae Nigrae, or Black Small Pox, with Some Account of the Great Mortality of the Small Pox Which Prevailed in 1837-8,

among the Indians of the North-west," *St. Louis Medical Surgical Journal,* 5 (1847/48), pp. 537–546.

39 See Adam Seybert, *Statistical Annals* (Philadelphia: Dobson, 1818), p. 52; C. F. Volney, *A View of the Soil and Climate of the United States,* ed. Charles Brockden Brown (Philadelphia: Conrad, 1804), pp. 389 ff.; Cooper, *Notions of the Americans,* p. 278; Albert Gallatin, "A Synopsis of the Indian Tribes . . . in North America," in "Archaeologia Americana," *Transactions and Collections,* American Antiquarian Society, 2 (1836), p. 135; George Catlin, *Letters and Notes on the Manners, Customs, and Condition of the North American Indians,* 2 vols., 3d ed. (London: Tilt and Bogue, 1842), Vol. 1, p. 6. Cooper pointed out that the numbers of the Indians "have always been exaggerated." In the late twentieth century the propensity for drawing up such estimates has extended to ethnohistorians using modern demographic techniques, but authorities continue to display little agreement. One of the most recent calculations, which has been criticized by several reviewers, postulates an Indian population of some 18 million in America north of Mexico around 1500, a number subsequently decimated by 93 known epidemics and unknown others. Henry F. Dobyns, *Their Number Become Thinned: Native American Population Dynamics in Eastern North America* (Knoxville: University of Tennessee Press, 1983), pp. 11–26.

40 Catlin, *North American Indians,* p. 6.

41 See "Summary View of Protestant Missions," *Missionary Herald,* 24 (1828), pp. 8–13.

42 One of the informative reports from the Lewis and Clark expedition was a chart by William Clark, "Statistical View of the Indian Nations Inhabiting the Territory of Louisiana and the Mountains Adjacent to Its Northern and Western Boundaries" (undated MS, at American Philosophical Society Library, Philadelphia). The seriousness with which that expedition regarded its record-keeping function is shown by the fact that not only the two leaders but seven of their men kept individual journals during the trip. See Paul Russell Cutright, *Lewis and Clark: Pioneering Naturalists* (Urbana: University of Illinois Press, 1969), pp. 44–45.

43 See "Pike's Journey to Explore Louisiana," *Medical Repository,* 11 (1808), pp. 297–300; and review, ibid., 15 (1812), pp. 256–264.

44 Heustis wrote that, of 2,000 troops sent for the defense of New Orleans, half died of scurvy at Camp Terre-aux-Boeufs in the summer of 1809, and 600 more died on boats while being evacuated up the Mississippi. Heustis, *Physical Observations of Louisiana,* esp. pp. 163–164; and Garret E. Pendergrast, *A Physical and Topographical Sketch of the Mississippi Territory, Lower Louisiana, and a Part of West Florida* (Philadelphia: Gazette of the United States, 1803).

45 The use and significance of this data will be discussed in Chapter 3.

46 Tobias Watkins, "Medical Report of Military Inspection Tour through the

Northern Division of the United States, 1818," MS at National Library of Medicine, Bethesda, Maryland.

47 William Beaumont, *Experiments and Observations on the Gastric Juice, and the Physiology of Digestion* (Plattsburgh, New York: Allen, 1833); J. H. Bill, "Notes on Arrow Wounds," *American Journal of the Medical Sciences,* n.s., 44 (1862), pp. 365–387.

48 See *Statistical Report on the Sickness and Mortality in the Army of the United States . . . from January, 1819, to January, 1839* (Washington: Gideon, 1840), passim.

49 *Statistical Report on the Sickness and Mortality in the Army of the United States . . . from Jan. 1855, to Jan. 1860* (Washington: Bowman, 1860), pp. 283–304; [Roberts] Bartholow, "Mormonism, in Its Physical, Mental and Moral Aspects," *Boston Medical and Surgical Journal,* 63 (1860/61), pp. 438–440.

50 Thomas Lawson, preface, [U.S. Army], *Meteorological Register for Twelve Years, from 1831 to 1842 Inclusive* (Washington: Alexander, 1851), p. 4.

## Chapter 3. Medical Geography of a Growing Nation

1 Timothy Dwight, *Travels in New England and New York,* ed. Barbara Miller Solomon, 4 vols. (Cambridge, Mass.: Harvard University Press, 1969), Vol. 4, pp. 77–82.

2 James H. Cassedy, *American Medicine and Statistical Thinking, 1800–1860* (Cambridge, Mass.: Harvard University Press, 1984), pp. 11–14.

3 D [Daniel Drake], "Miscellaneous Intelligence," *Western Journal of the Medical and Physical Sciences,* 11 (1837/38), p. 662. The interests of geographers and statisticians came together professionally in 1851 with the establishment of the American Geographical and Statistical Society.

4 Charles Caldwell, "A Physical Sketch of the City of Philadelphia," in his *Medical and Physical Memoirs* (Philadelphia: Thomas and Bradford, 1801), pp. 2–4.

5 Samuel Latham Mitchill, "Sketch of the Mineralogical History of New York," *Medical Repository,* 1 (1797/98), pp. 279–303, 431–439; ibid., 3 (1800), pp. 325–335; ibid., 5 (1802), pp. 212–214; Samuel Latham Mitchill, "Outlines of Medical Geography," ibid., 2 (1799), pp. 36–44.

6 See, for example, John H. Frisbre, "Sketch of the Medical Topography of the Military Tract of the State of New York," *Philadelphia Medical and Physical Journal,* 2, Part 2 (1806), pp. 69–71.

7 Jno P. Hiester, "Medical Topography of Berks County, Penn.," *Boston Medical and Surgical Journal,* 46 (1852), p. 118; Edmund Ravenel, "On the Medical Topography of St. John's, Berkeley, S.C., and Its Relations to

Geology," *Charleston Medical Journal,* 4 (1849), pp. 703–704; review, *Western Journal of Medicine and Surgery,* 2d ser., 7 (1847), p. 149.

8 J. B. Hiester, "Thoughts on the Study of Diseases with Reference to Geology," *Medical Examiner,* n.s., 8 (1852), p. 22; Edmund Ravenel, "Medical Topography," pp. 703–704.

9 E. H. Davis, *Report of the Committee on the Statistics of Calculous Diseases in Ohio* (Columbus: Medary, 1850); review, *Medical Examiner,* n.s., 7 (1851), pp. 370–371.

10 *Proceedings of the American Association for the Advancement of Science,* 2 (1849, published 1850), pp. 406–408; review, *Western Journal of Medicine and Surgery,* 2d ser., 7 (1851), pp. 370–371.

11 *Transactions of the Medical Society of the State of New York,* 1 (1832/33), appendix, pp. 41–45.

12 Hiester, "Medical Topography," p. 118. An 1866 report of the Kansas Geological Survey included a special section, by Dr. C. A. Logan, linking geology and health and calling for organized public health measures. Rex Buchanan, "Fighting the Ubiquitous Monarch, Disease: the 1866 Report on the Sanitary Relations of Kansas," *Journal of the History of Medicine,* 13 (1983), pp. 78–83.

13 David Arnell, "A Geological and Topographical History of Orange County, New York," *Medical Repository,* 12 (1809), p. 314; review, ibid., 13 (1810), pp. 153–158; John Stearns, "A Topographical Description of the County of Saratoga, N.Y.," ibid., 12 (1809), pp. 130–135; and David Ramsay, *A Sketch of the Soil, Climate, Weather and Disease of South Carolina* (Charleston: Young, 1796), p. 26. Ramsay, like many others of his generation, probably took his views on this subject from his mentor, Benjamin Rush. Rush's views were expressed in a 1785 paper, "An Enquiry into the Cause of the Increase of Bilious and Intermitting Fevers in Pennsylvania, with Hints for Preventing Them," *Transactions of the American Philosophical Society,* 2 (1786), pp. 206–212.

14 Robert Mills, *Statistics of South Carolina* (Charleston: Hurlbut and Lloyd, 1826), p. 139.

15 "A Letter from the Rev. Jedidiah Morse, D. D. to Mr. Smith, including a Topographical Account of Charlestown (Massachusetts), with Bills of Mortality, &c &c" (Feb. 10, 1798), *Medical Repository,* 2 (1799), pp. 7–12.

16 For seventeenth- and eighteenth-century beginnings of these interests and activities, see James H. Cassedy, "Meteorology and Medicine in Colonial America: Beginnings of the Experimental Approach," *Journal of the History of Medicine,* 24 (1969), pp. 193–204.

17 J. E. White, "A Few Remarks on the Weather and Diseases of 1805," *Medical Repository,* 11 (1808), pp. 12–24.

18 Joseph Kelso, "Meteorological Table, and Statement of Deaths . . . [for]

Harrisburgh," *Philadelphia Medical Museum,* 6 (1809), pp. 70–72; Samuel Agnew, "Observations on the Healthiness of Harrisburgh (Pennsylvania)," ibid., n.s., 1 (1810/11), pp. 190–199.

19 While Tilton's order was not enforceable during the War of 1812 or immediately thereafter, some individual medical officers, including most prominently Benjamin Waterhouse, did manage to keep weather diaries during this period. See Edgar Erskine Hume, "The Foundation of American Meteorology by the United States Army Medical Department," *Bulletin of the History of Medicine,* 8 (1940), pp. 202–206.

20 "Meteorological Observations Made at Nazareth, in Pennsylvania, for the Year 1793," *Philadelphia Medical and Physical Journal,* 1, Part 1 (1804), pp. 107–109; Richard Hazeltine, "An Abstract of a Series of Meteorological Observations, and of a History of Diseases for the Years 1803 and 1804," *Medical Repository,* 11 (1808), pp. 6–11; Garrett Elliott Pendergrast, *A Physical and Topographical Sketch of the Mississippi Territory, Lower Louisiana, and a Part of West Florida* (Philadelphia: Office of the Gazette of the United States, 1803), pp. 24–34; J. L. E. W. Shecut, *Medical and Philosophical Essays* (Charleston: Miller, 1819), pp. v–vi, 75.

21 Felix Pascalis, "Observations on the Yellow River," *Medical Repository,* 3 (1800), pp. 344–345; Adam Seybert, "Experiments and Observations on Land and Sea Air," *Transactions of the American Philosophical Society,* 4 (1799), pp. 262–276; Adam Seybert, "Experiments and Observations, on the Atmosphere of Marshes," ibid., pp. 415–430.

22 Editor, "Medical and Philosophical Register—Abstracts of Meteorological Observations," *Philadelphia Medical Museum,* 1 (1804/05), pp. 201–214. While Coxe acknowledged the influence of William Playfair, the former did not actually go very far along the lines of statistical representation, notably the use of graphs which Playfair had pioneered under the name of lineal arithmetic. Playfair introduced these methods in his *Commercial and Political Atlas* (London: J. Wallis, 1786). While nineteenth-century American statistical compilers used tables extensively, few if any adopted the use of graphs before midcentury.

23 Franklin Tuthill, quoted in editorial, "Registration of Births, Marriages and Deaths," *Buffalo Medical Journal,* 6 (1850/51), p. 693.

24 Unsigned editorial remarks, apparently by Daniel Drake, *Western Journal of the Medical and Physical Sciences,* 8 (1834/35), p. 323.

25 E. H. B. [Edward H. Barton], review, *New Orleans Medical and Surgical Journal,* 7 (1850/51), p. 69.

26 J. L. Dawson and H. W. Desaussure, *Census of the City of Charleston, South Carolina, for the Year 1848* (Charleston: Nixon, 1849), p. 183.

27 See, for instance, Thomas M. Logan, "Letters from California," *New Orleans Medical and Surgical Journal,* 7 (1850/51), p. 565.

28 George Engelmann, "The Meteorological Causes of Our Climatic Diseases," *St. Louis Medical and Surgical Journal,* 11 (1853), pp. 226–232.

29  B. F. Joslin, "On the Meteorology of Hemorrhage," *American Journal of the Medical Sciences,* n.s., 5 (1843), pp. 92–99.

30  Edward H. Barton, "Report upon the Sanitary Condition of New Orleans," in *Report of the Sanitary Commission of New Orleans on the Epidemic Fever of 1853* (New Orleans: Sanitary Commission of New Orleans), pp. 261–263, 269–284; E. H. Barton, Y. R. Lemonier, and T. G. Browning, "Annual Report on the Board of Health," *New Orleans Medical and Surgical Journal,* 6 (1849/50), pp. 667, 672.

31  Among earlier medical discussions of hygrometry, see Charles A. Lee, "On Hygrometrical Observations," *Boston Medical and Surgical Journal,* 26 (1842), pp. 69–77.

32  E. H. B., review, pp. 68–73; Edward Barton, resume of paper on yellow fever, *Boston Medical and Surgical Journal,* 55 (1856/57), pp. 432–434; Edward Barton to W. W. Morland, in "Dr. Barton on Meteorology," ibid., 44 (1851), pp. 504–505; H [Sanford B. Hunt], review, *Buffalo Medical Journal,* 10 (1854/55), pp. 76–81; *Boston Medical and Surgical Journal,* 52 (1855), pp. 122–124.

33  Lorin Blodget, *Climatology of the United States* (Philadelphia: Lippincott, 1857), p. 454; Josiah Nott, "Sketch of the Epidemic of Yellow Fever of 1847, in Mobile," *Charleston Medical Journal,* 3 (1848), p. 3; Bennet Dowler, "Researches on Meteorology," *New Orleans Medical and Surgical Journal,* 4 (1847/48), pp. 414–417. Nott, while discounting the possibility that meteorological observations would reveal much if anything about the etiology of yellow fever, came to feel by 1854 that microscopic observations, then only "in their infancy," might well eventually explain the causes and "erratic habits" of the disease. Josiah Nott, "The Epidemic Yellow Fever of Mobile in 1853," *New Orleans Medical and Surgical Journal,* 10 (1853/54), p. 581.

34  M. Morton Dowler, "On the Reputed Causes of Yellow Fever, and the So Called Sanitary Measures of the Day," *New Orleans Medical and Surgical Journal,* 11 (1854/55), pp. 56–57; M. Morton Dowler, "Letter on Yellow Fever," ibid., pp. 426–430; M. Morton Dowler, "Observations and Reflections on Yellow Fever," ibid., 16 (1859), pp. 314–315.

35  As late as 1857 a Virginia physician found it necessary to chide the backwardness and indifference of his colleagues with respect to compiling such statistics for that state. J. Stanley Beckwith, "On Climatology," *St. Louis Medical and Surgical Journal,* 15 (1857), p. 449.

36  [Richard H. Coolidge, Comp.], *Army Meteorological Register for Twelve Years, from 1843 to 1854, Inclusive* (Washington: Nicholson, 1855) p. v; Thomas Lawson, preface [U.S. Army], *Meteorological Register for Twelve Years, from 1831 to 1842 Inclusive* (Washington: Alexander, 1851) pp. 4–5.

37  Raw materials for the quarterly report were kept in diaries or journals. An early example of such diaries is Roger L. Nichols, Ed., *The Missouri Expedition, 1818-1820: the Journal of Surgeon John Gale with Related Documents* (Norman: University of Oklahoma Press, 1969).

38 [U.S. Army], *Meteorological Register for the Years 1826, 1827, 1828, 1829 and 1830* (Philadelphia: Haswell, Barrington, and Haswell, 1840), appendix, p. 103. Lovell's successor, Thomas Lawson, commented similarly in 1851 that observations made at posts far out ahead of the frontier, and "commenced while the adjacent country is still in its primitive wild and uncultivated state, will aid materially in determining the influences of the progress of civilization—that is, the effect of the improvement of a country—on climate, temperature, and atmospheric phenomena generally," [U.S. Army], *Meteorological Register, 1831–1842,* p. 5. See also Lovell to Messrs. Gales and Seaton (July 25, 1820), *Medical Repository,* 21 (1821), pp. 106 ff.

39 [U.S. Army], *Meteorological Register, 1826–1830;* [Samuel Forry, Comp.], *Statistical Report on the Sickness and Mortality in the Army of the United States . . . from January, 1819, to January, 1839* (Washington: Gideon, 1840). The Statistical Report is much fuller for the second 10-year period, 1829–1839, since it could then draw on data from the Adjutant-General's Office as well as from the Surgeon-General's Office. Although Forry is not listed on the title page as compiler, I shall refer throughout to the work as his. Two similar later reports on the army's disease and mortality were published before the Civil War; their compiler was Richard H. Coolidge.

40 Forry, *Statistical Report,* p. iii.

41 C. F. Volney, *A View of the Soil and Climate of the United States,* trans. and ed. Charles Brockden Brown (Philadelphia: Conrad, 1804).

42 Samuel Forry, *The Climate of the United States and Its Endemic Influences* (New York: Langley, 1842), pp. v–vi. The medical analyses in the Tulloch reports had been done principally by Henry Marshall. Forry's long review of the first two British reports is in the *American Journal of the Medical Sciences,* n.s., 1 (1841), pp. 431–473.

43 See review, probably by Daniel Drake, *Western Journal of Medicine and Surgery,* 4 (1841), pp. 271–272; Daniel Drake, *A Systematic Treatise, Historical, Etiological, and Practical, on the Principal Diseases of the Interior Valley of North America* (Cincinnati: Smith, 1850), p. 453; also, review, *New York Journal of Medicine,* n.s., 10 (1853), p. 252.

44 John B. Porter, extract in [Forry, Comp.], *Statistical Report on Sickness and Mortality in the Army, 1819–1839,* pp. 247–248.

45 "Death of Dr. Samuel Forry," *New Orleans Medical and Surgical Journal,* 1 (1844/45), p. 389; book review, *Medical Examiner,* n.s., 1 (1842), pp. 197–200; C. C. [Charles Caldwell], review, *Western Journal of Medicine and Surgery,* 7 (1843), pp. 142–153; editorial, "The Late Samuel Forry, M.D." *New York Journal of Medicine,* 4 (1845), pp. 7–16.

46 "Meteorological Observations," *New York Journal of Medicine,* 2 (1844), pp. 134–139; [U.S. Army], *Army Meteorological Register for Twelve Years, from 1843 to 1854, Inclusive* (Washington: Nicholson, 1855).

47 M. Morton Dowler, "Observations and Reflections on Yellow Fever," *New Orleans Medical and Surgical Journal,* 16 (1859), pp. 314–315, 322–323.

48 [U.S. Army], *Meteorological Register, 1843–1854,* pp. iii–vi; Smithsonian Institution, *5th Annual report, 1850* (Washington: Tippin and Streeper, 1850), p. 17. The 1840s also saw the rise of American microscopy, greatly stimulated in the same way by the emergence of native optical firms. See James H. Cassedy, "The Microscope in American Medical Science 1840–1860," *Isis,* 67 (1976), pp. 76–97.

49 The Belgian scientist L. A. Quetelet proposed simultaneous international observations of such phenomena as seasonal diseases, puberty, and sexual activity, as well as of the weather itself. Among the American bodies that received and discussed these proposals were the American Philosophical Society, the American Academy of Arts and Sciences, and the National Institute. See *Proceedings of the American Philosophical Society,* 2 (1844), pp. 235, 266; and "The Periodical Phenomena of Man," *Boston Medical and Surgical Journal,* 34 (1846), pp. 18–20. For the meteorological project of the British Association for the Advancement of Science, see Walter E. Gross, "The American Philosophical Society and the Growth of Meteorology in the United States, 1835–1850," *Annals of Science,* 29 (1972), pp. 326–329.

50 See the annual reports of the Smithsonian Institution for 1848–1851.

51 Elias Loomis, "Report on the Meteorology of the United States," *Report of the Board of Regents of the Smithsonian Institution, January 6, 1848* (Washington: Tippin and Streeper, 1848), p. 194.

52 [American Medical Association], "Report of the Committee on Hygiene," *Transactions of the American Medical Association,* 4 (1851), pp. 536–541; review, *New York Journal of Medicine,* n.s., 10 (1853), pp. 251–253; editorials on "The Smithsonian Institution," *Buffalo Medical Journal,* 10 (1854/55), pp. 306–309; 561–565; "Report of the Special Committee on Government Meteorological Reports," *Transactions of the American Medical Association,* 12 (1859), pp. 63–72. There was some feeling in the medical community during the mid-1850s that Henry had been obstructing the work of Blodget and was unsympathetic to the publication of the meteorological data accumulating at the Smithsonian.

53 Lorin Blodget, *Climatology of the United States and of the Temperate Latitudes of the North American Continent* (Philadelphia: Lippincott, 1857), passim.

54 Details of that practice are examined later in this chapter.

55 For an example, see H. M. Congar, "Monthly Meteorological and Pathological Report of the City of Buffalo, for January 1847," *Buffalo Medical Journal,* 2 (1846/47), pp. 600–610.

56 Review, *Boston Medical and Surgical Journal,* 52 (1855), p. 122.

57 Daniel Drake, *A Systematic Treatise, Historical, Etiological, and Practical, on the Principal Diseases of the Interior Valley of North America* (Cincinnati: Smith, 1850).

58 The second volume of Drake's work was edited and issued posthumously by S. Hanbury Smith and Francis G. Smith (Philadelphia: Lippincott,

Grambo, 1854). See also Daniel Drake, "Introductory Lecture for the Second Session of the Medical College of Ohio" (1821), in Henry D. Shapiro and Zane L. Miller, Eds., *Physician to the West: Selected Writings of Daniel Drake on Science and Society* (Lexington: University Press of Kentucky, 1970), pp. 170–171; Daniel Drake, "To the Physicians of the Western States," *Western Quarterly Reporter of Medical, Surgical, and Natural Science,* 1 (1822), pp. 307–311; Daniel Drake, "An Account of the Epidemic Cholera as It Appeared in Cincinnati," *Western Journal of Medicine and the Physical Sciences,* 6 (1832), pp. 349–350.

59  D [Daniel Drake], "Study of Botany by Young Physicians," *Western Journal of Medicine and Surgery,* n.s., 3 (1845), pp. 269–273; editorial announcement, ibid., 1 (1840), p. 79; Daniel Drake, "To the Physicians and Meteorological Observers of the Valley of the Mississippi and the Lakes," ibid., n.s., 4 (1845), pp. 541–542; Lunsford P. Yandell, review, ibid., 3d ser., 6 (1850), pp. 228–230.

60  D. F. C. [D. Francis Condie], review, *American Journal of the Medical Sciences,* n.s., 20 (1850), p. 109; review, probably by L. P. Yandell, *Western Journal of Medicine and Surgery,* 3d ser., 6 (1850), pp. 228–232.

61  Bennet Dowler, review, *New Orleans Medical and Surgical Journal,* 7 (1850/51), p. 56; Drake, *Systematic Treatise,* Vol. 1, pp. 453, 723–728.

62  Dowler, review, pp. 57, 61–66.

63  Drake, *Systematic Treatise,* Vol. 2, pp. 136, 533–534. Drake did make extensive use of the statistical reports of New Orleans' Charity Hospital.

64  D. F. C., review, p. 110.

65  Lemuel Shattuck, "Statistics of Consumption," *American Medical Almanac,* 2 (1840), pp. 109–113; George Hayward, "Statistics of Pulmonary Consumption in the Cities of Boston, New York and Philadelphia for Thirty Years," *American Journal of the Medical Sciences,* n.s., 5 (1843), pp. 506–508.

66  Among such studies, see Waldo I. Burnett, "A Consideration of Some of the Relations of Climate to Tubercular Disease," *Boston Medical and Surgical Journal,* 47 (1852/53) pp. 149–153; William F. Carrington, "Observations on the Effects of Climate on Disease," ibid., 49 (1853/54), pp. 441–448; James Wynne, "The Influence of the Gulf Stream upon the Summer Climate of the Atlantic Coast," *Proceedings of the American Association for the Advancement of Science,* 11 (1857, published 1858), Part 1, pp. 149–153; Samuel Forry, "Statistical Researches Relative to the Etiology of Pulmonary and Rheumatic Diseases, Illustrating the Application of the Laws of Climate to the Science of Medicine," *American Journal of the Medicine Sciences,* n.s., 1 (1841), pp. 13–54; Henry I. Bowditch, *Consumption in New England* (Boston: Ticknor and Fields, 1862); and Augustus A. Gould, "Climatology of Consumption," *Boston Medical and Surgical Journal,* 69 (1863/64), pp. 109–113; 71 (1864/65), pp. 449–451.

67  Austin Flint, "Annual Address of the Retiring President of the Buffalo Medical Association," *Buffalo Medical Journal,* 14 (1858/59), p. 138.

68 For a summary of then-current knowledge of and therapy for tuberculosis, see W. W. Gerhard, *Lectures on the Diagnosis, Pathology, and Treatment of the Diseases of the Chest* (Philadelphia: Haswell and Barrington, 1842).

69 An 1832 editorialist also pinpointed the extensive travel of businessmen, congressmen, participants in religious conventions, and medical students, and advised all to take extra precautions against change of climate and locality. "Medical Geography," *Journal of Health,* 4 (1832), pp. 1–3.

70 See "Travelling for Health," *Boston Medical and Surgical Journal,* 46 (1852), pp. 424–425.

71 See Samuel George Morton, *Illustrations of Pulmonary Consumption* (Philadelphia: Key and Biddle, 1834), pp. 144–160; Gerhard, *Diseases of the Chest,* pp. 112–113; "Winter Residence for Consumptive Patients," *Western Journal of the Medical and Physical Sciences,* 7 (1833/34), p. 487. Havana had a considerable colony of Americans throughout this period.

72 For the development of water-cure establishments or resorts, see Harry B. Weiss and Howard R. Kemble, *The Great American Water-Cure Craze, A History of Hydropathy in the United States* (Trenton, N.J.: Past Times Press, 1967).

73 "Medical Geography," p. 3.

74 Among many medical communications about some of these sites, see J. G. F. Wurdemann, "Climates of Florida and the West Indies," *Southern Journal of Medicine and Pharmacy,* 2 (1847), pp. 509–516; Daniel Drake, "The Northern Lakes a Summer Resort for Invalids of the South," *Western Journal of Medicine and Surgery,* 6 (1842), pp. 401–426; Alonzo Chapin, "Remarks on the Sandwich Islands," *American Journal of the Medical Sciences,* 20 (1837), pp. 43–59; Stephen W. Williams, "To Invalid Travellers in Pursuit of Health," *Boston Medical and Surgical Journal,* 46 (1852), pp. 376–383.

75 William Carrington, a naval surgeon, strongly deplored medically prescribed travel to distant places for consumptives, except those in the early stages of the disease. Available statistics, he said, showed that for most individuals this had "the almost uniform result of dying abroad," often alone, miserable, and depressed. It was far better for most advanced cases to remain home with their accustomed comforts, friends, and nursing care. William F. Carrington, "Observations on the Effects of Climate on Disease," *Boston Medical and Surgical Journal,* 49 (1853/54), pp. 441–448.

76 L. V. Bell, "St. Augustine, (E. F.) as a Resort for Invalids," *Medical Magazine,* 1 (1833), p. 724.

77 Ibid., pp. 723–732. Partly as a result of such criticism, St. Augustine gradually improved its facilities until, before midcentury, it was regarded as one of the more comfortable southern resorts.

78 "Medical Geography," p. 3.

79 Thomas M. Logan, "Letters from California," *New Orleans Medical and Surgical Journal,* 7 (1850/51), pp. 560 ff. As secretary of the California State

Medical Society, Logan was instrumental in the mid-1850s in having that body circularize its members to gather further medical-topographical information.

80 F. W. Hatch, "Malaria and Its Sources in the Valley of the Sacramento," *New York Journal of Medicine,* 3d ser., 4 (1858), pp. 363–384; G. L. Simmons, "Phthisis in California," *Boston Medical and Surgical Journal,* 61 (1860), pp. 469–473; Charles D. Cleveland, "Pulmonary Diseases in California," *Boston Medical and Surgical Journal,* 59 (1858), pp. 129–133; William Henry Doughty, "An Essay on the Adaptation of Climate to the Consumptive," *Southern Medical and Surgical Journal,* n.s., 15 (1859), pp. 291 ff.

## Chapter 4. Medicine and the Westward Movement

1 Benjamin Rush, "An Account of the Progress of Population, Agriculture, Manners, and Government in Pennsylvania," in his *Essays, Literary, Moral and Philosophical,* 2d ed. (Philadelphia: Bradford, 1806), pp. 213–215.

2 Timothy Flint concluded that the strongest motivations of New England migrants to the Ohio Valley after the War of 1812 were essentially poetic in nature. "Very few, except the Germans, emigrate simply to find better and cheaper lands." Timothy Flint, *Recollections of the Last Ten Years* (Boston: Cummings, Hilliard, 1826), pp. 214–242.

3 Edward Jarvis, "Autobiography," MS at Harvard University Library.

4 Edward Jarvis, "Concord to Louisville 1837," MS journal, Harvard University Library, p. 158.

5 Daniel Drake, *An Introductory Lecture, on the Means of Promoting the Intellectual Improvement of the Students and Physicians of the Valley of the Mississippi* (Louisville: Prentice and Weissinger, 1844), p. 15.

o Daniel Drake, arguing the need for more such hospitals in 1835, estimated that roughly 43,000 "hands" were then manning the various craft on the inland canals, lakes, and rivers of the West. He suggested 14 marine hospitals to serve this clientele; 9 were actually provided by 1860. Daniel Drake, "Report [on Western Commercial Hospitals]," *Western Journal of Medical and Physical Science,* 8 (1834/35), pp. 459–464.

7 Daniel Drake, letter, *Western Journal of Medicine and Surgery,* n.s., 1 (1844), pp. 546–553; "Buffalo City Hospital," *Buffalo Medical Journal,* 3 (1847/48), pp. 502–503; "St. Louis, Her Hospitals and Medical Schools," *St. Louis Medical and Surgical Journal,* 15 (1857), pp. 470–471. In 1850, Edward Jarvis urged states to locate their mental hospitals in accordance with population distribution rather than having single huge central institutions. Edward Jarvis, "The Influence of Distance from and Proximity to an Insane Hospital, on Its Use by Any People," *Boston Medical and Surgical Journal,* 42 (1850), pp. 209–222.

8 Daniel Drake, "On the Origin and Influence of Medical Periodical Literature; and the Benefits of Public Medical Libraries," in his *Discourses, Delivered by*

*Appointment, before the Cincinnati Medical Library Association, January 9th and 10th, 1852* (Cincinnati: 1852), pp. 82–83. Toner calculated that by the early 1870s the regulars alone had some 408 state and local medical societies in 35 states. J. M. Toner, "Statistics of Regular Medical Associations and Hospitals of the United States," *Transactions of the American Medical Association*, 24 (1873), pp. 288–313. See also the listing of pre-1860 orthodox societies in William G. Rothstein, *American Physicians in the Nineteenth Century: from Sects to Science* (Baltimore: Johns Hopkins University Press, 1972), pp. 327–331.

9 Henry B. Shafer, "Early Medical Magazines in America," *Annals of Medical History*, n.s., 7 (1935), pp. 480–491; John Shaw Billings, "The Medical Journals of the United States," *Boston Medical and Surgical Journal*, 100 (1879), pp. 1–14. Ebert calculated that a total of 249 journals had appeared by 1850. These included sectarian journals and society transactions as well as regular medical and dental journals. Ebert's 204 regular medical and dental periodicals were founded as follows:

| | | | |
|---|---|---|---|
| 1797–1809: | 7 | 1830–39: | 63 |
| 1810–19: | 8 | 1840–49: | 94 |
| 1820–29: | 32 | | |

Myrl Ebert, "The Rise and Development of the American Medical Periodical, 1797–1850," *Bulletin of the Medical Library Association*, 40 (1952), pp. 243–276.

10 Ebert, "American Medical Periodical," passim; "American Homoeopathic Review, 6 (1865/66), pp. 458–467; "Homoeopathic Journals," *Boston Medical and Surgical Journal*, 46 (1852), p. 525; James H. Cassedy, "The Flourishing and Character of Early American Medical Journalism, 1797–1860," *Journal of the History of Medicine and Allied Sciences*, 38 (1983), pp. 135–150.

11 D [Daniel Drake], "Western Periodicals," *Western Journal of Medicine and Surgery*, 5 (1842), pp. 472–474; review, ibid., 3d ser., 1 (1848), p. 42.

12 Edgar Erskine Hume, "Early Kentucky Medical Literature," *Annals of Medical History*, n.s., 8 (1936), pp. 324–347; Irwin H. Pizer and Harriet Steuernagel, "Medical Journals in St. Louis Before 1900, Background," *Bulletin of the Missouri Historical Society*, April (1964), pp. 221–256.

13 "New Medical Journals," *Medical Examiner*, n.s., 1 (1845), p. 147.

14 Drake, "Origin of Medical Periodical Literature," pp. 72–73.

15 "New Medical Journals," *Boston Medical and Surgical Journal*, 46 (1852), p. 325.

16 The number of schools existing in any given year was not, of course, the same as the total that had been created since 1765, since almost as many unsuccessful schools were launched as those that survived. Rothstein identified 85 schools that were established prior to 1860, but of those 38 did not survive. Rothstein,

*American Physicians,* p. 98. Figures on the numbers of physicians during this period are highly uncertain. Rough estimates have suggested a total of somewhere between 3,500 and 4,900 in 1790, while the 40,564 enumerated in the census of 1850 is not thought to be at all accurate. However, on the strength of these figures, the proportion of physicians to the population rose during these 60 years from between 1 in 800 and 1 in 1,100 to roughly 1 in 570 (based on census figures of 3.9 million for 1790 and 23.2 million for 1850). See C. A. Lee, "Statistics of the Medical Profession in the United States," *Buffalo Medical Journal,* 10 (1854/55), pp. 203–205.

17 Charles Caldwell, *Thoughts on the Impolicy of Multiplying Schools of Medicine* (Lexington: Clark, 1834), pp. 20–22.

18 Of the members of the American Institute of Homoeopathy in 1851, nine-tenths were reported to have received degrees from allopathic medical colleges. However, figures on the numbers of homeopathic practitioners were hard to come by. The institute's membership climbed from 238 in 1851 to 575 in 1865. Overall some spokesmen guessed 700–800 in 1845 and 4,000–5,000 a generation later, but nobody knew. While regulars did not necessarily agree with these figures, they allowed that the numbers were "not insignificant." See. F. R. McManus, letter to editor, Oct. 9, 1847, *American Journal of Homoeopathy,* 2 (1847/48), p. 135; ibid., 7 (1852/53), pp. 21–23; *Transactions,* American Institute of Homoeopathy, 18 (1865), pp. 103, 123–137; ibid., 6 (1849), p. 4; ibid., 18 (1865), p. 23; "The Progression of Homoeopathia," *American Journal of Homoeopathy,* 3 (1849), p. 147; "An Argument against Homoeopathy!!" ibid., 5 (1850/51), p. 107; "Homoeopathic Organization," *American Homoeopathic Review,* 6 (1865/66), p. 394.

19 Frederick C. Waite, "American Sectarian Medical Colleges before the Civil War," *Bulletin of the History of Medicine,* 19 (1946), pp. 148–166.

20 "Increase of Medical Schools," *Medical Examiner,* 2 (1839), pp. 780–781.

21 Editorial comment, "Army Medical Board," *Boston Medical and Surgical Journal,* 42 (1850), p. 208.

22 L. P. Yandell, "Medical Graduates in the United States in 1840," *Western Journal of Medicine and Surgery,* 1 (1840), p. 477; T. Romeyn Beck, "Statistics of the Medical Colleges of the United States," *Transactions of the Medical Society of the State of New York,* 4 (1838/40), pp. 166–228. Among other things, Beck also tried to prove that the number of New Yorkers enrolled in out-of-state medical schools was not excessive.

23 Editorial, "Medical Schools," *Western Journal of Medicine and Surgery,* 3d ser., 3 (1848), p. 85.

24 "Physicians in Buffalo," *Buffalo Medical Journal,* 1 (1845/46), pp. 162–163; ibid., 5 (1849/50), p. 359; "Science of Medicine in Missouri," *Boston Medical and Surgical Journal,* 31 (1844), p. 83. St. Louis was found to have 146 medical practitioners of all kinds in 1845 for a population of 40,000, or 1 for every 274 persons. Of these, about 100 had medical school diplomas, but only a third had substantial practices. Of the rest, most were reported to live precariously on

their medical practices in the city for one to three years, after which they quietly left the city for new opportunities elsewhere, usually in smaller towns. "The Medical Profession of St. Louis," ibid., 33 (1845/46), pp. 166–167. Quantities of immigrant physicians sometimes compounded the physician-supply problem.

25  C. A. Lee, "Statistics of the Medical Profession in the United States," *Buffalo Medical Journal,* 10 (1854/55), pp. 203–220; John K. Mitchell, "Numbers of Physicians Required in the United States," *Boston Medical and Surgical Journal,* 42 (1850), pp. 137–139; George Tucker, "On the Proportion of Graduates to the Population," *Buffalo Medical Journal,* 5 (1849/50), pp. 735–736; "Schools of Medicine and Medical Practitioners," *Boston Medical and Surgical Journal,* 50 (1854), p. 443; editorial by Y. Z., "Facts *vs.* Figures," *Medical Examiner,* n.s., 6 (1850), pp. 298–302.

26  "Health of the Sioux Indians," *Boston Medical and Surgical Journal,* 37 (1847/48), p. 45; "Schools of Medicine and Medical Practitioners," *Boston Medical and Surgical Journal,* 50 (1854), p. 443; Lee, "Statistics of the Medical Profession," pp. 203–205.

27  "Iowa Medical College," *Boston Medical and Surgical Journal,* 39 (1848/49), p. 305.

28  An amused Timothy Flint observed that by the 1820s the great Mississippi basin had already become "the paradise of puffers." America, he thought, had originally inherited its propensity for puffing from England, but "she has improved upon her model." Timothy Flint, *Recollections of the Last Ten Years* (Boston: Cummings, Hilliard, 1826), p. 185.

29  "Medical Graduations in Missouri," *Boston Medical and Surgical Journal,* 38 (1848), pp. 408–409; "New Medical Schools," *Buffalo Medical Journal,* 4 (1848), pp. 454–455; "Nashville vs. Philadelphia and the Rest of Creation," *St. Louis Medical and Surgical Journal,* 13 (1855), pp. 87–90.

30  G. S. W., "The West," *American Phrenological Journal,* 19 (1854), pp. 128–129.

31  Edward Everett, "Future of America," *American Phrenological Journal,* 17 (1853), p. 131.

32  Editorial, "Medical Geography," *Journal of Health,* 4 (1833), p. 1.

33  Austin Flint emphasized in 1841 that Americans ought to feel "the highest gratitude, that for a disease prevailing so generally over large portions of our country [i.e., malaria], and which, if not susceptible of relief, would be an almost insuperable obstacle in the development of the resources of our national domains, we have a specific [quinine] which, whenever it occurs or recurs, will almost invariably produce speedy relief." Austin Flint, "On the Treatment of Intermitting Fever," *American Journal of Medical Sciences,* n.s., 2 (1841), p. 292.

34  A. B. Shipman, "Professional Matters at the West—Malarious Fever," *Boston Medical and Surgical Journal,* 40 (1849), p. 69; M. H. Clark, "Mortality on the Platte River," *Boston Medical and Surgical Journal,* 47

(1852/53), p. 121; "Sad News from the Plains," *American Phrenological Journal,* 16 (1852), p. 65.

35 Timothy Flint, *Recollections,* pp. 240–241.

36 Ibid., pp. 40–41, 240–241, 251, 311.

37 J. V. Prather, "The Causes of Mortality among the Children of St. Louis," *St. Louis Medical and Surgical Journal,* 5 (1847/48), p. 123; McP [W. M. McPheeters], "Editorial—Health of St. Louis," ibid., pp. 152–154.

38 M. H. Clark, "Mortality on the Platte River," *Boston Medical and Surgical Journal,* 47 (1852/53), p. 121; "Sad News from the Plains," p. 65.

39 B. D. [Bennet Dowler], "Historical and Statistical Observations on Cholera," *New Orleans Medical and Surgical Journal,* 14 (1857), p. 6. See also "Professional Matters at the West—Malarious Fever," *Boston Medical and Surgical Journal,* 40 (1849), p. 69; "Sad News from the Plains," p. 65.

40 I. S. Briggs, "Medical History of a California Expedition," *Boston Medical and Surgical Journal,* 41 (1849/50), pp. 479–481.

41 Timothy Dwight, *Travels in New England and New York,* 4 vols., ed. Barbara Miller Solomon (Cambridge, Mass.: Harvard University Press, 1969), Vol. 4, pp. 77–79.

42 Thomas M. Logan, who served as physician to the Strangers' Friend Society in San Francisco during the winter of 1849–1850, estimated that 30 percent of the diarrhea sufferers were dying of the disease, but he was not able to obtain accurate data on this. Thomas M. Logan, "Letters from California," *New Orleans Medical and Surgical Journal,* 7 (1850/51), pp. 563, 565.

43 J. D. B. Stillman, "Observations on the Medical Topography and Diseases (Especially Diarrhea) of the Sacramento Valley, California, during the years 1849–50," *New York Journal of Medicine,* n.s., 7 (1851), p. 298.

44 J. P. Leonard, "Letter from California," *Boston Medical and Surgical Journal,* 41 (1849/50), pp. 52–55, 394–399; C. A. Lee, "Statistics of the Medical Profession in the United States," p. 205; G. R. B. Horner, "Remarks on California," *Medical Examiner,* n.s., 7 (1851), pp. 91–95; W. Taylor, "Cholera as It Appeared in California," *Boston Medical and Surgical Journal,* 46 (1852), pp. 509–513.

45 Thomas M. Logan, "Letters from California," p. 562.

46 See James H. Cassedy, *American Medicine and Statistical Thinking, 1800–1860* (Cambridge, Mass.: Harvard University Press, 1984).

47 Edward Jarvis, "Concord to Louisville 1837," MS journal, Jarvis papers, Countway Library, Boston, p. 92.

48 Samuel Cartwright, "Statistical Medicine or Numerical Analysis Applied to the Investigation of Morbid Actions," *Western Journal of Science and Surgery,* 3d ser., 1 (1848), pp. 196–197.

49 Andrew Stone, "Remarks on Diseases of the West—No. 1," *Boston Medical and Surgical Journal,* 33 (1845/46), pp. 476–480; A. B. Shipman, "Medical Matters at the West," ibid., 34 (1846), pp. 78–80; Daniel Stahl, "The Sectional Teachings of Medicine," *Southern Medical and Surgical Journal,* n.s., 5

(1849), pp. 545–550; Charles Caldwell, review, *Western Journal of Medicine and Surgery,* 1 (1840), pp. 32–55, 233–256; Charles Caldwell, review, ibid., 3 (1841), pp. 113 ff.

50 Southern medical sectionalism will be discussed in Chapter 5.

51 McP [W. M. McPheeters], "Sectional Medicine," *St. Louis Medical and Surgical Journal,* 5 (1847/48), pp. 363–365; "Western Journal of Medicine and Surgery," *Medical Examiner,* 7 (1844), pp. 201–202; B. Rush Mitchell, "Southern versus Northern Practice," ibid., n.s., 4 (1848), pp. 591–595.

52 Daniel Drake, *An Introductory Lecture, on the Means of Promoting the Intellectual Improvement of the Students and Physicians of the Valley of the Mississippi* (Louisville: Prentice and Weissinger, 1844), passim; D. Drake, "Western Medical Schools," *Western Journal of Medical and Physical Sciences,* 9 (1835/36), pp. 607–611; Henry D. Shapiro and Zane L. Miller, *Physician to the West: Selected Writings of Daniel Drake on Science and Society* (Lexington: University Press of Kentucky, 1970), passim.

53 E. J. [Edward Jarvis], review, *American Journal of the Medical Sciences,* n.s., 29 (1855), p. 408. In the South, New Orleans, Memphis, and Charleston were on the list.

54 Among these, Victor J. Fourgeaud, for a number of years, prepared such compilations of the vital statistics of St. Louis.

55 Passage of the Kentucky legislation owed much to the personal influence with the legislature of one man, Dr. William L. Sutton, who was the legislation's principal sponsor. Sutton devoted himself also to making the Kentucky system workable throughout much of the decade of the 1850s, until it was halted by the Civil War.

56 Stillman, "Medical Topography and Diseases of the Sacramento Valley," pp. 290, 298.

57 Ibid., pp. 289–302; J. P. Leonard, "Letter from California," *Boston Medical and Surgical Journal,* 41 (1849/50), pp. 394–399; F. W. Hatch, "Review of the Climate and Diseases of Certain Portions of the State of California," *New York Journal of Medicine,* n.s., 13 (1854), pp. 9–13, 30–33, 41–43; Albert F. Sawyer, "On the Vital Statistics and the Causes of Mortality in San Francisco," *Boston Medical and Surgical Journal,* 55 (1856/57), pp. 217–224; "Mortality Report of San Francisco," ibid., 58 (1858), pp. 323–325.

58 Hatch, "Climate and Diseases of California," pp. 9–10.

59 State of California, *Annual Report of the State Registrar for the Year 1859* (Sacramento: 1860), p. 3.

60 Levin S. Joynes, "Statistics of the Mortality of Baltimore, during a Period of Fourteen Years, from 1836 to 1849 (Inclusive)," *American Journal of the Medical Sciences,* n.s., 20 (1850), p. 313.

61 James H. Cassedy, "The Registration Area and American Vital Statistics," *Bulletin of the History of Medicine,* 39 (1965), pp. 221–231.

62 Franklin Tuthill, "Registration of Births, Deaths and Marriages," *Transactions of the Medical Society of the State of New York* (1853), pp. 14–15.

63 "New Lebanon; Its Physic Gardens and Their Products," *Southern Medical and Surgical Journal,* n.s., 7 (1851), pp. 699-701.

64 Karl J. R. Arndt, Ed., *A Documentary History of the Indiana Decade of the Harmony Society 1814-1824,* 2 vols. (Indianapolis: Indiana Historical Society, 1975), passim.

65 Edmund Wilson, *To the Finland Station* (New York: Farrar, Strauss, and Giroux, 1972). For a general account of New Harmony and its participants, see Richard W. Leopold, *Robert Dale Owen, a Biography* (New York: Octagon, 1969). The ideas of Robert Dale Owen on marriage and birth control will be considered in Chapter 8.

66 Etienne Cabet, *Voyage en Icarie,* 5th ed. (Paris: Bureau du Populaire, 1848) pp. 38, 362, 597.

67 Laureen R. Jaussi and Gloria D. Chaston, *Register of L.D.S. Church Records* (Salt Lake City: Deseret Book Co., 1968), pp. 61, 65, 341, 357; Andrew Jensen, *Encyclopedic History of the Church of Jesus Christ of Latter-Day Saints* (Salt Lake City: Deseret News Publishing Co., 1941), pp. 139-140; 338-339.

68 Lester E. Bush, Jr., "Birth Control among the Mormons: Introduction to an Insistent Question," *Dialogue: A Journal of Mormon Thought,* 10, 2 (Autumn 1976), pp. 13, 16-17, 34-37.

69 D. B. Slack, "Medical View of Marriage," *Boston Medical and Surgical Journal,* 41 (1849/50), pp. 260-262. Recent historians have estimated that between 8.5 percent and 12.6 percent of Mormon males averaged more than one wife during this period. James E. Smith and Phillip R. Kunz, "Polygny and Fertility in Nineteenth Century America," *Population Studies,* 30 (1976), pp. 465-480.

70 *Statistical Report on the Sickness and Mortality in the Army of the United States . . . from January, 1855, to January, 1860* (Washington: Gideon, 1860), pp. 283-304; [Roberts] Bartholow, "Mormonism in Its Physical, Mental and Moral Aspects," *Boston Medical and Surgical Journal,* 63 (1860/61), pp. 438-440. I. S. Briggs showed a somewhat less jaundiced view of the Mormons after his stop in Utah for several weeks in 1849. While confirming the community's practice of laying on hands, he found that "in reality they often make use of medicine." At the time, however, all of Salt Lake City's three trained physicians were away at once—one in Europe, another in Washington, and the third at the gold mines. I. S. Briggs, "Medical History of a California Expedition," *Boston Medical and Surgical Journal,* 41 (1849/50), p. 480.

71 Dr. [Charles H.] Furley, "The Effects of Mormonism," *American Journal of Insanity,* 20 (1863/64), pp. 366-367.

72 The following discussion (including quotes), except as otherwise indicated, has been drawn essentially from the various community documents which were collected and edited by Constance Noyes Robertson, *Oneida Community, An Autobiography, 1851-1876* (Syracuse: Syracuse University Press, 1970).

73 For a full statement of Perfectionist principles, see John Humphrey Noyes,

*The Berean. Male Continence. Essay on Scientific Propagation,* reprints (New York: Arno, 1969).

74 T. R. Noyes, "Report on Nervous Diseases in the Oneida Community," *Medical Gazette,* 5 (1870), pp. 253–258. One American editor commented that Noyes's paper, a "model of careful observation," provided persuasive evidence that the mental consequences of excessive sexual indulgence had been much exaggerated by the medical profession. Editorial, ibid., pp. 259–260. Noyes makes no mention of venereal disease, but other sources left the impression that it was not a problem at Oneida. Robertson, *Oneida Community,* pp. 270–271, 347–350. A contemporary clinical study confirmed that Oneida women suffered no unusual gynecological complications from the practice of male continence. Ely Van de Warker, "A Gynecological Study of the Oneida Community," *American Journal of Obstetrics,* 17 (1884), pp. 785–810.

75 Noyes, quoted in Robertson, *Oneida Community,* pp. 337, 350. Exactly what form these records took is not known, since the documents pertaining to the stirpiculture experiment were subsequently destroyed.

## Chapter 5. The Medical Arithmetic of Southern Regional Development

1 Alexis de Tocqueville, *Democracy in America,* 2 vols., ed. Phillips Bradley (New York: Vintage, 1954), Vol. 1, pp. 370–389.

2 In 1790, the whites were calculated to be approximately 1,271,000, the slaves 657,000, and the free colored 32,000; in 1860, the respective census figures were 7,034,000, 3,839,000, and 258,000. United States Bureau of the Census, *Historical Statistics of the United States, 1789–1945* (Washington: U.S. Department of Commerce, 1949), p. 27.

3 The devastating effect of these diseases on the Florida tribes is shown in Henry F. Dobyns, *Their Number Become Thinned: Native American Population Dynamics in Eastern North America* (Knoxville: University of Tennessee Press, 1983).

4 Robert Everest, "On the Influence of Social Degradation in Producing Pauperism and Crime, as Exemplified in the Free Coloured Citizens and Foreigners in the United States," *Journal of the Statistical Society of London,* 18 (1855), p. 229.

5 Curtin estimates that around 275,000 slaves were imported into the present area of the United States prior to 1790, another 70,000 between 1791 and 1807, and perhaps 54,000 between 1808 and 1866. Large additional numbers of slaves, of course, died along the way, with mortality ranging from 10 percent to as much as 55 percent on early eighteenth-century Danish slavers, and possibly somewhat less in the nineteenth century. Philip D. Curtin, *The Atlantic Slave Trade: a Census* (Madison: University of Wisconsin Press, 1969), pp. 72–75, 92, 143, 275–286.

6 Timothy Dwight, *Travels in New England and New York,* ed. Barbara Miller Solomon, 4 vols. (Cambridge, Mass.: Harvard University Press, 1969), Vol. 4, p. 367.

7 According to census enumerations, this population grew from around 60,000 in 1790 to nearly 500,000 in 1860, well over half of which was in the South. Bureau of the Census, *Historical Statistics,* p. 27.

8 Tocqueville, *Democracy,* Vol. 1, pp. 382–383. In 1783, Ezra Stiles had assumed that both the slave and free-black populations as well as the Indians were declining. ". . . The *Indians,* as well as the million *Africans* in America, are decreasing *as rapidly* [as the whites are increasing]. Both, left to themselves, in this way diminishing, may gradually vanish: and thus an unrighteous Slavery may at length, in God's good providence, be abolished and cease in this land of Liberty." Ezra Stiles, *The United States Elevated to Glory and Honor* (New Haven: Green, 1783), p. 14.

9 Nathaniel Niles and John D. Russ, *Medical Statistics* (New York: Bliss, 1827), p. 9; Gouverneur Emerson, "Medical Statistics," *American Journal of the Medical Sciences,* 9 (1831/32), pp. 34–36.

10 G. Emerson, "An Account of an Epidemic Fever, Which Prevailed among the Negroes of Philadelphia, in the Year 1821," *Phildelphia Journal of the Medical and Physical Sciences,* 3 (1821), pp. 193–216.

11 Charles A. Lee, "Medical Statistics," *American Journal of the Medical Sciences,* 19 (1836/37), p. 43. Even in death the black, whether free or slave, was degraded. Medical students needing bodies for anatomical dissection frequently dug up cadavers from potter's fields or spirited away bodies from the morgues of almshouses. Neither blacks nor white paupers had much defense against such practices. See David C. Humphrey, "Dissection and Discrimination: the Social Origins of Cadavers in America, 1760-1915," *Bulletin of the New York Academy of Medicine,* 49 (1973), pp. 819-827.

12 A summary of the mortality statistics from various Philadelphia prisons is given in Isaac Parish, "Report on the Sanitary Condition of Philadelphia," *Transactions of the American Medical Association,* 2 (1849), pp. 480–486; *A Vindication of the Separate System of Prison Discipline* (Philadelphia: Dobson, 1839); "Health and Mortality of Convicts," *Boston Medical and Surgical Journal,* 41 (1849/50), pp. 524-525.

13 James Fenimore Cooper, *Notions of the Americans,* 2 vols. (New York: Stringer and Townsend, 1850), Vol. 1, pp. 284-287.

14 George Tucker [Joseph Atterley, pseud.], *A Voyage to the Moon,* (New York: Elam Bliss, 1827), p. 53. See also Matthew Carey, "African Colonization," in his *Miscellaneous Essays* (Philadelphia: Carey and Hart, 1830), pp. 218 ff.; and Tocqueville, *Democracy,* Vol. 1, p. 393. By 1858, the American and Maryland colonization societies were reported to have sent out a total of 11,172 blacks to Liberia over the period of 38 years. Of these, some 3,500 had died. E. Ruffin, cited in a review, *New Orleans Medical and Surgical Journal,* 17 (1860), pp. 128-129.

15 Thomas Ewell, *Statement of Improvements in the Theory and Practice of the Science of Medicine* (Philadelphia: Bioren, for the author, 1819), p. 56.

16 Carey, "African Colonization," pp. 218–222.

17 David Ramsay, *The History of South Carolina,* 2 vols. (Charleston: Longworth, 1809), Vol. 2, pp. 556–557, 582; Joseph Johnson, *Oration Delivered before the Medical Society of South Carolina* (Charleston: Marchant, Willington, 1808), p. 23; J. E. White, "A Few Remarks on the Weather and Diseases of 1805," *Medical Repository,* 11 (1808), p. 22.

18 Adam Seybert, *Statistical Annals* (Philadelphia: Dobson, 1818), pp. 19, 52–53. For more on the shortcomings of official data on the blacks, see Chapter 9.

19 S. C. Farrar, "General Report on the Topography, Meteorology and Diseases of Jackson, the Capital of Mississippi," *Southern Medical Reports,* 1 (1849), pp. 349–353. For a similar view of changing southern therapeutics, see E. N. Fenner's editorial, "Health of the Country," *New-Orleans Medical Journal,* 1 (1844/45), pp. 247–248. Fenner pointed out that venesection had changed from the massive depletion which was carried out for fevers in the early decades to a much more selective "topical bloodletting." Ibid., p. 248.

20 See, for example, McP [W. M. McPheeters], "Sectional Medicine," *St. Louis Medical and Surgical Journal,* 5 (1847/48), pp. 363–365; "Nashville *vs.* Philadelphia and the Rest of Creation," ibid., 13 (1855), pp. 87–90; review, *New York Journal of Medicine,* 9 (1847), pp. 237–238; "Plea for Mobile as a Site for a Medical School," *St. Louis Medical and Surgical Journal,* 13 (1855), pp. 565–566.

21 Arnold to Milton M. Antony, Aug. 27, 1838, Richard H. Shryock, Ed., *Letters of Richard D. Arnold, M.D., 1808–1876* (Durham: Duke University Press, 1929), pp. 18–19.

22 [John Bell], "Dr. Cartwright's Address—State-Rights Medicine," *Bulletin of Medical Science,* 4 (1846), pp. 207–213.

23 J. C. Nott, "An Examination into the Health and Longevity of the Southern Sea Ports of the United States, with Reference to the Subject of Life Insurance," *Southern Journal of Medicine and Pharmacy,* 2 (1847), p. 1.

24 Robert Mills, *Statistics of South Carolina* (Charleston: Hurlbut and Lloyd, 1826).

25 Nott, "Health and Longevity of Southern Sea Ports," p. 121.

26 John LeConte, "Statistical Researches on Cancer," *Southern Medical and Surgical Journal,* n.s., 2 (1846), pp. 257–293.

27 L. A. Dugas, Professor of Anatomy at the Medical College of Georgia, was one of the earliest southern medical men to be persuaded of the "importance of . . . statistical observations." In 1837 he wrote: "The age in which we live is one of *positive* research; one in which facts are loudly called for, and theories laid prostrate. Let us then not be reluctant to contribute to truth, by yielding up our store of *facts.*" L. A. Dugas, "Medical Statistics: Being Tables, &c.

Relating to the Mortality of Augusta," *Southern Medical and Surgical Journal,* 1 (1836/37), p. 650.

28 Telfair to his overseer, June 11, 1832, in Ulrich B. Phillips, Ed., *Plantation and Frontier Documents 1649–1863,* 2 vols. (Cleveland: Clark, 1909), Vol. 1, p. 127. J. D. B. DeBow reminded planters that such records were as essential to their well-being as careful bookkeeping was to a factory owner. Editorial, *DeBow's Review,* 13 (1852), p. 194.

29 Review, *DeBow's Review,* 8 (1850), p. 98; Thomas Affleck, "On the Hygiene of Cotton Plantations and the Management of Negro Slaves," *Southern Medical Reports,* 2 (1850), pp. 429–436.

30 J. C. Simonds, letter to Edward Jarvis, Nov. 5, 1852, Jarvis papers, Harvard University; "Introductory Address," *New Orleans Medical Journal,* 1 (1844/45), pp. i–vi. Directly affected by this situation was the heavily statistical *DeBow's Review,* which had to be printed and published in Washington, D.C. Noted in Ottis Clark Skipper, *J. D. B. DeBow, Magazinist of the Old South* (Athens: University of Georgia Press, 1958).

31 Thomas M. Logan in 1847 asked Louisiana physicians to supply him with information on the "topography, geology, climate, diseases, and statistics of the state," but apparently he had scant response and was unable to produce anything substantial. Thomas M. Logan, "Medical History of Louisiana," *New Orleans Medical and Surgical Journal,* 3 (1846/47), pp. 683–684.

32 *Southern Medical Reports,* 1 (1849); and ibid., 2 (1850). A third volume was projected but had to be cancelled. This volume, had it appeared, would have included an exceptionally candid statistical report of the mortality of Memphis, Tennessee, in 1851, a year when it was higher than almost any other American city, South or North. Geo. R. Grant, "The Vital Statistics and Sanitary Condition of Memphis, Tenn.," *New Orleans Medical and Surgical Journal,* 8 (1851/52), pp. 689–705.

33 See, for example, DeBow's editorial, "The Science of Statistics," *DeBow's Review,* 3 (1847), p. 270; and his letters on "The Census of 1850," ibid., 8 (1850), pp. 194–206, 291–294. DeBow also did his bit to stress the relevance of Baconian methods to the general development of the South. Ibid., 2 (1846), pp. 101 ff.

34 S. Chaillé, "Anniversary Oration," *New Orleans Medical and Surgical Journal,* 12 (1855/56), p. 591.

35 E. A. Fenner, "Account of Yellow Fever in New Orleans in 1846," *New Orleans Medical and Surgical Journal,* 3 (1846/47), pp. 445–466; E. A. Fenner, "Fever Statistics," ibid., 5 (1848/49), pp. 48–53.

36 Bennet Dowler, "Contributions to the Hydrographical Thermology and Hygiene of the Mississippi River," *New Orleans Medical and Surgical Journal,* 15 (1858), pp. 448–484; Bennet Dowler, "Psychological and Hygienic Observations and Reflections on Rivers," ibid., 18 (1861), pp. 54–61.

37 Charles Caldwell, "Thoughts on the Probable Destiny of New Orleans in Relation to Health, Population, and Commerce," *Philadelphia Journal of the Medical and Physical Sciences,* 6 (1823), pp. 1–14.

38 Bennet Dowler, *Tableaux, Geographical, Commercial, Geological and Sanitary, of New Orleans* (New Orleans: Daily Delta, 1853), pp. 3–6, 17–35; Bennet Dowler, *Tableau of the Yellow Fever of 1853* (New Orleans: Picayune, 1854), pp. 29–34, 45–46; Bennet Dowler, "Researches upon the Necropolis of New Orleans, with Brief Allusions to Its Vital Arithmetic," *New Orleans Medical and Surgical Journal,* 7 (1850/51), pp. 275–300.

39 Dowler, "Researches upon the Necropolis of New Orleans," p. 292.

40 Bennet Dowler, "Researches upon the Vital Dynamics of Civil Government," *New Orleans Medical and Surgical Journal,* 5 (1848/49), p. 685.

41 See ibid., 8 (1851/52), pp. 606–620.

42 Another reason for the legislature's balking at a registration act in 1852 was the failure of the existing state bureau of statistics under DeBow to live up to expectations. One observer wrote, "Mr. DeBow has neglected his office so much that it will probably be abolished, and he informs me that he recommended its abolition, deeming it useless, as it certainly has been under his superintendence." J. C. Simonds to Edward Jarvis, Nov. 5, 1852, Jarvis papers, Harvard University.

43 E. H. Barton, *Report to the Louisiana State Medical Society, on the Meteorology, Vital Statistics and Hygiene of the State of Louisiana* (New Orleans: Davies, 1851), pp. 24–31, 42–46; Barton to Jarvis, Mar. 26, 1853, Jarvis papers, Harvard University. Samuel Cartwright published a favorable view of Dowler's statistics and an unfavorable one of Barton's in his review, *New Orleans Medical and Surgical Journal,* 8 (1851/52), pp. 237–253, 384.

44 J. C. Simonds, "A Comparison of the Weekly Bills of Mortality of New Orleans and Boston for 1851," *Charleston Medical Journal,* 7 (1852), pp. 289–293; see also J. C. Simonds, "Report on the Hygienic Characteristics of New Orleans, as Illustrated by Its Mortuary Statistics," ibid., 6 (1851), pp. 677–745.

45 Barton to Jarvis, Sept. 18, 1852, Jarvis papers, Harvard University. For a contemporary review and criticism of Morton Dowler's attack on Barton, see *Boston Medical and Surgical Journal,* 52 (1855), pp. 122–124.

46 *Report of the Sanitary Commission of New Orleans on the Epidemic Yellow Fever of 1853* (New Orleans: Picayune, 1854).

47 See Barton's letters to Jarvis, 1853–1857, Jarvis papers, Harvard University. See also review, *Medical Examiner,* n.s., 11 (1855), pp. 309–313; editorial, "The Sanitary Commission of 1853 and the City of New Orleans," *Boston Medical and Surgical Journal,* 56 (1857), pp. 144–145; and M. Morton Dowler, review, *New Orleans Medical and Surgical Journal,* 11 (1854/55), pp. 523–526.

48 [S.] Chaillé, "Review of the Report of the Board of Health for 1857," *New Orleans Medical and Surgical Journal,* 15 (1858), pp. 270–275. See also *Report of the Board of Health to the Legislature of the State of Louisiana, January 1857* (New Orleans: Claiborne, 1857); and ibid., 1861.

49 Josiah C. Nott, "On the Pathology of Yellow Fever," *American Journal of the Medical Sciences,* n.s., 9 (1845), pp. 277–293; J. C. Nott, "Sketch of the Epidemic of Yellow Fever of 1847, in Mobile," *Charleston Medical Journal,* 3

(1848), pp. 1–19; Josiah C. Nott, "Yellow Fever Contrasted with Bilious Fever," *New Orleans Medical and Surgical Journal*, 4 (1847/48), pp. 563–601; J. C. Nott, "The Epidemic Yellow Fever of Mobile in 1853," ibid., 10 (1853/54), pp. 577–583.

50 J. C. Nott, "Thoughts on Acclimation and Adaptation of Races to Climates," *American Journal of the Medical Sciences*, n.s., 32 (1856), p. 325.

51 William Stanton, *The Leopard's Spots: Scientific Attitudes toward Race in America* (Chicago: University of Chicago Press, 1960).

52 Josiah C. Nott, "Statistics of Southern Slave Population, with Especial Reference to Life Insurance," *DeBow's Review*, 4 (1847), pp. 275–289; J. C. Nott, "Acclimation," in Josiah C. Nott and Geo. R. Gliddon, Eds., *Indigenous Races of the Earth* (Philadelphia: Lippincott, 1857), pp. 353–401.

53 J. C. Nott, "The Mulatto a Hybrid," *American Journal of the Medical Sciences*, n.s., 6 (1843), pp. 252–256. George Tucker, by contrast, considered mulattoes to be longer-lived than either the Caucasian or the black races.

54 Stanton argues that among the scientists North and South there was little disagreement with the doctrine, and that such a defender of the Biblical account as John Bachman of Charleston was an exception. Stanton, *The Leopard's Spots*, passim.

55 Samuel A. Cartwright, "Report on the Diseases and Physical Peculiarities of the Negro Race," *New Orleans Medical and Surgical Journal*, 7 (1850/51), pp. 697–698.

56 The Editor [Samuel Forry], "Vital Statistics Furnished by the Sixth Census of the United States, Bearing upon the Question of the Unity of the Human Race," *New York Journal of Medicine*, 1 (1843), pp. 151–167.

57 Y [Yandell], "Professor Dickson on the Intermarriage of the Races," *Western Journal of Medicine and Surgery*, n.s., 4 (1845), pp. 91–92.

58 "Western Journal of Medicine and Surgery," *Medical Examiner*, 7 (1844), pp. 201–202. For an extended recent study of antebellum southern medical self-consciousness, see John Harley Warner, "A Southern Medical Reform: the Meaning of the Antebellum Argument for Southern Medical Education," *Bulletin of the History of Medicine*, 57 (1983), pp. 364–381.

59 "Introduction," *Southern Medical and Surgical Journal*, 1 (1836/37), pp. 1–4; "Introductory Address," pp. i–vi.

60 See, for example, "Southern Medical Students," *Medical Examiner*, n.s., 6 (1850), pp. 662–664; "Exodus of Southern Medical Students," *North American Medical and Chirurgical Review*, 4 (1860), pp. 188–189, 571–572.

61 Samuel A. Cartwright, "Cartwright on Southern Medicine," *New Orleans Medical and Surgical Journal*, 3 (1846/47), pp. 259–272; B. Rush Mitchell, "Southern versus Northern Practice," *Medical Examiner*, n.s., 4 (1848), pp. 591–595; "The Medical Examiner on 'Sectional Medicine,'" *Southern Medical and Surgical Journal*, n.s., 4 (1848), pp. 699–704; [John Bell], "Dr. Cartwright's Address—State-Rights Medicine," *Bulletin of Medical Science*, 4 (1846), pp. 207–213.

62 Samuel A. Cartwright, "Statistical Medicine, or Numerical Analysis Applied to the Investigation of Morbid Actions," *Western Journal of Medicine and Surgery*, 3d ser., 1 (1848), pp. 185–206.

63 Samuel A. Cartwright, "Remarks on Statistical Medicine, Contrasting the Result of the Empirical with the Regular Practice of Physic, in Natchez," *Western Journal of Medicine and Surgery*, 2 (1840), pp. 1–21; Samuel A. Cartwright, "Hygienics of Temperance," *Boston Medical and Surgical Journal*, 48 (1853), pp. 373–377, 494–499; ibid., 49 (1853), pp. 9–13.

64 Samuel A. Cartwright, "Proofs of the Health-preserving Properties of the Jussieua Grandiflora or Floating Plant," *Western Journal of Medicine and Surgery*, 1 (1840), pp. 428–452.

65 Samuel A. Cartwright, "Prevention of Yellow Fever," *New Orleans Medical and Surgical Journal*, 10 (1853/54), pp. 316–317.

66 Editorial, "Excessive Slave Population—the Remedy," *DeBow's Review*, 12 (1852) pp. 182–185.

67 E. D. Fenner, "Acclimation; and the Liability of Negroes to the Endemic Fevers of the South," *Southern Medical and Surgical Journal*, n.s., 14 (1858), pp. 452–460; review, *Western Journal of Medicine and Surgery*, 4th ser., 1 (1854), pp. 279–293, 354–361.

68 Edward H. Barton, *Introductory Lecture on Acclimation* (New Orleans: Commercial Bulletin Printers, 1837); "Diseases of New Orleans," *Boston Medical and Surgical Journal*, 17 (1837), pp. 47–49; E. J. [Edward Jarvis], review, *American Journal of the Medical Sciences*, n.s., 37 (1859), pp. 480–481.

69 "Address of Samuel A. Cartwright before the Medical Convention, in the City of Jackson, January 13, 1846," *New Orleans Medical and Surgical Journal*, 2 (1845/46), pp. 724–733; Cartwright, "Cartwright on Southern Medicine."

70 Daniel Drake, "Diseases of the Negro Population," *Western Journal of Medicine and Surgery*, 2d ser., 3 (1845), p. 166.

71 Samuel Hazard, "Statistical Observations on the Number of Blind in Pennsylvania and the United States." *Transactions of the Medical Society of the State of New York*, 4 (1838/40), pp. 44–58.

72 Samuel A. Cartwright, "Report on the Diseases and Physical Peculiarities of the Negro Race," *New Orleans Medical and Surgical Journal*, 7 (1850/51), pp. 691–715; ibid., 8 (1851/52), pp. 187–194.

73 Editorial, "Dr. Cartwright on 'Drapetomania,'" *Buffalo Medical Journal*, 10 (1854/55), pp. 438–442; James T. Smith, "Review of Dr. Cartwright's Report on the Diseases and Peculiarities of the Negro Race," *New Orleans Medical and Surgical Journal*, 8 (1851/52), pp. 228 ff.; "Cartwright on the Diseases, etc., of the Negro Race," *Charleston Medical Journal*, 6 (1851), pp. 829–843; 7 (1852), pp. 89–98; Morton Dowler, "On Yellow Fever," *New Orleans Medical and Surgical Journal*, 11 (1854/55), p. 375.

74 H. V. Wooten, "Dysentery among Negroes," *New Orleans Medical and*

*Surgical Journal,* pp. 449; [E. D. Fenner], "State Medical Society of Louisiana," *Southern Medical Reports,* 2 (1850), pp. 295–297; D. W. B., review, *New Orleans Medical and Surgical Journal,* 6 (1849/50), pp. 224–235.

75 S. L. Grier, "The Negro and His Diseases," *New Orleans Medical and Surgical Journal,* 9 (1852/53), pp. 752–763; A. P. Merrill, "An Essay on Some of the Distinctive Peculiarities of the Negro Race," *Memphis Medical Record,* 4 (1855/56), pp. 1–17, 65–77, 129–139, 321–330.

76 "Mortality Statistics of the Seventh Census," *Southern Medical and Surgical Journal,* n.s., 12 (1856), pp. 127–128. Samuel Forry earlier pointed out that few blacks kept family registers or had records of their birth. The Editor [Samuel Forry], "Vital Statistics Furnished by the Sixth Census of the United States," p. 155.

77 Alfred G. Tebault, "Practical Remarks on Diseases of the Spleen," *American Journal of the Medical Sciences,* n.s., 31 (1856), p. 350; E. M. Pendleton, "On the Susceptibility of the Caucasian and African races to the Different Classes of Disease," *Southern Medical Reports,* 1 (1849), pp. 336–342; E. M. Pendleton, "General Report on the Topography, Climate and Diseases of Middle Georgia," ibid., pp. 314–335.

78 Grier, "The Negro and His Diseases," passim.

79 Still another aspect of the regional controversy over health-related factors was the higher rates that were charged southerners for life insurance, on the basis of the greater mortality and morbidity in that region. See discussion in Chapter 9.

80 T. Romeyn Beck, "Statistics of the Deaf and Dumb in the State of New York, the United States, and in Various Countries in Europe," *Transactions of the Medical Society of the State of New York,* 3 (1836/37), p. 337.

81 Niles and Russ, *Medical Statistics,* pp. 9–10.

82 Samuel Forry, "Statistical Researches Elucidating the Climate of the United States and Its Relation with Diseases of Malarial Origin," *American Journal of the Medical Sciences,* n.s., 2 (1841), p. 42; Samuel Forry, *The Climate of the United States and Its Endemic Influence,* 2d ed. (New York: Langley, 1842), pp. 326–328.

83 J. D. B. DeBow, *Mortality Statistics of the Seventh Census of the United States, 1850* (Washington: Nicholson, 1855), passim. Bennet Dowler, while carefully pointing out the instances of southern superiority, also reflected that the job of analyzing the deaths of "several hundred thousand compatriots might make any one sick, désolé, or at least, triste, melancholy as the moonbeam which strays through the crevice of a delapidated tomb into the eyeless sockets of a death's head." Review, *New Orleans Medical and Surgical Journal,* 12 (1855/56), pp. 679–683.

84 [Samuel Forry, Comp.], *Statistieal Report on the Sickness and Mortality in the Army of the United States . . . from January 1819, to January 1939* (Washington: Gideon, 1840); James B. Colegrove, "Frequency of Consumption in Different Parts of the United States," *Boston Medical and Surgi-*

*cal Journal,* 54 (1856), pp. 69–72; Bennet Dowler, "Statistical Researches on the Ratio of Mortality from Pulmonary Consumption in the Northern and Southern States . . .," *New Orleans Medical and Surgical Journal,* 14 (1857), pp. 312–323; E. Andrews, "The Relations of Cancer and Consumption to Climate in the United States," ibid., 19 (1867), pp. 643–646; C. A. L. [Charles A. Lee], "Consumption in Massachusetts," *Boston Medical and Surgical Journal,* 54 (1856), pp. 186–187. See also the discussion of tuberculosis in Chapter 3.

85 Edward Jarvis, "Statistics of Insanity in the United States," *Boston Medical and Surgical Journal,* 27 (1842), pp. 116–121, 281–282.

86 Ibid.

87 "Reflections on the Census of 1840," *Southern Literary Messenger,* 9 (1843), pp. 340–352.

88 Bowditch to I. Hays, Oct. 1, 1843, Isaac Hays papers, American Philosophical Society Library, Philadelphia; Bowditch to Jarvis, Oct. 1, 1843, Bowditch papers, Countway Library, Harvard University; Edward Jarvis, "Insanity among the Coloured Population of the Free States," *American Journal of the Medical Sciences,* n.s., 7 (1844), pp. 71–83.

89 Smith's memorial was published in *The Liberator,* May 31, 1884.

90 E. Jarvis, "Insanity among the Colored Population of the Free States," *American Journal of Insanity,* 8 (1851/52), p. 281; J. D. B. DeBow, *Statistical View of the United States* (Washington: Nicholson, 1854), pp. 75–77.

91 B. Dowler, "The Vital Statistics of Negroes in the United States," *New Orleans Medical and Surgical Journal,* 13 (1856/57), pp. 164–175. Dowler found considerable support for his views in the comments of army surgeons on the degeneration and decline of western Indian tribes in the course of the latters' contacts with the white race. Bennet Dowler, "Researches into the Sanitary Condition and Vital Statistics of Barbarians," ibid., 14 (1857), pp. 335–352. At the same time, southern health officers generally echoed Dowler's conclusions throughout the 1850s. See Chaillé, "Review of the Report of the Board of Health for 1857," pp. 272–273.

92 George Fitzhugh, *Sociology for the South, or the Failure of Free Society* (Richmond; Morris, 1854), p. 222; James H. Hammond, "Letters on Slavery," in *The Pro-Slavery Argument* (Charleston: Walker, Richards, 1852; reprinted New York: Negro Universities Press, 1968), p. 154.

93 S. H. Dickson, "Statistics of Height and Weight in the South," *Charleston Medical Journal,* 12 (1857), pp. 607–613. In a sequel to this study, Dickson analyzed the measurements of 946 students from nine institutions in different sections of the United States and compared them with European figures, chiefly those of Quetelet. Among his findings, no differences in stature from one social class to another were observed in the United States, contrary to findings in Europe. More striking, while Quetelet found that only 2 percent in a sample of 900 European men had reached 5′10″ in height or more, Dickson found that over 20 percent of his sample of 780 Americans exceeded 6′. S. H.

Dickson, "Some Additional Statistics of Height and Weight," ibid., 13 (1858), pp. 494–506.

94 Hinton Rowan Helper, *The Impending Crisis of the South; How to Meet It* (New York: Burdick, 1857), pp. 28–33, 298–303.

95 Horace Bushnell, *The Census and Slavery* (Hartford: Hunt, 1860).

96 Ibid., p. 9.

97 S. B. Hunt, "The Cranial Characteristics and Powers of Human Races," *Boston Medical and Surgical Journal,* 51 (1854), pp. 69–74.

## Chapter 6. Manifest Destiny and Medicine

1 For various contemporary accounts of the heavy migration into Texas after 1821, see Ulrich B. Phillips, *Plantation and Frontier Documents 1649–1863,* 2 vols. (Cleveland: Clark, 1909), Vol. 2, pp. 251–257.

2 Samuel Forry, *The Climate of the United States and Its Endemic Influences* (New York: Langley, 1842), p. 22.

3 William B. Herrick, "Medical and Surgical Reports from the Army in Mexico," *Southern Medical and Surgical Journal,* n.s., 3 (1847), p. 299; George Johnson, "Remarks on the Medical Topography of Texas, and on the Diseases of the Army of Invasion," *St. Louis Medical and Surgical Journal,* 10 (1847), pp. 433–439; Robert Newton, "Constitution and Diseases of Mexicans," *Western Journal of Medicine and Surgery,* 3d ser., 2 (1848), pp. 519–526.

4 "Statistics of the War with Mexico," in [R. H. Coolidge, Ed.], *Statistical Report on the Sickness and Mortality in the Army of the United States . . . from January, 1839, to January, 1855* (Washington: Nicholson, 1856), pp. 605–621; W. B. Herrick, "The Medical Department of the Army, and the Effects of Marching and a Camp Life in Producing and Modifying Disease," *Boston Medical and Surgical Journal,* 37 (1847/48), p. 241; "Report of the Surgeon General," *New Orleans Medical and Surgical Journal,* 3 (1846/47), pp. 765–767.

5 "Report of the Surgeon General," pp. 765–767; "Statistics of the War with Mexico," pp. 605–606. Enlisted soldiers of this period came mostly from cities and were drawn heavily from among immigrants. By the 1840s the army recruiting service kept records of the national origins and occupations of all applicants, of reasons for rejections, and of a few physical characteristics, such as height, weight, complexion, and hair color. Ibid., pp. 625–633.

6 Thos. N. Love, "Diseases among the U.S. Volunteers in the Late War," *Boston Medical and Surgical Journal,* 39 (1848), pp. 49–53; H. R. Robards, "The Diseases of the Army of Occupation in the Summer of 1846," *Western Journal of Medicine and Surgery,* 2d ser., 7 (1847), pp. 185–196.

7 "Report of the Surgeon General," pp. 764–767; Johnson, "Medical Topography of Texas," pp. 433–437; William G. Proctor, "On the Diseases of the United States' Army on the Rio Grande," *Western Journal of Medicine and Surgery,* 3d ser., 1 (1848), pp. 461–466; "Health of the Army on the

Rio Grande," *New Orleans Medical and Surgical Journal,* 3 (1846/47), pp. 276–277.

8 "Effects of Climate on Northern and Southern Troops," *Boston Medical and Surgical Journal,* 65 (1861/62), p. 127.

9 Herrick, "Medical Department of the Army," pp. 242–244.

10 John B. Porter, "Medical and Surgical Notes of Campaigns in the War with Mexico, during the Years 1845, 1846, 1847, and 1848," *American Journal of the Medical Sciences,* n.s., 26 (1853), pp. 330–331.

11 E. D. Fenner, "An Account of the Yellow Fever at New Orleans, in the Year 1848," *New Orleans Medical and Surgical Journal,* 5 (1849/50), pp. 9–29; "Sickness in the U.S. Army in Mexico," ibid., 4 (1847/48), pp. 138–141; "Introductory Address," *New Orleans Medical Journal,* 1 (1844/45), p. ii; E. D. Fenner, "The Yellow Fever Quarantine at New Orleans," *Transactions of the American Medical Association,* 2 (1849), pp. 630–631.

12 John G. F. Wurdemann, *Notes on Cuba* (Boston: Thurston, Torry, 1844), pp. 1, 252; "The Cuban Expedition," *Eclectic Medical Journal,* 9 (1850), pp. 339–341. A much larger number of physicians participated in the Canadian uprising of 1837. See Eugene P. Link, "Vermont Physicians and the Canadian Rebellion of 1837," *Vermont History,* 37 (1969), 7 pp.

13 I. Moses, "Military Surgery and Operations following the Battle of Rivas, Nicaragua, April, 1856," *American Journal of the Medical Sciences,* n.s., 33 (1857), p. 26; "Excess of Physicians—Opening in the East," *Boston Medical and Surgical Journal,* 51 (1854/55), pp. 484–485; "American Physicians in Russia," *Southern Medical and Surgical Journal,* n.s., 12 (1856), p. 255; C. R. Parke, "American Surgeons in the Russian Army in the Crimea," *American Journal of the Medical Sciences,* n.s., 39 (1860), pp. 570–572.

14 As early as 1837, caravans were also "continually travelling" across the Mexican isthmus from Veracruz on their way to Hawaii and various other Pacific points. Alonzo Chapin, "Remarks on the Sandwich Islands," *American Journal of the Medical Sciences,* 20 (1837), p. 57.

15 J. P. Leonard, "Medical Matters at Panama," *Boston Medical and Surgical Journal,* 40 (1849), pp. 455–456; "Loss of Health and Life in Crossing the Isthmus of Panama," ibid., 44 (1851), p. 164; John A. Lidell, "Upon the Medical Topography and Diseases of the Isthmus of Panama," *New York Journal of Medicine,* 8 (1852), pp. 242–259; Delta, "Panama Fever," *Boston Medical and Surgical Journal,* 46 (1852), pp. 155–156; Wm. P. Buel, "Notes on the Medical Topography, Climate, and Diseases of Panama, N. G.," *American Journal of the Medical Sciences,* n.s., 37 (1859), pp. 131–136; G. R. B. Horner, "Observations on the Isthmus of Panama, and on the Hospitals of Havana," ibid., pp. 359–364. Other names given to Panama Fever included congestive, typhus bilious, and pernicious fevers. H. Doty, "On Panama Fever, as Modified by Climate," *Eclectic Medical Journal,* 12 (1853), p. 298.

16 Horner, "Observations on Panama," p. 359; "Loss of Health and Life in Panama," p. 164.

17 "Naval Surgeons," *Medical Examiner,* n.s., 4 (1848), pp. 41–42.

18  Richard McSherry, "On the Influence of Sea Life upon Health," *American Journal of the Medical Sciences,* n.s., 18 (1849), pp. 404–407; Edward R. Squibb, "Summary Report on the Hospital Department of the U.S. Frigate Cumberland, during a Cruise to the Mediterranean, from July 19th 1849, to July 9, 1851," ibid., n.s., 23 (1852), pp. 54–57; J. H. Wright, "Medical Statistics of the U.S. Ship Constellation, on Her Present Voyage," *Boston Medical and Surgical Journal,* 26 (1842), pp. 309–315.

19  See for example, W. S. W. Ruschenberger, *Narrative of a Voyage Round the World, during the Years 1835, 36 and 37,* 2 vols. (London: Bentley, 1838); G. R. B. Horner, *Medical Topography of Brazil and Uruguay* (Philadelphia: Lindsay and Blakiston, 1845).

20  J. M. Foltz, "Medical Statistics of the United States Frigate Potomac, Commodore John Downes, Commander, during a Three Years' Voyage of Circumnavigation of the Globe," *New York Journal of Medicine,* 1 (1843), pp. 189–207; D. C. McLeod, "On the Topography of Singapore," *American Journal of the Medical Sciences,* n.s., 11 (1846), pp. 361–362; Samuel George Morton, *Crania Americana* (Philadelphia: Dobson, 1839).

21  George Clymer, "Notices of the African Station," *American Journal of the Medical Sciences,* n.s., 38 (1859), pp. 378–379.

22  News note, *Boston Medical and Surgical Journal,* 33 (1845/46), p. 125; "Missionary Physicians," ibid., 25 (1842), p. 403; "Medical Missions," in Henry O. Dwight, H. Allen Tupper, and Edwin M. Bliss, Eds., *The Encyclopedia of Missions,* 2d ed., (New York: Funk and Wagnalls, 1904), p. 445.

23  O. R. Bacheler, "Health and Longevity of Missionaries in India," *Boston Medical and Surgical Journal,* 35 (1846), pp. 289–295; editorial comment, ibid., 33 (1845/46), p. 525; J. W. Lugenbeel, "The Acclimating Fever of Western Intertropical Africa," ibid., 37 (1847/48), p. 411.

24  Letter from Mrs. J. H. Hanoford, "Hydropathy for Foreign Missionaries," *Water-Cure Journal,* 18 (1854), pp. 29–30; "The Water-Cure in India," ibid., 12 (1851), p. 90; summary of a letter to the editor from George Thompson, ibid., 19 (1855), p. 104; "Homoeopathy in Siam," *American Homoeopathic Review,* 1 (1858/59), p. 528; editorial comment, ibid., 19 (1855), p. 104; A. Curtis, "Mortality of Missionaries," *Thomsonian Recorder,* 2 (1833/34), pp. 374–375; "A Missionary Gone," *Botanico-Medical Recorder,* 12 (1843/44), p. 318. So far as I have discovered, most medical missionaries supported by the American Board of Commissioners for Foreign Missions and by other American missionary societies seem to have been orthodox in their medical beliefs. But nonphysician missionaries undoubtedly were often devotees of various of the irregular therapies. The head of the Oregon mission in the 1830s and 1840s was Marcus Whitman, an orthodox physician. However, both his wife and father-in-law were confirmed Thomsonians. The party thus ended up carrying along large supplies of lobelia and cayenne pepper as well as Whitman's own orthodox drugs. Related in Clifford M. Drury,

*Marcus Whitman, M.D., Pioneer and Martyr* (Caldwell, Idaho: Caxton, 1937), p. 135.

25 Ruschenberger, *Voyage Round the World,* Vol. 2, pp. 66–68, 350–351.

26 See Peter Parker's instructions, in George B. Stevens and W. Fisher Markwick, Eds., *The Life, Letters, and Journals of the Rev. and Hon. Peter Parker, M.D.* (Boston: Congregational Sunday School and Publications Society, 1896), p. 82; editorial comment, *Missionary Herald,* 23 (1827), p. 139; "Diseases of Tahiti," *Boston Medical and Surgical Journal,* 34 (1846), p. 185.

27 "Medical Practice in China," *Boston Medical and Surgical Journal,* 31 (1844/45), p. 521; "Physicians in Foreign and Domestic Missionary Service," ibid., 15 (1836/37), p. 384; "Medical Missionary Service," ibid., 18 (1838), pp. 81–82; "American Missionary Physicians," ibid., 35 (1846–47), p. 540; "Colored Physicians for Africa," ibid., 48 (1853), p. 264.

Ruschenberger noted a practice among missionaries in Bangkok of having verses of scripture printed on the back of prescription slips. He thought that this was a dubious procedure scientifically, for "the patients have acquired the notion that this is an important part of the treatment," Ruschenberger, *Voyage Round the World,* Vol. 2, p. 71. At the same time, it was readily apparent that the "relief of bodily ills . . . affords the readiest access to [people's] confidence and esteem. The medical missionary, therefore, while practicing his profession entirely incidentally to the great object of his mission, is silently breaking down the strongest barriers to his success." Review, *New York Journal of Medicine,* n.s., 10 (1853), pp. 88–89.

28 O. R. Bacheler, "Medical Missionary Operations at Balasore, India," *Boston Medical and Surgical Journal,* 40 (1849), pp. 76–77; "American Surgery in India," ibid., 38 (1848), pp. 103–104; Ruschenberger, *Voyage Round the World,* Vol. 2, pp. 40–43, 261–264. Merle Curti has noted the many scholarly contributions of nineteenth-century missionaries generally, in ethnology, linguistics, geography, and other fields. Merle Curti, *American Philanthropy Abroad: a History* (New Brunswick: Rutgers University Press, 1963), pp. 138–174.

29 Ruschenberger, *Voyage Round the World,* Vol. 2, pp. 68–71; "Sandwich Island Anatomy," *Boston Medical and Surgical Journal,* 20 (1839), pp. 125–126; O. R. Bacheler, "Medical Missionary Operations at Balasore, India," p. 76; "Medical Practice in China," ibid., 31 (1844/45), pp. 520–521.

30 "Medical Books for Liberia," ibid., 37 (1847/48), pp. 324–325; *The First and Second Reports of the Medical Missionary Society in China* (Macao: Williams, 1841), p. 53; "American Surgery in India," p. 103; Bacheler, "Medical Missionary Operations at Balasore, India," pp. 73–76; John J. Kerr, "Medicine in China," *North American Medical and Chirurgical Review,* 3 (1859), pp. 293–297; Edward V. Gulick, *Peter Parker and the Opening of China* (Cambridge, Mass: Harvard University Press, 1973), pp. 56–57.

31 "Medical Practice in China," *Boston Medical and Surgical Journal,* 31

(1844/45), p. 520; Bacheler, "Medical Missionary Operations at Balasore, India," pp. 73–76; *First and Second Reports, Medical Missionary Society in China,* passim.

32 John G. Kerr prepared a statistical article on the operations at Canton for removal of bladder stones. "Cases Treated at the Medical Missionary Society's Hospital at Canton, China," *American Journal of the Medical Sciences,* n.s., 44 (1862), pp. 99–102.

33 The editor of the *Boston Medical and Surgical Journal,* for example, hoped that Robert H. Wood, newly arrived in Oahu, would send back details about climatic features, medical botany, prevalent diseases—particularly syphilis, native modes of treatment, and other matters. "Sandwich Islands," *Boston Medical and Surgical Journal,* 19 (1838), p. 209.

34 "Negroes in the Medical College at Boston," *Southern Medical and Surgical Journal,* n.s., 7 (1851), pp. 125–126; "Colored Physicians for Liberia," *Boston Medical and Surgical Journal,* 48 (1852), pp. 264–265; ibid., 50 (1854), p. 284.

35 James L. Day, "Medical Department of the National Institute," *Boston Medical and Surgical Journal,* 30 (1844), pp. 371–375; J. W. Lugenbeel, "Influence of Climate, in Western Africa, on the Mind," ibid., 33 (1845/46), pp. 18–22; J. W. Lugenbeel, "The Acclimating Fever of Western Intertropical Africa," ibid., 37 (1847/48), pp. 409–412; William H. Clark, "African Fevers —Intermittent and Remittent," *Southern Medical and Surgical Journal,* n.s., 15 (1859), pp. 172 ff.; Clymer, "Notices of the African Station," pp. 372–373.

36 Similarly, Wilkes and his physician-scientists looked with much interest into the enormous population decreases among Tahitians and other South Pacific islanders since the first visits by European explorers and sailors.

37 Chapin, "Remarks on the Sandwich Islands," p. 55; "Depopulation of the Sandwich Islands," *Boston Medical and Surgical Journal,* 48 (1853), p. 308; ibid., 54 (1856), p. 448.

38 C. F. Winslow, "Intermarriage among the Sandwich Islanders," *Boston Medical and Surgical Journal,* 63 (1860), pp. 329–335; Chapin, "Remarks on the Sandwich Islands," pp. 43–59; A. Chapin, "Remarks on the Venereal Disease at the Sandwich Islands," *Boston Medical and Surgical Journal,* 42 (1850), pp. 89–93.

39 Luther H. Gulick, "On the Climate, Diseases, and Materia Medica of the Sandwich (Hawaiian) Islands," *New York Journal of Medicine,* n.s., 14 (1855), pp. 169–211; "Mortality of Children at the Sandwich Islands," *Boston Medical and Surgical Journal,* 24 (1841), p. 397; "Diseases in the South-Sea Islands," ibid., 34 (1846), p. 325; Horace Bushnell, *Christian Nurture* (New York: Scribner, 1863), pp. 209–211.

40 *First and Second Reports, Medical Missionary Society in China,* pp. 25, 31, 38, 62; *Report of the Medical Missionary Society in China for the Year 1845* (Victoria: Hong Kong Register Press, 1846), p. 35; *Report of the Medical Missionary Society in China, 1862* (Hong Kong: n.p., 1863), pp. 8–9.

41 *The Hospital Reports of the Medical Missionary Society in China, for the year 1839* [Macao]: Chinese Repository, 1840), p. 1–3, 11–16; Medical Missionary Society, *Report of the Medical Missionary Society in China, 1860* (Hong Kong: n.p., 1861) pp. 17, 19. Two British firms which long subscribed to the society through their Canton offices were the Jardine and Dent companies. Nathan Allen, *An Essay on the Opium Trade* (Boston: Jewett, 1850), pp. 12–13. The American firm of Olyphant and Company heavily supported Parker and the China mission during the early years. It provided free passage to many missionaries and their families, furnished a ship to distribute tracts along the China coast, and contributed to the medical society. However, Allen did not find any evidence that it was involved in the opium trade.

42 Allen, *Opium Trade,* passim; review, *New York Journal of Medicine,* 4 (1845), pp. 395–396; Ruschenberger, *Voyage Round the World,* Vol. 2, p. 211; "The Opium Trade," *Boston Medical and Surgical Journal,* 42 (1850), p. 277; "Prophylactic and Curative Powers of Tobacco," *Boston Medical and Surgical Journal,* 20 (1839), p. 316.

43 "Opium Eating," taken from *The New York Organ,* in *Water-Cure Journal,* 15 (1853), p. 85; Oliver Wendell Holmes, "Currents and Counter Currents in Medical Science" (1860), in his *Medical Essays* (Boston: Houghton, Mifflin, 1889), pp. 200–201. Actually, as early as 1841, a temperance speaker estimated that the city already had some 3,000–5,000 habitual opium users. Noted in David T. Courtwright, *Dark Paradise: Opiate Addiction in America before 1940* (Cambridge, Mass: Harvard University Press, 1982), pp. 45–46.

## Chapter 7. The Medical Demography of Immigration and Industrialism

1 Among the early anti-Chinese tracts, see Arthur B. Stout, *Chinese Immigration and the Physiological Causes of the Decay of a Nation* (San Francisco: Agnew and Deffebach, 1862). Total *recorded* immigration from Asia between 1820 and 1860 was around 42,000, all but a handful of which was from China between 1854 and 1860. U.S. Bureau of the Census, *Historical Statistics of the United States, 1789–1945* (Washington: Department of Commerce, 1949), p. 36.

2 For the influx of black populations and its ramifications, see Chapter 5. For treatments of the epidemiological interactions of European, African, and American populations, see Alfred W. Crosby, *The Columbian Exchange: Biological and Cultural Consequences of 1492* (Westport, Conn.: Greenwood, 1972); and William H. McNeill, *Plagues and Peoples* Garden City, N.Y.: Anchor/Doubleday, 1976).

3 Annual recorded immigration from Europe climbed from 7,691 in 1820 to 405,542 in 1854, but fell back, under the influence of nativist agitation, to fewer than 200,000 annually from 1854 until 1860, except for the 216,000 of

1857. Each year the figures for Europe were a vast proportion of the total immigration from all continents. Bureau of Census, *Historical Statistics,* p. 34.

4 James H. Cassedy, *American Medicine and Statistical Thinking, 1800–1860,* (Cambridge, Mass.: Harvard University Press, 1984), pp. 25–51, 178–229.

5 Franklin Tuthill, "Registration of Births, Deaths, and Marriages" (Albany: Van Benthuysen, 1853), p. 14 (offprint from *Transactions of the Medical Society of the State of New York,* June 1852).

6 "Report of the Charity Hospital, New Orleans," *Western Journal of Medicine and Surgery,* 7 (1843), pp. 159–160; "Charity Hospital Monthly Reports for 1844," *New Orleans Medical and Surgical Journal,* 1 (1844/45), pp. 100–103; Samuel Cartwright, communication in *Report of the Select Committee of the Senate of the United States on the Sickness and Mortality on Board Emigrant Ships* (Washington: Tucker, 1854), p. 135.

7 For an account of Shattuck's contributions to statistics and public health, see Cassedy, *American Medicine,* pp. 194–198, 217–219, 223–224.

8 The Charleston, South Carolina, census of 1848 emulated the Boston census in various respects. The more typical city censuses of this period, however, were somewhat more closely geared to commercial and booster interests than to social or scientific purposes; many, as in Syracuse (1844) and Savannah (1848), were carried out in connection with the preparation of city directories. Other early censuses which showed broadened ranges of inquiries included the New York State census of 1845 and the federal census of 1850, the latter as a result of recommendations by Shattuck, Jarvis, and other consultants.

9 Lemuel Shattuck, *Report to the Committee of the City Council Appointed to Obtain the Census of Boston for the Year 1845* (Boston: Eastburn, 1846), pp. 1, 11–16, 62, 73, 125, 126–177.

10 [Lemuel Shattuck, et al.], *Report of a General Plan for the Promotion of Public and Personal Health . . . Relating to a Sanitary Survey of the State* (Boston: Dutton and Wentworth, 1850), pp. 200–206.

11 "Annual Reports of the Hospitals, Dispensaries, and Public Charities of New York City," *New York Journal of Medicine,* n.s., 15 (1855), p. 300; John H. Griscom to Lemuel Shattuck, Jan. 8, 1844, Shattuck papers, Huntington Library, Pasadena, California; Joseph Garland, "Jerome Van Crowninshield Smith," *New England Journal of Medicine,* 283 (1970), pp. 303–304. The effects of immigration on the insane asylums are examined in Norman Dain, *Concepts of Insanity in the United States, 1789–1865* (New Brunswick: Rutgers University Press, 1964), pp. 97–104, 122–130; and Gerald Grob, *Mental Institutions in America* (New York: Free Press, 1973), pp. 229–243.

12 For one review of immigrant health and disease, see William P. Buel, "Report of the Diseases of Females Treated at the New York Dispensary, from May 1842 to May 1843," *American Journal of the Medical Sciences,* n.s., 7 (1844), pp. 96 ff.

13 J. E. White, "A Few Remarks on the Weather and Diseases of 1805 [at Savannah]," *Medical Repository,* 11 (1808), pp. 22–23; Henry P. Russell, *An Official Register of the Deaths Which Occurred among the White Population in the City of Savannah, during the Extraordinary Season of Sickness and Mortality Which Prevailed in the Summer and Fall Months of the Year 1820* (Savannah: Russell, 1820).

14 *A Brief Account of the New-York Hospital* (New York: Collins, 1804), pp. 5–6, 64–65; "New York Hospital Returns for 1802–3," *Medical Repository,* 7 (1804), p. 293.

15 Charles A. Lee, "Medical Statistics," *American Journal of the Medical Sciences,* 19 (1836/37), pp. 26–27.

16 Charles Bowles Fripp, "Statistics of the City of New York," *Journal of the Statistical Society of London,* 2 (1839/40), p. 8; Matthew Carey, *Miscellaneous Essays* (Philadelphia: Carey and Hart, 1830), pp. 122, 321–322.

17 "Cholera," *Western Journal of Medicine and Surgery,* 3d ser., 3 (1849), pp. 362–363; editorial, ibid., pp. 142–144; "Progress of Cholera," ibid., 3d ser., 4 (1849), pp. 89, 180–183, 270–273.

18 Stephen Smith, "Report on the Progress of Epidemic Cholera," *New York Journal of Medicine,* n.s., 13 (1854), pp. 368–377. For more on cholera record-keeping, 1832–1855, see Cassedy, *American Medicine,* pp. 184–189.

19 For one such instance, see John W. Monette, "Observations on the Epidemic Yellow Fever of Natchez, and of the South-west," *Western Journal of Medicine and Surgery,* 5 (1842), pp. 422–426.

20 John H. Griscom, "Notice of a Malignant Disease Generated on Ship-Board by Filth, Imperfect Ventilation, &c," *American Journal of the Medical Sciences,* 12 (1833), pp. 272–273. By 1853, however, Griscom could report even more gruesome horrors in the lower steerage of some of the three-decker ships, to which little fresh air descended, where "almost perpetual night reigns," and accordingly, where "cleaning is impossible." See *Report of the Select Committee of the Senate of the United States on the Sickness and Mortality on Board Emigrant Ships* (Washington: Tucker, 1854), p. 66 (33d Congress, 1st Session, Senate, Reports of Committees No. 386). The following recent article, which discusses immigrant mortality as reflected in the records of 1,077 ships, provides detailed estimates on variations caused by sex, season, port of origin, and other factors. Raymond L. Cohn, "Mortality on Immigrant Voyages to New York, 1836–1853," *Journal of Economic History,* 44 (1984), pp. 289–300.

21 A. C. Castle, "A Common-Sense Talk about 'Ship Fever,'" *Boston Medical and Surgical Journal,* 40 (1849), pp. 290–297; "Anniversary Dinner . . . 1848," *Annalist,* 3 (1848/49), p. 107.

22 "Health of the City," *New Orleans Medical and Surgical Journal,* 4 (1847/48), pp. 683–684; Dan Drake, "The Irish Immigrants' Fever," *Boston Medical and Surgical Journal,* 37 (1847/48), pp. 149–157; Elizabeth Blackwell, "Ship Fever," *Western Journal of Medicine and Surgery,* 3d ser., 3 (1849),

pp. 347-357; "Report of Committee on Typhus, Typhoid, or Ship Fever," *Annalist*, 1 (1846/47), pp. 509-512.

23 [Joseph M. Smith, Chairman], "Report of the Committee on Public Hygiene," *Transactions of the American Medical Association*, 3 (1850), pp. 223-225, 233, 244-246.

24 *Senate Report of Mortality on Emigrant Ships*, pp. 8, 25, 55.

25 For examples, see "Ship Fever," *Boston Medical and Surgical Journal*, 46 (1852), pp. 105-106; "Ventilation of Passenger Vessels," ibid., 38 (1848), pp. 163-164; "Physicians for Emigrant Ships," *Medical Examiner*, n.s., 9 (1853), pp. 431-433; Andrew Combe, "Sanitary Regulations on Board Emigrant Ships," *Water-Cure Journal*, 6 (1848), pp. 89-92, 117-120.

26 *Senate Report of Mortality on Emigrant Ships*, passim. For a review of Griscom's view and his large role in this legislation, see Duncan R. Jamieson, "Towards a Cleaner New York: John H. Griscom and New York's Public Health," Ph.D. Diss., Michigan State University, 1971, Chapter 2.

27 Not a few considered the British Industrial Revolution to have been an unfortunate development for the British people. Among them, Matthew Carey observed, "If the true art of government, and the duty of governors, is to produce the greatest happiness of the greatest number of the governed, then the extraordinary extent of the so-much-lauded improvements in machinery, is anything but a blessing to *a country with a crowded population, especially when there is a difficulty of egress."* Carey, *Miscellaneous Essays*, pp. 122, 321-322.

28 Benjamin W. M'Cready, "On the Influence of Trades, Professions, and Occupations, in the United States, in the Production of Disease," *Transactions of the Medical Society of the State of New York*, 3 (1836/37), pp. 91-150. M'Cready, like most other writers of the early nineteenth century, had no doubts that the building of canals and railroads, and any other initial clearance of the soil, was generally accompanied by serious outbreaks of disease, particularly remitting and intermitting fevers. However, actual experience varied to some extent. The original construction of New York's Erie Canal during the 1820s was accompanied by a heavy incidence of agues and bilious fevers along its route; moreover, when the canal was enlarged in the early 1840s, it brought diseases that were of a "much higher grade, and more difficult to cure than they were previously." Ohio observers, by contrast, found that the building of the Ohio and Erie Canal in the 1830s did not have the adverse effect on the health of the region that had been feared. Ibid., pp. 93-96; Joseph M. Smith, "Report on the Medical Topography and Epidemics of the State of New York," *Transactions of the American Medical Association*, 13 (1860), pp. 221-222; D. Hempstead, "A History of the Topography, Climate and Diseases of the County of Scioto, from Its Settlement to the Present Time," *Western Journal of Medicine and Surgery*, 7 (1843), pp. 429-439.

29 "Our Country and Its Prospective Greatness," *American Phrenological Journal,* 20 (1854), pp. 13–14; "Fast Living," *Boston Medical and Surgical Journal,* 55 (1856/57), p. 454.

30 J. Curtis, "Public Hygiene of Massachusetts; but More Particularly of the Cities of Boston and Lowell," *Transactions of the American Medical Association,* 2 (1849), pp. 515–516; Lewis Rogers, "A Lecture on Sanitary Reform," *Western Journal of Medicine and Surgery,* 3d ser., 8 (1851), pp. 530–531.

31 Franklin Tuthill, "Registration of Births, Deaths, and Marriages," *Transactions of the Medical Society of the State of New York* (1853), pp. 14–15.

32 M'Cready, "On the Influence of Trades," pp. 109–112.

33 Elisha Bartlett, *A Vindication of the Character and Condition of the Females Employed in the Lowell Mills, against the Charges Contained in The Boston Times, and the Boston Quarterly Review* (Lowell: Huntress, 1841). Most of Bartlett's material appeared originally in the *Lowell Courier* in 1839. For Bartlett's early mill investigation, however, see his "Contributions to Pathological Anatomy," *Medical Magazine,* 3 (1834), pp. 671–673.

34 John O. Green, *The Factory System, in Its Hygienic Relations* (Boston: Damrell, 1846); Nathan Allen, "Health of Factory Operatives," *Boston Medical and Surgical Journal,* 55 (1855/56), pp. 342–345.

35 Curtis, "Public Hygiene of Massachusetts," pp. 487–554.

36 "Diseases of the Season," *Boston Medical and Surgical Journal,* 12 (1835), pp. 288–289.

37 "Hospital Reports: Charity Hospital," *New Orleans Medical Journal,* 2 (1845/46), p. 114; letter from Harriet Beecher Stowe, *Godey's Lady's Book,* 23 (1841). While Mark Twain faithfully gathered a great variety of statistics pertaining to the Mississippi River, he did not quantify steamboat accidents beyond the assertion that there had been "many a disaster" of this sort. Mark Twain, *Life on the Mississippi* (New York: Bantam, 1945), p. 159.

38 Between 1856 and 1860, 683 deaths and 624 injuries were reported on New York railroads alone. "Dr. Arnold on Medical Provision for Railroads," *Boston Medical and Surgical Journal,* 68 (1863), pp. 105–108. See also "Health Promoted by Railroads," ibid., 39 (1848), pp. 63–64; Edw. Warren, "Rail Road Accidents," ibid., 48 (1853), pp. 330–333; "Fresh Air for the Working Class," ibid., 72 (1865), pp. 164–165; "Remuneration for Injuries by Accidents upon Railroads," ibid., 52 (1855), pp. 364–366; "Effects of Rail Roads on Surgery," *Botanico-Medical Recorder,* 12 (1843/44), p. 360; "Railway Traveling a Cause of Disease," *St. Louis Medical and Surgical Journal,* 20 (1864), pp. 90–92.

39 James H. Cassedy, "Why Self-Help? Americans Alone with their Diseases 1800–1850," in Guenter B. Risse, Ronald L. Numbers, and Judith W. Leavitt, Eds., *Medicine Without Doctors: Home Health Care in American History* (New York: Science History Publications/USA, 1977), pp. 45–46.

40 [William Farr], *English Life Table. Tables of Lifetimes, Annuities, and Premiums* (London: Longman, Green, Longman, Roberts and Green, 1864), pp. xiii, cxxxix–cxlii.

### Chapter 8. Women in Antebellum Medical-Demographic Change

1 Sarah J. Hale, "An Appeal to American Christians on Behalf of the Ladies' Medical Missionary Society," *Godey's Lady's Book,* 44 (1852), pp. 186–187.
2 Ibid.
3 Paulina Wright Davis, "Female Physicians," *Boston Medical and Surgical Journal,* 41 (1849/50), pp. 520–522. Mary Gove (Nichols) gave such lectures as early as 1838, followed by Paulina Wright Davis, Jane Hitchcock Jones, and others.
4 For concise accounts of many of these individuals, see the sketches in Edwin T. James, Ed., *Notable American Women 1607–1950* (Cambridge: Harvard University Press, 1971), particularly those of the Blackwells, Ann Preston, Maria Zakrzewska, Paulina Wright Davis, Lydia Folger Fowler, Harriot K. Hunt, and Mary Gove Nichols.
5 Editorial, "Female Physicians," *Buffalo Medical Journal,* 3 (1847/48), p. 496; Jno. Stainback Wilson, "Female Medical Education," *Southern Medical and Surgical Journal,* n.s., 10 (1854), pp. 6–10; B. Dowler, "Female Physicians, Medical Colleges, and Medical Ethics," *New Orleans Medical and Surgical Journal,* 17 (1860), pp. 908–911. Sarah Hale urged widows of her day to go into medicine rather than into school teaching, since the former was more remunerative. Editorial, *Godey's Lady's Book,* 47 (1853), pp. 273–274.
6 "Female Doctors," *Buffalo Medical Journal,* 13 (1857/58), p. 191; "Females as Physicians," *Boston Medical and Surgical Journal,* 53 (1855/56), pp. 292–294; [Samuel Gross], editorial, "Female Medical Colleges and Female Doctors," *North American Medico-Chirurgical Review,* 1 (1857), pp. 942–947; Dan King, *Quackery Unmasked* (Boston: Clapp, 1858), pp. 210–215, 333.
7 The Boston Female Medical College was established in 1848, the Female Medical College of Pennsylvania in 1850, the Women's College of the New York Infirmary in 1868.
8 By 1852 female medical-education societies had been formed in several cities to help raise such support, among them the Ladies' Medical Missionary Society of Philadelphia. The latter society had the energetic and dedicated support of the editor of *Godey's Lady's Book,* Sarah J. Hale, who used her editorial columns extensively in its behalf. "Ladies' Medical Missionary Society," *Boston Medical and Surgical Journal,* 47 (1852/53), p. 104; Wm. M. Cornell, "The Medical Education of Women," ibid., 49 (1853/54), pp. 421–422.
9 "Female Medical Schools," *Boston Medical and Surgical Journal,* 51 (1854/55), pp. 263–264; "Female Medical Education," *Buffalo Medical*

*Journal,* 12 (1856/57), pp. 112–115; King, *Quackery Unmasked,* p. 333; Sarah J. Hale, "Doings of the Ladies' Medical Missionary Society," *Godey's Lady's Book,* 46 (1853), pp. 553–554; editorial, ibid., 44 (1852), p. 228.

10 William Henry Channing solicited statistics of this type from Charlotte Fowler Wells for use in his 1851 speech to the Woman's Rights Convention at Worcester. Madeleine B. Stern, "William Henry Channing's Letters on Woman," *Cornell Library Journal,* Autumn (1968), pp. 56–58.

11 An American admirer of the phrenologist Franz Joseph Gall proposed that dispensary physicians encourage their patients to keep such observations. "Law of Menstruation," *Boston Medical and Surgical Journal,* 14 (1836), pp. 190–191. The considerable extent of such records that were actually kept was kindly brought to my attention by Janet Farrell Brodie.

12 These matters have been discussed in detail in Regina Markell Morantz, "Nineteenth Century Health Reform and Women; a Program of Self-Help," in Guenter B. Risse, Ronald L. Numbers, Judith W. Leavitt, Eds., *Medicine Without Doctors: Home Health Care in American History* (New York: Science History Publications, 1977), pp. 73–93.

13 D. Meredith Reese, "Report on Infant Mortality in Large Cities, the Sources of Its Increase, and Means of Its Diminution," *Transactions of the American Medical Association,* 10 (1857), pp. 93–107; Thos. W. Carter, "The Morbid Effects of Tight Lacing," *Western Journal of Medicine and Surgery,* 2d ser., 5 (1846), pp. 166–171.

14 Edward Delony, "Topography and Diseases of Talbot County, Ga.," *Southern Medical and Surgical Journal,* 1 (1836/37), pp. 605–606; "A Cause of Ill Health in Females," *Boston Medical and Surgical Journal,* 61 (1859), pp. 23–24.

15 Bartlett's arguments about female workers at Lowell are discussed in Chapter 7.

16 A. K. Gardner, "Hygiene of the Sewing Machine," *American Medical Times,* 1 (1860), pp. 420–421, 435–437.

17 Samuel Cartwright, "Statistical Medicine or Numerical Analysis Applied to the Investigation of Morbid Actions," *Western Journal of Medicine and Surgery,* 3d ser., 1 (1848), pp. 198–205.

18 Catherine E. Beecher, *Letters to the People on Health and Happiness* (New York: Harper, 1855) pp. 7–11, 120–133.

19 Henry C. Carey, *Principles of Political Economy* (Philadelphia: Lea and Blanchard, 1840); Gouverneur Emerson, review, *American Journal of the Medical Sciences,* 26 (1840), pp. 434–437.

20 Yasukichi Yasuba, *Birth Rates of the White Population in the United States, 1800–1860, an Economic Study* (Baltimore: Johns Hopkins Press, 1962).

21 "Report of the City Registrar of Boston," *Boston Medical and Surgical Journal,* 42 (1850), p. 26; "Bills of Mortality," ibid., 1 (1828), p. 109; William B. Bibbins, "A Registry of Births," *American Medical Times,* 1 (1860), p. 196.

22 Edwin M. Snow, *Report on Registration, Presented to the Quarantine and Sanitary Convention, Fourth Annual Meeting* (Boston, 1860), p. 4.
23 G. Emerson, "Causes of the Greater Mortality of Male Children, and the Relative Proportion of the Sexes at Birth," *Boston Medical and Surgical Journal,* 42 (1850), pp. 129–131. The same article appeared under a slightly different title in the *Medical Examiner,* 6 (1850), pp. 147–150. A variation of Emerson's theory stated simply that the proportion of the sexes at birth depended upon the sanitary condition of a community. However, American analysts did not uniformly support this. Edwin M. Snow, for one, felt that the Providence experience of 1860 did not bear this theory out. *Sixth Annual Report of the Births, Marriages, and Deaths in the City of Providence, for the Year 1860* (Providence: Knowles, Anthony, 1861), p. 3.
24 Edwin M. Snow confirmed for the United States Villermé's conclusion that birth differentials by season were greater in rural areas than in large cities.
25 Gouveneur Emerson, "Medical Statistics," *American Journal of the Medical Sciences,* 9 (1831/32), pp. 21–25.
26 *Sixth Annual Report of Providence Births, Marriages, and Deaths, 1860,* p. 88.
27 See the comments on this problem by Charles V. Chapin, in *Thirty-Sixth Annual Report on the Births, Marriages, and Deaths, in the City of Providence, during the Year Ending December 31, 1890* (Providence: Snow and Farnham, 1891), p. 1.
28 Henry C. Carey, *Principles of Social Science,* 3 vols. (Philadelphia: Lippincott, 1858–1865), Vol. 1, p. 295, footnote; Lemuel Shattuck, *Memorials of the Descendants of William Shattuck* (Boston: Dutton and Wentworth, 1855), p. 34.
29 Orson S. Fowler, *Matrimony,* 61st ed. (New York: Fowlers and Wells, 1851); Orson S. Fowler, *Hereditary Descent* (New York: Fowlers and Wells, 1848), p. 15; O. S. Fowler, *Works on Phrenology, Physiology, and Kindred Subjects* (London: Watson, 1851), p. 2.
30 Edward Jarvis, *Production of Vital Force* (Boston: Clapp, 1849), pp. 31–34; Samuel Jackson, et al., "Registration of Marriages and Births," *Western Journal of Medicine and Surgery,* 3d ser., 2 (1848), pp. 61–65.
31 Ezra Read, "The Mortality Statistics of the Census of 1850," *North American Medico-Chirurgical Review,* 2 (1858), pp. 334–335.
32 R. T. Trall, *Sexual Physiology,* 5th ed. (New York: Miller, Wood, 1867), esp. pp. 197 ff. For Perfectionist views on this subject, see Chapter 4.
33 Samuel Gridley Howe, *Report Made to the Legislature of Massachusetts on Idiocy* (Boston: Coolidge and Wiley, 1848); Samuel Gridley Howe, *Dr. Howe's Report on Idiocy* (Boston: 1850) (State of Massachusetts, Senate Document no. 38).
34 John Bartlett, "Circular," *Boston Medical and Surgical Journal,* 52 (1855), p. 208; Charles Brooks, "Laws of Reproduction, Considered with Particular Reference to the Intermarriage of First-Cousins," *Proceedings of the Ameri-*

*can Association for the Advancement of Science,* 9 (1855, published 1856), pp. 236–246; Alexander Walker, *Intermarriage* (Philadelphia: Lindsay and Blakiston, 1851).

35 S. M. Bemiss, "On the Evil Effects of Marriages of Consanguinity," *North American Medico-Chirurgical Review,* 1 (1857), pp. 97–107; S. M. Bemiss, "Report on Influence of Marriages of Consanguinity upon Offspring," *Transactions of the American Medical Association,* 11 (1858), pp. 321–425; "Marriages of Consanguinity," *Boston Medical and Surgical Journal,* 57 (1857), pp. 343–344.

36 Isaac Ray, *Mental Hygiene* (Boston: Tichnor and Fields, 1863), pp. 37–40, 44–45.

37 John Bell, "The Effects of the Consanguinity of Parents upon the Mental Constitution of the Offspring," *Boston Medical and Surgical Journal,* 60 (1859), pp. 473–484. Bell also considered Bemiss's estimate of 5,000 consanguinous marriages to be far too low. He thought that 50,000 would be a much closer guess. For Bemiss's defense of his figures, see his "Marriages of Sanguinity," ibid., 61 (1859), pp. 29–32.

38 Trall, *Sexual Physiology,* pp. 265–270; C. F. Winslow, "Intermarriage among the Sandwich Islanders," *Boston Medical and Surgical Journal,* 63 (1860), pp. 329–335; Lewis H. Morgan, "Laws of Descent of the Iroquois," *Proceedings of the American Association for the Advancement of Science,* 11 (1857), Part 2, pp. 132–147.

39 Greeley carried on a heated newspaper exchange on the subject with such reformers as Stephen Pearl Andrews, Robert Dale Owen, and Henry James, Sr. See especially Stephen Pearl Andrews, Ed., *Love, Marriage, and Divorce, and the Sovereignty of the Individual* (New York: Stringer and Townsend, 1853); and *Divorce: Being a Correspondence between Horace Greeley and Robert Dale Owen* (New York: DeWitt, 1860).

40 Robert Dale Owen, *The Moral Physiology* (New York: the author, 1836); Charles Knowlton, *Fruits of Philosophy,* reprinted in Charles Bradlaugh and Annie Besant, *A Treatise on the Population Question, 2d ed. (Garden City, N.Y.: Garden City Publishing Co., 1880), pp. 6–7, 21; "An American Physician", Reproductive Control* (Cincinnati: [the author?], 1855).

41 Owen, *Moral Physiology; Knowlton, Fruits of Philosophy.*

42 Trall, *Sexual Physiology,* p. 208; James Ashton, *The Book of Nature* (New York: Brother Jonathan Office, 1863), p. iii.

43 [William A. Alcott], *The Physiology of Marriage, by an Old Physician* (Boston: Jewett, 1856), pp. 180–186.

44 A Boston physician suggested in 1842 that Knowlton was probably "the only [regular] medical man in New England, if not in America" who had ever publicly advocated contraceptive measures. "Fruits of Philosophy," *Boston Medical and Surgical Journal,* 27 (1842/43), p. 256.

45 E. M. Pendleton, "On the Comparative Fecundity of the Caucasian and African Races," *Charleston Medical Journal,* 6 (1851), pp. 351–356. Pendle-

ton's case records from his own practice for eight years also showed that white women were more liable than blacks to most of the disease conditions which brought about sterility. Of these, natural abortions did occur somewhat more often among the blacks, but Pendleton concluded that these were readily explained by the physically demanding occupations of the latter.

46 William A. Alcott, *The Physiology of Marriage* (Boston: Dinsmoor, 1866), pp. 185–186.

47 Stephen W. Avery, "Observations on the Causes of the Large Proportions of Still-born Children in Our Large Cities over Those of London," *Transactions of the Medical Society of the State of New York,* 3 (1836/37), pp. 179–206. London had one stillbirth out of every 27.5 reported deaths between 1815 and 1824, while New York averaged one in 17 between 1816 and 1829, Boston 1 in 13.8 between 1820 and 1829, Philadelphia 1 in 18.1 between 1807 and 1826. Ibid., pp. 182–184.

48 Thomas Ewell, *Statement of Improvements in the Theory and Practice of the Science of Medicine* (Philadelphia: Bioren, 1819), p. 65; John B. Beck, *An Inaugural Dissertation on Infanticide* (New York: Seymour, 1817), p. 35.

49 John B. Beck, "Infanticide," in Theodric Romeyn Beck, *Elements of Medical Jurisprudence,* 7th ed. (London: Longman, et al., 1842), pp. 253–266; "Conviction of an Abortionist," *Southern Medical and Surgical Journal,* n.s., 15 (1859), p. 578; "Criminal Abortions," *Buffalo Medical Journal,* 14 (1858/59), pp. 247–251, 309–313; "Abortion Advertisements," *Boston Medical and Surgical Journal,* 57 (1857/58), p. 206; "Health of the City," *St. Louis Medical and Surgical Journal,* 16 (1858), pp. 280–282; D. M. Reese, "Report on Infant Mortality in Large Cities," *Transactions of the American Medical Association,* 10 (1857), p. 95; John Humphrey Noyes remarked that by the 1860s abortion had grown "almost to a distinct profession." John Humphrey Noyes, *Male Continence* (Oneida: The Circular Press, 1866), p. 2.

50 D. M. Reese, "Report on Infant Mortality," p. 95.

51 Storer's report was published in summary form in the *Transactions of the American Medical Association,* 12 (1859), pp. 75–78, and in full in the *North American Medico-Chirurgical Review,* 3 (1859). The latter was reissued separately under the title *On Criminal Abortion in America* (Philadelphia: Lippincott, 1860). See also a related editorial, "Criminal Abortion," *Boston Medical Surgical Journal,* 62 (1860), pp. 65–67. Storer's exposé of the abortion evil was subsequently carried to the general public through a number of popular works.

## Chapter 9. The Length of Lives in Antebellum America

1 John Sinclair, *An Essay on Longevity* (London: Strahan, 1802); "Longevity," *Medical Repository,* 6 (1803), pp. 351–352.

2 "The Stages of Human Life," *Boston Medical and Surgical Journal,* 4 (1831), pp. 289–291; Edward Jarvis, *The Increase of Human Life* (Boston: Clapp, 1872), p. 55.

3 "Health and Longevity in America," *Boston Medical and Surgical Journal,* 58 (1858), pp. 265–266.

4 B. F. Joslin, "On the Use of Chemical and Mechanical Means and Large Doses, in connection with Homoeopathic Practice," *American Journal of Homoeopathy,* 3 (1848/49), p. 72.

5 A. Clark, "The Claims of the Medical Profession," *Transactions of the Medical Society of the State of New York, 1852/53* (Albany: Van Benthuysen, 1853), pp. 287–289. Clark drew upon statistical records of the New York Hospital and the Pennsylvania Hospital.

6 W. Byrd Powell, "A Discovery of the Means of Determining the Comparative Length or Duration of Human Life, and Other Important Physiological Facts," *Boston Medical and Surgical Journal,* 51 (1854/55) pp. 309–314. Powell's figures were taken by extending a line "from the external occipital protuberance to the most prominent part of the external orbitar process of the os frontis" and measuring the distance from that line to the "meatus auditorius externis." Ibid., p. 310.

7 "Medical Statistics of the Moravian Society, Established at Bethlehem, Penn.," *American Journal of the Medical Sciences,* 8 (1831), p. 258; "Longevity of the Shakers," *Boston Medical and Surgical Journal,* 23 (1840/41), p. 117; "Medical Statistics," ibid., 10 (1834), p. 418.

8 J. E. Worcester, "Remarks on Longevity and the Expectation of Life in the United States, Relating More Particularly to the State of New Hampshire, with Some Comparative Views in Relation to Foreign Countries," *Memoirs of the American Academy of Arts and Science,* n.s., 1 (1833), pp. 1–44. Italics added.

9 A detailed summary of the specific inquiries of the first 11 censuses, together with their legislative histories and administrative arrangements, may be found in Carroll D. Wright, *The History and Growth of the United States Census* (Washington: Government Printing Office, 1900).

10 Analysts found that the mortality figures collected in the 1850, 1860, and 1870 censuses fell short of actuality each time by as much as 40 percent. James H. Cassedy, "The Registration Area and American Vital Statistics," *Bulletin of the History of Medicine,* 39 (1965), pp. 222–231.

11 J. D. B. DeBow, *Mortality Statistics of the Seventh Census of the United States, 1850* (Washington, Nicholson, 1855), esp. pp. 4–16. See also Jarvis's letters to DeBow, 1853–1856, in the Jarvis letterbooks, Jarvis Collection, Harvard University Library. Jarvis submitted a bill of $1,500 for an estimated five months of consultant labor on the mortality statistics, but he never received payment despite the efforts of DeBow, Kennedy, and several congressmen over a period of years. For a contemporary critique of Jarvis's

arrangement of diseases, see Ezra Read, "The Mortality Statistics of the Census of 1850, and a Review of the Letter of Dr. Edward Jarvis upon the classification of Diseases," *North American Medico-Chirurigical Review,* 2 (1858), pp. 334–340.

12 The quotation is from E. J. [Edward Jarvis], "Review," *American Journal of the Medical Sciences,* n.s., 29 (1855), p. 410.

13 Charles Caldwell, "Thoughts on the Probable Destiny of New Orleans, in Relation to Health, Population and Commerce," *Philadelphia Journal of the Medical and Physical Sciences,* 6 (1823), p. 12.

14 Edward Jarvis, *Production of Vital Force* (Boston: Clapp, 1849), pp. 49–51; Robert C. Davis, "An Early American Experiment in Health Insurance," *Bulletin of the Cleveland Medical Library,* 14 (1967), pp. 4–12.

15 Jarvis, *Production of Vital Force,* pp. 49–51; Edward Jarvis, "Sanitary Condition of Massachusetts and New England," *Transactions of the American Medical Association,* 3 (1850), pp. 253–254; "Assurance against Sickness," *Boston Medical and Surgical Journal,* 37 (1847/48), pp. 23–24; "The Law of Sickness and its Application to Health Insurance and Benefit Societies," *Merchants Magazine,* 19 (1848), pp. 605 ff.; "Medical Invalid Assurance Office," *Boston Medical and Surgical Journal,* 31 (1844/45), pp. 484–485.

16 J. Owen Stalson, *Marketing Life Insurance, Its History in America* (Cambridge, Mass.: Harvard University Press, 1942), pp. 44–50; John A. Fowler, *History of Insurance in Philadelphia for Two Centuries (1683–1882)* (Philadelphia: Review Publishing and Printing Co., 1888), pp. 605–627.

17 Mutual Life Insurance Company of New York, *The Agent's Manual of Life Assurance* (New York: Mutual Life Insurance Company of New York, 1867), pp. 23–24. These great business successes were partly due to aggressive new sales methods. At the same time, the American public demonstrated a new receptivity to life insurance, in part because of a greatly increased sense of insecurity brought on by such factors as changing family patterns, the decreased availability of free land, and new social and economic configurations.

18 Edward H. Barton's 1851 sanitary report for New Orleans included extensive mortality statistics supplied by H. G. Heartt, actuary of a Louisiana life insurance firm. The 1850 cholera mortality experience among the selected policyholders of Heartt's firm provided a striking contrast to that of the populace as a whole. In the general population, 9.83 percent of the whites and 3.44 percent of the blacks died of the disease, while of those insured by the firm, only .77 percent of the 266 whites and 1.72 percent of the 716 blacks succumbed. Barton considered these differentials to be a strong testimony to the value of morality and hygienic habits. Edward H. Barton, *Report to the Louisiana State Medical Society, on the Meteorology, Vital Statistics and Hygiene of the State of Louisiana* (New Orleans: Davies, 1851), pp. 56–66.

19 Mutual Life Insurance Company, *Agent's Manual of Life Assurance,* pp. 45,

85; J. V. C. Smith, "Physical Indications of Longevity in Man," in T. S. Lambert, et al., *Longevity,* 2d ed. (New York: Wood, 1869), separate pagination, p. 23.

20 Review, *Medical Repository,* 15 (1812), pp. 47–49; review, *New York Journal of Medicine,* 5 (1845), pp. 110–111; "Life Policies," *Boston Medical and Surgical Journal,* 40 (1849), p. 404; "Lectures on Life Insurance," ibid., 48 (1853), pp. 224–225; review, *New Orleans Medical and Surgical Journal,* 9 (1852/53), pp. 819–820.

21 "Fallacy of Life Insurance," *Boston Medical and Surgical Journal,* 42 (1850), pp. 123–124; "Life Insurance," ibid., 48 (1853), pp. 386–387.

22 Iatros, "Information Given to Life Insurance Companies," *Boston Medical and Surgical Journal,* 65 (1861/62), pp. 417–419; B, "Life Insurance Companies, and Their Treatment of the Medical Profession," ibid., 52 (1855), pp. 465–467; "Fallacy of Life Insurance," p. 123.

23 Theodric Romeyn Beck, "Contributions in Medical Jurisprudence, No. 1," *New York Medical and Physical Journal,* 5 (1826), p. 29; Mutual Benefit Life Insurance Company, *Life Insurance, Its Nature, Origin and Progress* (New York: Gray, 1858), pp. 44 ff.

24 "Life Insurance and Irregular Practitioners," *Boston Medical and Surgical Journal,* 39 (1848/49), p. 483.

25 "A New Feature in Life Insurance," *American Homoeopathic Review,* 6 (1865/66), pp. 196–197; H. M. Paine, "Albany County Homoeopathic Medical Society," ibid., pp. 396–397. Homeopaths continued to find their system actuarially as well as medically superior at least through the 1880s. See. R. T. Trall, "Homoeopathic Life Insurance," in DeWitt Clinton Moore, *The Science of Health Conservation . . .* (San Francisco: Bancroft, 1880), p. 15.

26 "Life Insurance and Irregular Practitioners," p. 483; "Fallacy of Life Insurance," p. 124. Forfeiture provisions became such a scandal as to be among the principal targets of antebellum life insurance reformers. Massachusetts, largely through the efforts of the abolitionist and actuary Elizur Wright, eliminated much of this abuse in its insurance reform legislation of 1861. For a summary of Wright's contribution, see his sketch in *Dictionary of American Biography,* 10 (1964), pp. 548–549.

27 In 1847, Josiah Nott pointed to the fact that "all the life insurance companies of the United States are north of the Potomac, as are nearly all the writers on vital statistics." [Josiah C. Nott], "Life Insurance at the South," *DeBow's Review,* 3 (1847), p. 362; Frederick L. Hoffman, "Life Insurance in the South," in J. C. Ballagh, Ed., *The South in the Building of the Nation,* Vol. 5, *Economic History, 1607–1865* (Richmond: Southern Historical Publication Society, 1910), pp. 638–645.

28 J. C. Nott, "An Examination into the Health and Longevity of the Southern Sea Ports of the United States, with Reference to the subject of Life Insurance," *Southern Journal of Medicine and Pharmacy,* 2 (1847), p. 145;

Hoffman, "Life Insurance in the South," p. 650. The New York firm reported the following regional financial losses due to the differences of mortality experience in 1859:

| | Premiums | Losses |
|---|---|---|
| *North* | *$2,556,929* | *$904,941 (or 35.5 percent of the premiums)* |
| *South* | *$580,225* | *$309,870 (or 53.5 percent of the premiums)* |

29 The census of 1830 showed, for instance, that the proportion of white centenarians reported for North Carolina was 15 times greater than in Massachusetts. Sylvester Graham, noting this, along with the greater (7 to 1) proportion of black centenarians in Massachusetts than in North Carolina, attributed the variations to dietary differences. Sylvester Graham, *Lectures on the Science of Human Life,* 2 vols. (Boston: Marsh, Capen, Lyon, and Webb, 1839), Vol. 1, p. 459; Vol. 2, pp. 36–41.

30 Review, probably by Samuel Forry, *New York Journal of Medicine,* 3 (1844), pp. 209–215; S. Chaillé, "Longevity," *New Orleans Medical and Surgical Journal,* 71 (1864/65), pp. 422–423; "Old Age," *Boston Medical and Surgical Journal,* 71 (1864/65), pp. 446–447; Nott, "An Examination into the Health and Longevity of the Southern Sea Ports," pp. 9–13.

A more objective New Orleans physician agreed that many of the southern instances of great longevity had to be considered suspect. "A credulous census taker or any body can get over half of the dried up old darkies in Louisiana, for an extra chew of tobacco, to answer to any age desired. If the cue had been given beforehand, the venerable centennarian [*sic*] would recall with gusto the landing of Columbus, or the burial of De Soto." Stanford E. Chaillé, *Life and Death in New Orleans from 1787 to 1869, and More Especially during the Five Years, 1856 to 1860* (New Orleans: The Bronze Pen, 1869), p. 66.

31 Nott's Boston statistics, as well as his methods of comparing the two cities, were drawn from Shattuck's 1845 report on the census of Boston. Nott also wrote Shattuck several times to obtain further data on longevity and mortality in New England port cities. See Nott to Shattuck, Oct. 2, 1846, Shattuck papers, Massachusetts Historical Society, Boston.

32 An 1846 study of climate by the New York City physician James M'Cune Smith, concluded, by contrast, that "the climate of New England is more favorable to longevity than the climate of the old Southern states, in the vast disproportion of 274 to 116, or 5½ to 2!" James M'Cune Smith, "The Influence of Climate on Longevity, with Special Reference to Life Insurance," *Merchants' Magazine,* 14 (1846), p. 412.

33 Nott, "An Examination into the Health and Longevity of the Southern Sea Ports," pp. 1–19, 121–145; Nott, "Life Insurance at the South," pp. 357–376; ibid., p. 376.

34 Josiah C. Nott, "Statistics of Southern Slave Population, with Especial Reference to Life Insurance," *DeBow's Review,* 4 (1847), p. 287.

35 Nott, "Statistics of Southern Slave Population," pp. 275–289; Hoffman, "Life Insurance in the South," pp. 641–644.

36 "Does a Man Shorten His Life by Insuring It?" *Merchants' Magazine,* 25 (1856), p. 110.

37 *Fifth Annual Report of the Registrar-General of Births, Deaths, and Marriages, in England* (London: General Register Office, 1843), pp. 16–19; Noel A. Humphreys, Ed., *Vital Statistics: a Memorial Volume of Selections from the Reports and Writings of William Farr* (London: Stanford, 1885), pp. 450–453.

38 *Vital Statistics,* p. 492.

39 For further discussion of these and other late eighteenth-century life calculations, see James H. Cassedy, *Demography in Early America* (Cambridge, Mass.: Harvard University Press, 1969), pp. 243–273.

40 J. Ingersoll Bowditch, "Tables Exhibiting the Number of White Persons in the United States, at Every Age, Deduced from the Last Census," *Memoirs of the American Academy of Arts and Sciences,* n.s., 1 (1833), pp. 345–347.

41 Firms using the Wigglesworth tables into the 1840s included, among others, the Massachusetts Life Insurance Company and the New England Mutual Life Insurance Company. Lemuel Shattuck, "Laws of Human Mortality," in J. V. C. Smith, Ed., *American Medical Almanac* (Boston: Marsh, Capen, Lyons, and Webb, 1840), pp. 106–107; Lemuel Shattuck, "Letter to the Secretary," appendix to John G. Palfrey, *Fourth Annual Report to the Legislature, Relating to the Registry and Returns of Births, Marriages, and Deaths in Massachusetts, for the Year Ending April 30th, 1845* (Boston: Dutton and Wentworth, 1845), pp. 28–29; James M'Cune Smith, "Influence of Climate on Longevity, with Special Reference to Life Insurance," *Merchants' Magazine,* 14 (1846), p. 403.

42 Shattuck, "Letter to the Secretary," p. 28.

43 "Registration of Births, Marriages and Deaths," *Buffalo Medical Journal,* 6 (1850/51), p. 692; Franklin Tuthill, "Registration of Births, Deaths and Marriages," *Transactions of the Medical Society of the State of New York* (Albany: Van Benthuysen, 1853), pp. 16–17; [Stephen G. Hubbard], "Registration the Basis of Sanitary Reform," *Buffalo Medical Journal,* 11 (1855/56), p. 509; James M'Cune Smith, "Influence of Climate on Longevity," pp. 403–404.

44 C. F. M'Cay, "The Mortality of Baltimore," *Merchants Magazine and Commercial Review,* 22 (1850), pp. 35–44; C. F. M'Cay, "On the Laws of Human Mortality," *Proceedings of the American Association for the Advancement of Science,* 10 (1856, published 1857), pp. 21–27.

45 [J. C. G. Kennedy], *The Seventh Census. Report of the Superintendent of the Census for December 1, 1852, [and] for December 1, 1851* (Washington: Armstrong, 1853), pp. 10–13.

46 E. B. Elliott, "On the Law of Human Mortality That Appears to Obtain in Massachusetts, with Tables of Practical Value Deduced Therefrom,"

*Proceedings of the American Association for the Advancement of Science,* 11 (1858), pp. 51–82; E. B. Elliott, "Vital Statistics," ibid., 10 (1856, published 1857), pp. 50–101; Oliver Warner, *Sixteenth Report to the Legislature of Massachusetts, Relating to the Registry and Return of Births, Marriages, and Deaths in the Commonwealth, for the Year Ending December 31, 1857* (Boston: White, 1858), pp. vii–viii, 193–214; "Massachusetts Registration Report," *Boston Medical and Surgical Journal,* 60 (1859), pp. 144–147.

47  "Mortality among the Blind," *Boston Medical and Surgical Journal,* 63 (1860/61), pp. 66–67. Elliott's paper, "Vital Statistics of the Blind, with an Approximate Life Table," was presented in August 1860 at the Newport meeting of the American Association for the Advancement of Science, but was not published in the meeting's proceedings.

48  "Vital Mortuary Statistics of the Alumni of Harvard College," *Boston Medical and Surgical Journal,* 57 (1857), pp. 65–66; "Longevity of Graduates of Colleges," ibid., 59 (1858), pp. 24–25. Peirce used a recent Prussian life table as a basis for comparisons.

49  [Sheppard Homans], *Report Exhibiting the Experience of the Mutual Life Insurance Company of New-York, for Fifteen Years Ending February First, 1858* (New York: Mutual Life Insurance Company of New York, 1859).

50  James Wynne, *Report on the Vital Statistics of the United States, Made to the Mutual Life Insurance Company of New York* (New York: Baillière, 1857).

51  "Life Assurance Convention at New York, 1860," *Journal of the Statistical Society of London,* 23 (1860), pp. 542–543.

## Epilogue: Demography and Medicine at Midcentury

1  The discussion that follows draws upon material presented earlier in this book together with general findings from my *American Medicine and Statistical Thinking, 1800–1860* (Cambridge, Mass.: Harvard University Press, 1984).

2  Richard H. Shryock, *Medicine and Society in America: 1660–1860* (Ithaca: Cornell University Press, Great Seal Books, 1962), p. 166.

3  With few other good data sources for the period at their disposal, modern demographers have also generally agreed that the figures for Massachusetts have to be accepted as providing fairly close approximations of the general life expectancy for the entire country. Some, however, point out that the figures for much of the rest of the United States may well have been somewhat higher, since Massachusetts had, during that time, gone further than most other states toward urbanization as well as toward vital registration. In any case, the overall figures given here do not reflect the sharp differentials in life expectancy between women and men, the native stock and recent immigrants, whites and blacks, rich and poor, or other population segments. See Louis B. Dublin, Alfred J. Lotka, Mortimer Spiegelman, *Length of Life,* rev. ed. (New York:

Ronald, 1949), pp. 35–41; W. S. Thompson and P. K. Whelpton, *Population Trends in the United States* (New York, 1933), p. 239; Yasukichi Yasuba, *Birth Rates of the White Population in the United States, 1800–1860: an Economic Study* (Baltimore: Johns Hopkins Press, 1962), pp. 86–96.

4 For the now well-known twentieth-century expression of these views, see Thomas McKeown, *The Modern Rise of Population* (New York: Academic Press, 1976); and Thomas McKeown, *The Role of Medicine: Dream, Mirage or Nemesis?* 2d ed. (Princeton: Princeton University Press, 1979).

# Bibliographical Note

This volume is based predominantly upon my examination of original materials, almost all of which are to be found in American libraries and are cited in detail in the footnotes. These materials include manuscript collections, newspapers, and government documents, as well as the book-length monographs of individuals who have been discussed. I have relied most heavily upon the periodical literature of the period. Searches for relevant material were made in a number of economic, religious, social reform, and other periodicals. Particularly extensive and systematic examinations, however, were made of a large proportion of early nineteenth-century American medical and scientific journals, including almost all of those that were published for periods of five years or longer. My research was greatly facilitated by the availability of most of these latter specialty periodicals in the collections of the National Library of Medicine. The others were found in general and academic libraries.

I have also consulted a wide range of secondary works. Since my book is interdisciplinary in nature, these have included not only works in general history but in the history of medicine, demography, statistics, and several related specialties. Although my reading of these works over the past 20 years or so has contributed immeasureably to my understanding of the United States and its history for the period under consideration, it has not been feasible to give credit to them in the footnotes except where I drew upon specific material from them. However, I have prepared a separate classified bibliography of selected secondary sources which I shall be glad to send to scholars upon request.

# Index

Abolition, 99, 125, 238$n8$

Abortion, 184–87, 210, 260

Accidents: among males, 8; in California, 77; among immigrants, 156; in industry 167; in transport, 167, 255$n38$; and stillbirth, 184; of slaves, 202–3; and the blind, 206; mentioned, 91, 163

Acclimation: in the South, 119–20, 201, 202; during the Mexican War, 132; in Liberia, 144. *See also* Seasoning, environmental

Achenwall, Gottfried, 3

Actuaries. *See* Insurance; Life Insurance

Adams, John, xv, 10

Advertising: of health resorts, 57–58; of abortion, 185

Africa: source of epidemic disease, 29, 251$n2$; and slave trade, 97; colonization in, 100, 143–44; and U. S. Navy, 136, 137–38

Agassiz, Louis, 31, 37, 116

Age: of slaves, 122; aging of women, 174; in census, 191. *See also* Longevity

Agrarianism, 148, 161, 209

Agriculture: and statistics, 6, 7; and War of 1812, 20; in Louisiana, 30; and health, 34, 37, 38, 119; surveys of, 35; and meteorology, 40, 45; and migration, 61, 72; physicians as farmers, 63;

healthfulness of, 163; mentioned, 85, 86, 119, 140

Ague, 36

Akerly, Samuel, 22, 219$n15$

Alabama, 72

Alcohol: and male mortality, 9; and Indians, 29; and Army troops, 32, 123; statistics of use, 118; in Navy, 137; and Hawaiians, 145; in West, 147; on ships, 160; and artisans, 163; and slaves, 203; and insurance, 203

Alcott, William A.: and health reform, 171; statistics of, 172; on birth control, 183, 184

Alexander, W. P., 144

Allen, Nathan: on opium, 146–47; and health of Lowell, 166

Allopaths. *See* Medicine; Physicians

Almshouses: and seamen, 16; creation of, 63; and immigrants, 152, 154; and typhus, 158; mentioned, 80. *See also* Philanthropy; Public welfare

Amenorrhea, 155

American Academy of Arts and Sciences, 227$n49$

American Association for the Advancement of Science, 37, 266$n47$

American Board of Commissioners for Foreign Missions, 248$n24$

271

COVER DESIGNED BY TOM ESSER
TEXT DESIGNED BY MIKE BURTON
COMPOSED BY THE COMPOSING ROOM, INC., APPLETON, WISCONSIN
MANUFACTURED BY EDWARDS BROTHERS, INC., ANN ARBOR, MICHIGAN
TEXT IS SET IN TIMES ROMAN
DISPLAY LINES ARE SET IN SNELL ROUNDHAND AND TIMES ROMAN

Ⓦ

Library of Congress Cataloging-in-Publication Data
Cassedy, James H.
Medicine and American growth, 1800–1860.
(Wisconsin publications in the history of
science and medicine; no. 5)
Bibliography: p. 269.
Includes index.
1. Medicine—United States—History—19th century.
2. Demographic transition—United States—History—
19th century. 3. United States—Population. I. Title.
II. Series. [DNLM: 1. History of Medicine, 19th Cent.—
United States. WI WI805 no.5/WZ 70 AA1 C27m]
R151.C37   1986     362.1'0973     86-40047
ISBN 0-299-10900-3
ISBN 0-299-10904-6 (pbk.)